THE WHEAT AND THE CHAFF

FRANÇOIS MITTERRAND

THE WHEAT

AND

THE CHAFF

WEIDENFELD AND NICOLSON LONDON

CONTENTS

TO EDMONDE and GASTON DEFFERRE

PART I

THE WHEAT
AND
THE CHAFF

TRANSLATED BY
RICHARD S. WOODWARD

PREFACE

I have no intention of writing my memoirs, nor do I keep a journal of the events I live through or anticipate. But what I do fairly often is jot down notes about something I feel strongly about or am involved with emotionally, or in an effort to record accurately as to time and context either an impression or a fact which, for a variety of reasons, I may feel is important. All of which, of course, is very subjective. These notes, as a whole, suffer varying fates. Some never see the light of day. Others appear, often in slightly or more than slightly different form, in various magazines, reviews, and newspapers.

The present volume consists of a rather arbitrary and random selection from the material thus recorded over a period of almost a decade. In it I practice a hybrid genre, neither diary, nor, strictly speaking, chronicle, though I have penned both words at one time or another.

In my jottings, I express whatever comes to mind, on any subject that captures my fancy, depending on my mood and the time of day. The reader should be forewarned that I do some editing and arranging, because I have little taste for indiscretion and because of my profound distaste for show of any kind.

I chose the title "The Wheat and the Chaff" because it summarizes reasonably well what I think of my work. I do not classify chaff as base matter while elevating grain to some noble position. Each to its own use. If, in the course of these pages, the reader discovers something that helps fill a need or satisfy a desire—that I share—to go beyond reality, to transcend appearances, as it were, I shall be pleased indeed to have helped him or her in that effort.

1971

In France, if defeat and anarchy are fatal to the Republics, they offer golden opportunities for famous men that the ruling class—landed gentry, men of the cloth, or wealthy businessmen of one kind or another—seems to have held in reserve over the past two centuries, and brings out at the opportune moment. The role of savior, which through a resurgence of devotional language we also refer to as "Man of Providence," is part and parcel of the national repertory. It is true that there is a kind of devotion in the way the bourgeoisie defends its interests. In earlier times the king was the Lord's anointed. Today the Civil Code acts as an intermediary between the two. Through an implicit reference to the decrees of Providence, the established fact takes on the value of law. What backs it up is just, since it is useful. Therefore, perish the Republic that fails to protect the established order.

In 1799, money was worthless. The powers-that-be went looking for an available sword among the generals of the Revolution. They had hoped for Hoche, Jourdan, Moreau. Napoleon Bonaparte appeared, and that was the end of the First Republic. In 1848 they trembled before a revolution that had dared utter the word "socialism." Cavaignac no longer a possible contender, they asked

Changarnier and Joinville to take charge. But Louis-Napoleon took matters into his own hands and settled the fate of the Second Republic. People rushed to join his banner.

In 1940 it was the "divine surprise." This expression, which we owe to Charles Maurras, expressed the opinion of those segments of the population who thought that the mirage of the Popular Front had drawn the wrath of God upon France. Beaten, occupied, humiliated, our country sacrificed the Third Republic and clothed itself with Marshal Pétain. Yet the First Republic had changed the face of the earth, the Second had dreamt great dreams, the Third had reestablished national unity. By their radiance, they had compelled the victors to pretend that they took their inspiration from their principles. The Fourth Republic, which lacked such luster, died not with a bang but a whimper. It had resorted to an outmoded political system. It had failed to solve the colonial crisis. It no longer stood for what the ruling class expected from the State. It was doomed. To be sure, de Gaulle was no more the desired savior than the two Bonapartes had been. But like them he knew how to seize the opportunity when the time was ripe and how to anticipate various conflicting ambitions. The wealthy bourgeoisie, long accustomed to marriages of reason, accepted the one who saved the essential. The Fifth Republic had a clear field. Clear? Not quite: its limitations were readily apparent.

General de Gaulle strikes me as being more remarkable for what he was than for what he did. At the risk of shocking my readers, let me say that in my view he was the last of the wide-ranging political minds of the nineteenth century rather than the commonly accepted precursor of the year 2000. Less than a year after his death, Gaullism is dead and gone too. Institutions are buckling under the weight of the thrusts and currents set free by the death of their founder. Not content to adapt his policies to evolving events, his successors distance themselves from the ideals that guided them.

Are they wrong? The world has once again become what it was before Charles de Gaulle invented it to suit his own purpose. In that sense, they are realists. De Gaulle was strong-willed and had strong opinions. He spoke the language that dreams are made of. When he spoke, you had the feeling that he had great plans in every area he touched upon, and that he was convinced they would come true. This frame of mind and basic characteristic convinced his contemporaries that his vision was greater than theirs. And yet it seems to me that most of the major ideas of his time escaped him completely. But I cannot forget that his sovereign imagination did cause history to pause for a moment, that it forced certain harsh realities to submit to its law, and that it remains one of the basic givens of our national life.

Many have tried to define just who de Gaulle, the man, was. I saw him for the first time in Algiers, on December 3 or 4, 1943. I had arrived from London the night before, via Bristol and Gibraltar. My memory of Algiers in those days—an Algiers that "smelled of goats and jasmine"—is of a city behind the lines, a place for soldiers on leave where life was hectic but precious. I was received by General de Gaulle accompanied by Henry Frenay, the Commissioner of War Prisoners. My route to this office in the Villa des Glycines had been long and arduous, through the routes of Germany, France, and England, and here he was sitting across from me, with his strange head, too small for his tall body, his *condottiere* face well-scrubbed by the priests, his long legs tucked under the table, the man I had so often pictured in my mind. I took heart by thinking of Stendhal. No shadow of a doubt: it was de Gaulle all right. He was friendly enough. But his opening remark, ridiculous, was to say, half seriously and half jokingly, "I understand you arrived here on an English aircraft." As he spoke, his beautiful, slightly soft hand swayed to the rhythm of some unheard lullaby. He questioned me about the state of the Resistance, its methods and moods. And although his tone remained nonchalant, it hardened as soon as he came to the heart of the matter. In his eyes, it was vitally important that propaganda in the POW camps be maintained, and that prisoners who had escaped become involved in political activities. The return of a million and a half prisoners of war was going to pose serious problems that needed study without delay. He also felt that immediate steps should be taken to stop competing Resistance units from quarreling with one another and dispersing their energies. After their unification—a step he intended to bring about through the leadership of Michel Charette, who turned out to be his nephew—they would then, and only then, be sent money and weapons. Not before. What objection could I raise to the obvious rules of national discipline? I answered that however useful that discipline might be, the fact remained that the Resistance inside France worked according to its own laws and could not easily be reduced to the simple carrying out of orders emanating from the outside and that, regarding the various networks he was referring to, his instructions were simply not applicable. The meeting was over. He got up and shook my hand. Back in France almost three months later I was informed by Alexandre Parodi that I had, with the concurrence of Algiers, been named by the government-in-exile head of POWs, deportees, and refugees in the future administration. It was in this capacity that I participated in the first plenary session of the Free French Government, presided over by General de Gaulle, on August 27, 1944. I can still hear the monologue he delivered that day. I listened, I observed, I admired. From the experience of having lived through various historic moments, the memory of which tends all too quickly to fade and be forgotten, I have learned to treasure this kind of emotion. But I was twenty-seven years old, still full of enthusiasm, and with a certain propensity to see events larger than they really were. Then, too, there was good reason to be somewhat wide-eyed: it was the beginning of an era, and this was General de Gaulle.

I often wonder why it is that special moment did not bring me any closer to him from whom I learned such important lessons. Aside from one meeting granted in May or June 1945 to the directors of former prisoner-of-war organizations, fourteen years were to pass before I found myself again in the presence of General de Gaulle. There are times when I've regretted this long hiatus.

I was a friend of and minister in the cabinets of both Robert Schuman and Pierre Mendès France, two heads of government in the Fourth Republic who tried to infuse that period with both style and ideas. De Gaulle unquestionably had more style, perhaps fewer original ideas, but no one could speak the language of State as he could. Mendès France was consumed with a passion for being right. Schuman was prey to the same kind of scruples, except that with him it was always a fear of being wrong.

De Gaulle did not pose the problem in these terms. He existed.

His acts created him, and his conviction that he *was* France, that
he was the manifest expression of her truth, that he incarnated a
moment in some eternal destiny, moved me more than it annoyed
me. I have never found this conviction laughable or ridiculous.
The visceral, exclusive love he felt for France impelled de Gaulle
to take up arms against shadows. He was a direct political descen-
dant of Richelieu, though Pitt, Metternich, and Bismarck also in-
fluenced his thinking, and for him the Czar was still in power in
Moscow. The homeland was a mystical plot of earth, drawn by
the hand of God and inhabited by a people of workers and soldiers. Whenever this sacred plot of ground was in mortal danger,
this predestined land naturally secreted the required hero. This
time, he was the hero. Both his temperament and education led
him to view events as the personal adventure of the happy few
chosen to act, speak, and decide in the name of all.

I was never a Gaullist, at least in the way that, no matter what
period of the movement, one was supposed to be in order to
deserve that title. The special figure of the head of Free France
both seduced and chilled me. In my view, our resistance to the
Nazis inside France, and our constant contact with torture and
death, was quite different from the resistance carried out from
abroad, and I did not accord the latter the preeminence it presumed for itself. I questioned whether the word "resistance" was
really applicable to the combat carried on from London or Algiers, simply another episode in a traditional war. I admired that
handful of men who, with de Gaulle at their center, affirmed the
French presence on every front simultaneously, not the least of
which was the insolence of our Allies. But I felt different, and I
was proud of a fight whose glory, I felt, was being taken away
from the people—of whom I was one.

Be that as it may, de Gaulle-as-hypothesis, by becoming reality,
erased competing ones, and today it is that reality with which
historians will have to grapple. So it will be forgotten that the
Resistance was not born of him alone, and that it often grew
without him, as it will be forgotten that defenders other than de
Gaulle, legitimized by combat, would have come forth to fight for
and protect the rights of France, no matter what the course of
events had been. This said, it would be only fair to concede, to de

Gaulle and the Gaullist movement, during the period 1940–1944, what it did accomplish and what it was. That is the determinant role of a man who throws himself across the path of destiny, seizes it by the throat, forces it to change its path, and creates, by virtue of his forewarning and will, a new path for it to follow. No meaning beyond that is possible or warranted.

A meditative soldier, an unforgiving patriot, de Gaulle dared through an initial act of insubordination to turn his back on his own social class which, in the embarrassment of defeat at the hands of the Germans, had opted, as is often the case, to deal with its victors in its own self-interest. And what victors! But when the sons of the bourgeoisie proudly choose a military career, it tends to untie the bonds that link them to their background. The career soldier has no material possessions, disdains them and is proud of it. By vocation and by condition, he has to justify life by values other than profit. De Gaulle saw his mother weep over the French defeat of 1870, and he cured himself of that grief by breaking with the established order—not only his mother's but his own—as soon as that established order turned traitor. I was no stranger to that tradition. When my grandparents reminisced about the surrender of Sedan it was as though an old wound had been reopened. Disciples of Clemenceau, they accused the colonial expeditions of having diverted the attention of the French people away from the real problem, which was revenge against the Germans. At night we used to recite Victor Hugo's "Terrible Year." The victory of 1918 did not erase the stigmata of misfortune. One loved France, earth and flesh, with a love filled with pain and anguish. God, how we suffered when she suffered! And we were just as concerned about the happy times, for fear they might allow us to forget the others.

Molded by this old-school mentality, de Gaulle was closer to the Napoleonic soldiers of the Year II and the recruits of 1914 than he was to the bourgeois of his own generation. From that anachronism stemmed his propensity to speak like a visionary. His backwardness became advance. By removing himself from his inheritance, he met the people. Neither he nor they ever fully parted company.

Thus, it is from that perspective that the Republic under de

Gaulle should be viewed, if one is to understand it. Reading Pierre
Viansson-Ponté's recent history of that era gives me the chance to
express my own views on the subject.

SUNDAY, SEPTEMBER 19

The other day I wrote that the person of General de Gaulle will
ultimately count more than what he has left behind. Having read
the second volume of Pierre Viansson-Ponté's *The Gaullist Republic*, I learn that the author largely shares my views. Clearly, the
hero whose history he is relating fascinates him. But that fascina-
tion ceases as soon as he shifts his focus from the actor to the acts.
Thus, whether in the realm of Franco-German politics, of economic policies, or social policies, what seems to stand out above
all is vanity. And if he notes that the referendum electing the
president of the Republic by universal suffrage marks a break
with parliamentary democracy and announces the arrival of a new
regime, one senses that in his eyes the history of the Gaullist
Republic forms a self-contained aside, which should not be confused with the history of the Fifth Republic.

In the flood of works dedicated to General de Gaulle—which
since his death has grown to such a degree that it leaves far behind the standard cluster of best-sellers including Jesus, Marx,
and Lenin—Viansson-Ponté's work stands out for its clarification
and explanation of the facts, and for an internal logic which the
writers of memoirs have too often neglected. The one notable
exception, it should be said, is de Gaulle's own *Memoirs*, which
deserve a critical supplement. *The Gaullist Republic* is the work of
an historian who remains a journalist.

We all know how difficult it is for any writer preoccupied with
daily deadlines to adapt to the rhythm of a longer period, as we
know the dangers he runs when writing about events as they
happen while trying to place them in their proper perspective.
Viansson-Ponté does not escape the problem. I believe, for instance, that he underestimates the full significance, which I deem

decisive, of France's withdrawal from NATO and its return to the sources of our foreign policy. He fails to realize the importance of France's refusal to join the Common Market at a time when Germany had not yet regained its full strength. And he yields more than he should to the temptation of judging the Left's opposition by fashionable, rather than reasoned, criteria.

To turn one's back on Gaullism was not the same thing as turning one's back on one's own time. The Left was not, as Viansson-Ponté would have it, simply that tired old thing, peopled with old fogeys futilely reciting their beads in front of dusty altars. After 1958, it took a full four years for a new generation to evolve new parties and clubs. In 1962 and 1963 there were a great many conflicting and contradictory initiatives, but no lack of fresh ideas. The circumstances were fast approaching which would channel these tendencies into a vast assembly. The coherence of the movement which, from 1965 to the present day—and despite the setback of '68—prepares and announces the shift of the majority in France, was not readily apparent.

All of a sudden, the decline of the Gaullist Republic can be explained by a growing incompatibility between de Gaulle and the French people, which greatly tends to minimize its real significance.

I have no quarrel with any historian's preferences, as long as they are not based on any preconceived system or mold. False objectivity is the worst way of choosing and the surest way of boring the reader. Viansson-Ponté chooses, gives his opinion, approves or disapproves, and never bores, except when he must lead the uninformed reader into the labyrinthine network of legislative or constitutional processes, or follow the intricate intrigues of the high command. I savor his freedom of time and style.

What a task he has undertaken in separating the real from the counterfeit, of putting the jigsaw puzzle of history into its proper place and perspective! He knows how to linger on a setting, a scene, or a portrait when the subjects interest him, and in such moments he is at his best.

I will not say that Viansson-Ponté chose the wrong subject when he focused on the Gaullist era, but at the very moment when this period was at its height, one can see the author observing with meticulous and impassioned attention the imperceptible movements which not long thereafter were to dictate the future course of events. These pages are among the best in a work which is of a remarkably high quality throughout. The conflict, and what must be termed the break between de Gaulle and Pompidou, lend both chapters three and five—"The Disappearance" and "The Last Hurrah"—an element of high drama. We are here listening to a silence broken by a few subtle words, a watchful, worried silence, and—did I make it up?—a painful silence.

Let me add that when he is dealing with the end of that reign, the journalist brings to the historian a solid body of unpublished source material which the latter uses with great effectiveness. "In a century or two history will accord de Gaulle the place he truly merits and we will then learn whether the man of day-before-yesterday was also the man of day-after tomorrow." That remark by Viansson-Ponté in no way detracts from his obvious desire to enter a debate of that basic question without any delay. Nor does he doubt any more than I do that in a century or two France will remember this exceptional personage whom it simultaneously misunderstood, fawned upon, endured, loved, rejected, and whom it now looks upon as among the greatest heroes of its entire history. But as to the question he raises: will the eleven years of the Gaullist era have a lasting effect on the future, his book answers, perhaps without the author's wanting to, that he does not think so.

To be sure, "nothing any longer is, nothing can any longer be, nothing will any longer be quite the same as it was before," and the time of de Gaulle was a time of rupture and disagreement. But if institutions did change through him, and methods and technology without him, the manners and morals of the French people changed against him. As for the economic structures, they remained essentially as they were before he came to power.

De Gaulle bequeathed to France a new set of political rules. That is important. Does anyone believe that legalization of the referendum, of the election of the president by direct vote, and the fact of majority rule had any deep or lasting effect on the French people? I very much doubt it. For those who think as I do that political life—however active, diverse, or unexpected it may

be—is dictated by the economic relationships among various social groups and entities, and mainly by those related to production, that is not enough. For millions of French people looking for
a decent job and housing, chained to an implacable socio-eco-
nomic system, Viansson-Ponté could have written an entirely different story. The quality of life of the French was dependent on
other masters than Charles de Gaulle. These men in power do not
like to be upset or inconvenienced. When, in April 1969, the
powers that be were threatened, they didn't shilly-shally to get rid
of the problem. Valéry Giscard d'Estaing looked up and saw the
Big Bosses with their thumbs pointing down, and finished off the
colossus.

FRIDAY, SEPTEMBER 24

How many of my contemporaries could sum up thirty years of
their lives with a "De Gaulle and me!" I refuse to fall into this
trap. I saw and sensed a France in need of no one. But one has to
yield to popular opinion, and my "De Gaulle and me" will doubtless endure as the most often quoted expression used to describe
a long moment in our national history.

Like most of the French at the time, I did not hear the call on
June 18, 1940. There were a number of good reasons why a man of
my generation was in no position to hear Radio London that mo-
mentous day. War had torn two million men from their homes,
and the disaster of defeat had at that time hurled five or six million civilians onto the roads of France, trying to keep one step
ahead of the advancing German armies.

So it was that on June 18, 1940, I reached the town of Bruyères,
in the Vosges mountains, having been pushed there on a wheeled
stretcher. Wounded near Verdun, I had wandered about in the
maelstrom of the pocket in Lorraine which the German armies
were reducing hour by hour. I had been taken from one hospital
to another, seven in all, before I had finally been granted a mat-
tress in Vittel, and some perfunctory medical help by a nurse. As

soon as I had crossed the moving line of what was really no longer "the front," I had come upon the caterpillar-like wave of fleeing civilians whose haste to reach some mythical haven made them jostle one another and argue over their places in the line, so much so that the line seemed not to move at all. From time to time German or Italian planes would appear in the cloudless sky—for it was one of the most beautiful summers we had seen in a long time—peel off, and dive on that crowd, which would run for cover in the neighboring fields or in the ditches beside the road, while the pilots would amuse themselves by machine-gunning at will this hapless game that war had created. After they had left, the snake would re-form and wind its way slowly onward. In those days portable radios were unknown, and I don't remember seeing any crystal set or hearing its crackling noises. Besides, no one spoke except in case of extreme necessity. Thus, as everyone else, I was unaware of the BBC. The Germans reached Bruyères. I was a prisoner of war. At the hospital, civilians and soldiers had but one thought in mind—for an armistice that would allow them to return home.

I watched that world crumble. France had been so quickly and so completely defeated that it seemed pointless to continue fighting. All that remained was a captive army and a dog-tired civilian population. I had lived through the phony war of 1939–40 and felt totally removed from a system and order for which I felt nothing but disdain. What I had seen of the declining days of the Third Republic had taught me that there was nothing about it I could like or relate to. Nothing to hope for, either. It was feeding upon its own decadence, and derived from that source enough strength to believe itself eternal. The day would come, however, I thought, when it would fall without being pushed, of its own weight— exhausted, ruined, emptied. But when? Its outlines were such that it was hard to get a real grip on it. It had escaped from the coup d'état in 1934 because its opponents of the extreme Right so closely resembled the people in power. Class lines are as important as family ties. The Leaguers of February 6 who had stopped in front of the iron gates of the Palais Bourbon, when the only obstacle between them and the seizure of power were those iron bars, had somehow understood that there were some things you didn't do within the confines of your own family. They had shouted, "Down with the damn thieves!" but their moral conscience had not snuffed out their political conscience. After all, the "thieves" had stolen from them no more than a modicum of reputation and small change. Certainly not enough to overturn the whole system. They contented themselves with exchanging Edouard Daladier for Paul Doumergue as prime minister. La Rocque had furled his flags, Maurras had brandished his kitchen knife. And that was called a revolution! The holy union had buried its differences and joined forces against the other threat, the real one, the one brewing in the factories and workers' suburbs, among those who were banding together because they realized that it was they who had been taken—their bread had been taken, their freedom, and soon their precarious peace would be stolen, too—and that knowledge was fueling their increasing anger. In those days I belonged to neither group. The former—those in power—because I knew them all too well; the latter, because I didn't know them at all. But in the absence of knowledge, I was beginning to sense the truth. Unaware that the current regime was actually in its death throes, I thought that France was condemned to be forever subjected to the endless round of ministerial crises, pompous rhetoric, and the mediocrity of its political leaders, and I was alarmed and upset about this dead period in the life of a great people.

Then war broke out. I had seen the officers of my regiment who in May would die bravely, play poker in April without worrying about the soldiers under their command who were paying dearly for the Popular Front. They did not like Germany, but they did admire the Third Reich. They loved France, but not the French people. They were nothing more or less than the residue of a society that had outlived its time and was rushing down the path of its own destruction.

It was at Lunéville, at the camp where we were waiting to be shipped off to Germany, that I heard the name Charles de Gaulle spoken for the first time. A friend of mine, an aspiring young actor who was also an amateur astrologer, told me that an unknown general whose name he told me had taken refuge in London and refused to admit that the Germans had won the war. "What a beautiful name for a beautiful story!" he exclaimed. I agreed, and dreamed of the future.

I ended up in Stalag 1515 in Schaala, in Thuringia. There were two hundred and fifty of us there. We had been labeled intellectuals, doubtless because among us there was a high proportion of priests, Jews, teachers, commissioned officers, lawyers, and Spanish Republicans. Our days as POWs were spent bundling hay and straw, building a road, and repairing railroads. The flattering designation "intellectual" did not increase our productivity to any marked degree. Cut off from the rest of the world, we set about building our own society. I discovered that my fellow Frenchmen were primarily cooks and jurists. One of them, a notary public, drew up in October 1940 the statutes of the future war veterans' association of the Schaala Stalag. Another, a Jesuit priest, cooked up some extraordinary gourmet dishes using shoe polish for fat. A school teacher was in charge of parceling out among the inmates the tons of potatoes that we managed to pilfer from the enemy and hide beneath the floorboards of our prison barracks. In spite of the scarcity of books, clothing, and calories, neither our souls nor our bodies lacked the necessities. The order of the early months had been based on the domination of the knife and the law of the jungle. That order was soon swept away and the knife became, by its use as an instrument to cut the loaf of bread into precisely equal portions, the instrument of justice. Paris had scarcely scraped away the education I had received at my local school down to its raw finish; I had traveled very little, but it is fair to say that I learned far more from this introverted society than I had from all the teachers of my adolescent years. I would not go so far as to say that we had built the ideal society. But I have never known a more well-balanced community than that POW camp. The winter was harsh; Hitler controlled the whole of Europe. Defeated soldiers, anonymous workers, we were captives in the center of his empire. He promised us a thousand years of a new regime. What had become of our friends, of our youth and its world weariness of times gone by? Our destinies were governed by powers black and red—Hitler, Mussolini, France, and, farther away, Stalin. In order to live, to find the courage to live and keep on going, we had to relearn some simple things. Freedom, for example.

I escaped from the stalag. Six hundred kilometers and twenty-two days of walking brought us—for there were two of us, another

POW and I—to the Swiss border, or more precisely to a solid prison
in South Württemberg. Along the way we had been hungry and
dreamt of bread, milk, honey. In my cell, I dreamt of the tall grass
along the Charente River where my father went fishing for chub,
and of the reflections of the clear sky in the still water. It seemed
that my entire life would not suffice to see and find in this familiar
circle a certain lost truth. But at the Schaala POW camp the voice of
General de Gaulle had reached our ears. Old country, old adventure, old future. That voice announced the springtime with a new
love. It called for a renewed effort on our part, and the will to
resist. I had no problem understanding that what that voice was
saying to me, as it was saying to the others, was as simple as
bread, milk, and honey.

That is why I, who have never been a Gaullist, have always
refused to be an anti-Gaullist.

FRIDAY, OCTOBER 15

A passage from the Goncourt brothers' *Journals* reminds me that
the Society for the Protection of Animals was founded in 1845.
Three years before the abolition of slavery.

SUNDAY, OCTOBER 17

Often when I contemplate nature I experience moments of happiness that compel me to exclaim this is the most beautiful place in
the world. The earth, our friend, lavishes its marvels upon us. I
have gazed upon it repeatedly ever since childhood without ex-
hausting the astonishment which the contemplation of beauty can
arouse, and which somehow makes you vaguely want to thank
someone. That is what just happened to me in Trébeurden, a
Breton village overlooking the sea. Actually, very little happened.

From the hills of Bihit I gazed out at the curving shore, the play of the islands and water, the slow round of hours in the sky. At sunset I walked to the little strait that separates the mainland from Milhaud Island. At each step the horizon changed. At times a fishing village came into view, with its upright sails and its boats pulled up on the shore; at others, the view opened to reveal a spit of land with its unusual architecture of gleaming granite surrounded by the ocean. I sat down and waited for night to fall, breathing in the odor of seaweed and iodine the way one drinks, listening to the tide rush to shore. An equinoctial light such as can only be found in Brittany, in the tread of its tempests, colored the countryside from Beg An Fry to Ploumanach. It was so clear that I could make out, a full league away, the break in the land where the estuary lay. I let the elements dictate my train of thought. Nearby, a cormorant slept on a pink rock. The wind gently lifted its wing.

MONDAY, NOVEMBER 15

Have I sufficiently looked at the portrait of the earth? Whenever I can carve out an evening from my Parisian obligations, I open my atlases—I have at least three or four—and compare the various colors and typefaces that make the same country seem so different, and I make up all kinds of itineraries. My real voyages have always confirmed the intuitions I had about them before I went to the country, except for India, whose lovely triangular design in the atlases flatters her. In short, I love to read a country's fate in the map of the world. Minor game, major game, depending on the choice. From page to page before my eyes parade the countries which, tomorrow or the day after, will be candidates as world powers: Brazil, Germany, Japan, Iran, Nigeria. As for Canada, what will remain once its immense natural resources have become exhausted? Indonesia is a century or two behind. Argentina will find its way if the people have a chance to guide it. Zaire will suffer for a long time to overcome the consequences of colonial exploitation. India loves death too much. No historian I know has ever adequately explained the basic reasons that move a people to become great or why it ceases to be so, nor the impetus, positive or negative, that lies behind a country's growth or decline. I can see the motives of small countries, overpopulated, geographically restricted, their destinies inextricably bound to their land and who derive their energies from hardship: Israel, Holland, Vietnam, Cuba. Less obvious are the reasons that dictate major powers either to dominate history or refrain from so doing. As we know, those who possess large populations, plenty of space, oil, water, metals and minerals, belong to the circle of strong nations. But something else is needed to reach the center. The human species obeys laws that derive from chemistry. Not that I deny the role of the individual, of ideas, of symbols; but they merely fix what is already there. Like the volcanologist Haroun Tazieff, bent over a volcano, I observe the places where the earth, in its depths, is at the melting point, and from its boiling, seething state try to extract the formula that will explain it.

So it is that tonight I have my maps spread out in front of me, opened to Siberia. I will not exclaim, as Salvador Dali once did at the Perpignan train station: "It is obvious that Siberia is the center of the universe," but I do know for sure that a new world will arise there.

My interest is long-standing. Siberia casts a veritable spell on my mind. It is one of those very decorative regions of the world, such as the Mediterranean or the Sunda Isles. Siberia, a captive within the land mass of the Asian continent, is less apparent at first glance. But when you look at it from the opposite viewpoint, that is, from the North Pole, it is impossible not to be overwhelmed by the immense shoreline that unfolds along the length of the Arctic Ocean, whose shape resembles an open wing covering half the globe. And besides, I like its name, like Borneo, Abyssinia, and Labrador, without knowing exactly why. This power of syllables will seem a waste of time to many, but it is rare that poetry does not uncover earthy powers. And finally, at home Siberia was referred to so often as a mysterious and formidable country—the planet Siberia, colder than cold, with its snow, its sleighs, its wolves, its bears, and its rough and ready men with their frosted breath—that if someone had asked me, What country would you choose if you could pick only one? I would surely have chosen Siberia. Literature reinforced my thinking, starting with Michael Strogoff, before Dostoevsky peopled my dreams of space and solitude. In the Charente, where I come from, people refer to a slope that faces north, or a field beneath which deep waters lie, as Siberia. Along the route from Auxerre to Clamecy, which I know very well, natives call the low-lying area that you travel through just before you reach Courson-les-Carrières, Siberia. In winter one is sure to run into fog and frost, and during the autumn equinox one has to be especially careful when driving through the area. In fact, the other day as I was driving back to Paris from Château-Chinon, I skidded "in Siberia," at the spot where the lowest point in the road makes a sharp curve, and after crossing the soft shoulder only managed to stop the car when the front end was stuck in a hedge. Happy misfortune! The air was so fresh, so sparkling, the sky so vast above, that for a long time I paced back and forth in all directions, my hands in my pockets and the collar of my coat turned up, before it occurred to me that I ought to call a garage for help. The memory of Siberia—the real one—came back to me then, for ten years before I had gazed down on its vast, flat landscape from a plane that was taking me from Moscow to Irkutsk. I had spent hours gazing through the double-glassed window, which at times took on every color of the rainbow, with emphasis on the purple, looking down at the tracks and signs of that earth where the eye slides across the landscape to the far horizon and perceives no end, as one does at sea. Here and there the edge of a forest, a lake, a road in the steppes, a river drew some simple geometric figures. After a while a magnetic spell wove itself around me, absorbing my every thought. So total was my concentration that I could feel myself dissolving and becoming part of some limitless being, and I found myself repeating the line from Tennyson I had read years before and which now seemed clear to me: "It is the limpid of the limpid, the certain of the certain, the strange of the strange, totally beyond language—where death is an almost laughable impossibility." When night fell, I could no longer tell where earth ended and sky began. The rising mist blurred the horizon. One imagined rather than saw a land drenched with water, vast swamps that the fires of the setting sun turned rosy, unless it was the reflection of dusk on a cloud. As we landed at Irkutsk, all I saw of Lake Baikal was a black hole.

I was on my way to China. In Peking, people talked about Siberia as they would have about a trial. In a show of ill temper, they spoke in acid tones, blaming Russia for breaking treaties and violating borders. When they uttered the word "revisionist," you could tell they were thinking rather of "revenge." Who could help casting a covetous eye on that territory that is larger than all of North America, whose population is less than thirty million souls? Japan feigns indifference but secretly mourns the loss of Manchuria. The United States would love to see that Lomonosov's prediction, through the intermediary of some third party, was proved wrong: "The power of Russia," he claimed, "will ultimately stem from Siberia." While Russia itself, the legitimate owner of the area, makes plans to develop it in all kinds of ways. It was not that long ago that the Tungus gave up their tools and weapons made of flint and bone. Now my various atlases are filled with more signs and symbols than space allows to show: gold, copper, nickel, uranium, lead, tungsten, coal, manganese, diamonds; or dams, industrial complexes, pipelines, be they for gas or oil, oil, oil. The subsoil of Siberia holds 80 percent of the world's reserves of energy. Places which a few years ago were mere hamlets, or empty space, have overnight mushroomed into major cities. Remember their names: Tiumen, Bratsk, Ust-Ilymsk, Samotlor, Medvezkye. Novosibirsk boasts more than a million and a half residents. Akademgorodok aligns its streets straight, parallel to one another, to meet at science's infinity.

Brezhnev, breaking with the diplomacy of suspicion, invites the Western nations to invest their capital and technological knowhow in exchange for raw materials. It's a race, the match of the twenty-first century. Peace and war always occur in the same place. I see them advancing, both, toward a rendezvous at which the fate of the universe will be decided. An amazing adventure, as yet scarcely begun—and meanwhile mosquitoes rule the summer and ice the winter in the silence of the tundra.

1972

TUESDAY, FEBRUARY 8

An article by Vercors appears in *Le Monde*, entitled "Hitler Won the War." A cry of anger and disgust in order to denounce the repression being visited upon the Czechoslovakian Communists guilty of not following Mr. Husak's line of political thought. In the next column of the same newspaper Jiri Pelikan, former head of the Czech Communist Youth Movement, former member of the Central Committee of the Czechoslovakian Communist Party, former chairman of the Foreign Affairs Commission of Parliament, who emigrated to Italy after the Russian intervention, announces "we intend to instigate a trial," and the accused "are Dubcek, Smrkovski, Kriegel and their 1968 policies." He opportunely points out that Husak himself was sentenced by Novotny in 1954, "as an enemy of the Republic who, under the guise of nationalistic slogans, wanted to restore capitalism with the help and collaboration of reactionary émigrés." *Sic transit.* We are back again in Prague, and its springtime without a summer.

What can be done? "We all have strength enough to endure other people's misfortunes," La Rochefoucauld once remarked. Are we going to leave these men—who are now gagged if not bound—defenseless, men whose only guilt is having dreamt of a

socialism in their own country that the current situation would
not allow? International etiquette calls for silence. Oblivion is a
pleasant accomplice. The misfortune of others is always so far
away. And yet a point of light in the darkness: the French Socialist
Party did react. Let it continue to do so, ever more vigorously;
may it take the initiative in calling for a solemn, urgent protest.
No walls will be thick enough to stifle its voice.

MONDAY, FEBRUARY 21

I shall add nothing to the political analyses appearing virtually
everywhere about the "meeting of the century," that between
Nixon and Mao, except to note that our generation, with its taste
for historical hyperbole, will have experienced many "meetings of
the century" in less than twenty-five years. While I am perfectly
willing to acknowledge its importance, I am somewhat more hesi-
tant about assessing its possible ramifications.

Is it essentially a tactical maneuver on the part of China, a
means of ending its isolation vis-à-vis a Russia that it fears? Or is
it rather, on the part of the United States, a way of telling Brezhnev that the balance of world power is not necessarily at the end
of a red telephone? Or does it relate to the post-Yalta conference
period, which announced the reappearance of Germany and Japan
on the world scene? Or is it a meeting of two good businessmen
working out a mutually favorable deal? Or could it simply be that
two world leaders were aware of what was incumbent on men in
their positions? All these possible explanations intertwine and
complement one another. There are doubtless others of which I
am unaware.

The Americans, I fear, have not finished paying for the major
political blunder they committed in 1946 during General Mar-
shall's unsuccessful effort at mediation in China. It is true that at
about the same time Stalin committed the same error. "In our
opinion," he cabled Mao, "the revolt in China cannot be successful, and therefore an accommodation with Chiang Kai-shek must
be sought." And so saying, he stopped supplying arms to the

Communists in Yenan who were fighting the nationalists in Chungking.

I went to China in January 1961. I spent about a month there, traveling the classic itinerary from Shenyan to Canton that the Chinese authorities reserve for their guests. I think I was the first Frenchman—the atomic physicist Pierre Joliot-Curie may have preceded me—to visit Mao in his home outside Hangchow. At my Peking hotel, a formal delegation (there is nothing more imperious than extreme politeness) had woken me at five in the morning to inform me with great reticence that Chairman Mao (Ah, those metallic syllables!) was expecting me.

At dawn, a plane filled with parcels had taken off with me and my inseparable companions—the interpreter and the Party secretary—and carried us throughout the entire morning over a goodly portion of Central China, a country turned in upon itself, an earth cultivated from one end to the other, a crowded world criss-crossed by immense indentations where the rivers—those transporters of alluvial soil—flow. Mao Tse-tung's house was a few kilometers from Hangchow. A lake, a secondary road, two stone stacks, a driveway flanked by trees, and we were there.

Our Cadillac (war booty taken from Chiang Kai-shek twelve years before) stopped. I almost bumped into my host as I got out of the car, for he was waiting for me on his doorstep, his hand outstretched. Actually, I had run into Chairman Mao throughout the preceding three weeks, everywhere I went. In marble, bronze, copper, ivory; in silk, cotton, and paper; in statues, photos, posters, stamps, ashtrays, and umbrella handles; in the guise of miner, mechanic, gardener, factory worker, thinker, swimmer. Less physiognomist than some, however, I didn't recognize him right away. Of medium height, wearing a gray Sun Yat-sen uniform, one shoulder lower than the other, slow of step, his face round and peaceful, short of breath and soft of voice, he was at that time sixty-seven.

In my book China Defied, I gave a full account of our meeting, with its setting, its ritual, the light tobacco Mao smoked, his small, well-tended hands, his laugh, and above all the serenity that pervaded the room. By comparison, what a bunch of marionettes our Western dictators are, with their flashy uniforms, their strident voices, their theatricality. Mao spent two-thirds of the year away from the capital, the army, the party, the administration. He raised chrysanthemums, of which there are 250 varieties, and at times bred them. He wrote, by which I mean that he painted letters and signs on lovely scrolls with the jealous care of his country's artists (I still have the one he gave me, in my office in Paris).

He also wrote other things, as we all know.

What has he become today? This week's edition of *Le Nouvel Observateur* contains an article on him by his old friend, the American Edgar Snow. It seems that Mao, though he is keeping a somewhat more watchful eye on Peking than in the past, continues to spend a good deal of time growing vegetables in his little plot of ground and studying and recording his agricultural experiments. He is also worried about the cult of personality. Among all the many superlative titles bestowed upon him, the only one he wants to acknowledge is that of teacher, "because, even before he became a Communist, he was a primary grade school teacher in Changsha." Realism of intransigence. In earlier times, he promised his people to chase the American lackeys from the continent of Asia, "their tail between their legs." And here he is welcoming Nixon, the very incarnation of monopoly capitalism.

Eleven years after my meeting with him, I picture the old man in his garden. A word from him moves me and sets me dreaming. "He said to me," Snow writes, "that he wasn't a very complicated person, but on the contrary really quite simple, that he was merely a solitary monk traveling through the world beneath an umbrella full of holes."

MONDAY, MARCH 6

> By slow degrees I caught the ear of kings
> And soon they whispered, Hark, the oracle sings.
> —*Athalie*, Act III, Scene 3

What an amazing document. I refer to the interview that André Malraux recently granted Jean Mauriac, which was widely disseminated by the French Press Agency. The author of *Anti-Memoirs* offers us his own transcription of the dialogue that might have taken place between Mao and de Gaulle if the two had ever met. "The shorthand," he assures us, "would have been Shakespearean."

So saying, our soothsayer changes into a stenographer. "Well now," says de Gaulle to Mao, "when you were China there wasn't any China." To which Mao answers, "When you were France, there wasn't any France." And he goes on: "I made the Long March. What did you do?" And de Gaulle replies, "I was in the Resistance." At that point in the article I was still able to contain my laughter until the following sentence. "Mao, that emperor of bronze, thought that de Gaulle was something out of the *Iliad*." All right for the *Iliad*, but bronze?

Fontenelle relates that Demosthenes found fault with the Delphic oracles, which he claimed followed too closely the policies and interests of Philip of Macedon. I will not go so far as to accuse Malraux of "Philipizing" (the neologism is Demosthenes') the messages from the other side of the grave, and I am willing to admit that the high priestess of Apollo at Delphi is indeed obscure, since such is the Pythian condition. I therefore leave it to my readers to translate into the language of their choice the following sentences, culled by the pious Jean Mauriac from the mouth of the inspired latter-day oracle: "Mao said to us, we have no appointed successor. If there is one, he will be a Maoist." Or: "Stalin told me, 'People thought that we would be saved by the European revolution, but in fact it is the European revolution that will be saved by the Red Army.'" Or: "The error is to think that the Long March was as if we went to see Stalin with bank robbery in mind."

Most intriguing is the "when you were China—when you were France," which is a way of writing history that I had thought had become impossible since Marx. Thus, in the eyes of André Malraux, France did not exist at the time of de Gaulle. Absorbed through consubstantiation, melted into the real person of its leader. One can guess how the theological explanation prepares the return in full force of the old myths.

It is so easy, and so tempting, to expel a people from its own

historical adventure by reducing its work and struggle to the lin-
ear tale of the births and deaths of kings, the marriages of princes
and princesses, and the dates of major battles. An important
leader arrives on the scene, and everything begins and ends with
him. A dubious over-simplification that obviates the necessity of
seeking out the real laws which make human society move and
change. I believe in the importance of de Gaulle, not in his necessity. A given situation produced him, not the opposite. Predesti-
nation is not part of history. Taken even further, no people needs
anyone to become what it is.

I would perhaps not even have bothered to comment on the
interview in question were it not for the fact that this morning I
learned from L'Express that Malraux is currently shooting, with
Claude Santelli as director, a mammoth ten-hour television program—"the most ambitious undertaking of its kind in the history
of the medium"—entitled "The Legend of the Century." The author of the article in L'Express ecstatically describes the venture as
"the most fascinating of guides," "an extraordinary visionary,"
and "a fantastic carousel in time." Malraux parades through the
film in the familiar company of Robespierre and Gandhi, Lenin
and Saint Bernard, Michelet and Alexander the Great, not to mention of course the subtle Bronze Emperor referred to above.

For men of my age who read Man's Fate and Man's Hope in their
twenties and did not reread them when in their forties, there remains a certain image of Malraux, despite his more recent work,
which ranges from unfortunate to abysmal. Those earlier works
were, for us, masterpieces. But then came The Royal Way, which
I couldn't help laying aside. A dogged piety made me forget
my momentary ill-humor, as it made me temper my dismay on
reading Museum Without Walls, the disbelief caused by his Anti-
Memoirs, and the boredom experienced when I read The Fallen
Oaks. My reserves of belief are not exhausted, however, since I
still keep going back to him. After all his master, Barrès, who was
also Aragon's, published more than his fair share of dull and
useless books. The fact also remains that Malraux is an incom-
parable storyteller, whom I had the good fortune to hear at Crans-
sur-Sierre one warm, pleasant evening in June 1956. In the light of
the flickering candles in the Swiss chalet where we dined that

night, you could hear the sound of the Mongol horses striking the ground at Samarkand.

Speaking of which, I wonder if Malraux does not belong to that group of writers whose genius is best expressed in conversation and disappears on the written page. Chamfort's contemporaries thought him the best among them. Chateaubriand reserved this honor for Joubert; Léon Daudet dazzled his listeners. But once they could no longer impress with the spoken word, what happened to their special role and position? In 1933 our Malraux, with his syncopated rhythm of the cinema which was already into "talkies," and his novel-like reporting, was very much in tune with the times. But then the person eclipsed the work; all we could see after a certain point was the man, and we mistook one for the other. A regrettable mistake.

THURSDAY, MARCH 16—JERUSALEM

Golda Meir is seventy-four and looks like her photographs: a large woman with piercing eyes, simply dressed in a gray and black dress, with her hair in a tight chignon at the base of her neck. She talks, smokes, grows excited, and ends up keeping us with her for two hours instead of the three-quarters of an hour that protocol requires. "The day when history will write its final book," said David Ben-Gurion referring to her, "the world will know that a Jewess allowed the Jewish state to come into being." When we saw her she had just returned from a short visit to the United States, where she had raised fifty million dollars from major bankers of the Jewish community, most of whom were apathetic to the cause of Israel but were unable to resist the blandishments of that low, slightly hoarse voice that kept telling them over and over again, "We will fight, and we will continue to fight! It's not up to you to decide whether or not we ought to keep on fighting, but simply who will win that fight."

She had a long, militant past on which to draw when she made such pronouncements. An immigrant from the Ukraine, at the age of seventeen she had raised money in the streets of Denver, Colorado, for the victims of the pogroms. In Jerusalem, for years her house was one of the focal points for the Jewish underground movement. And it was she who, on November 29, 1947, when word arrived that the United Nations had voted in favor of the division of Palestine, had shouted to the worried crowd gathered in front of the Jewish Agency: "For two thousand years we've been waiting for our deliverance. Now that it's here, good luck, fellow-Jews!"

For the French Socialists she is receiving, and whose thoughts she tries to guess—the Israeli press, much given to exaggeration, blew up a statement I had made voicing concern about the fate of the Palestinian Arabs—she suddenly adopts a peremptory tone. "France is always in the forefront of those who are against us," she throws out, as though we were responsible for the acts of our government. To the classic matters of dispute she adds a new reproach: France is the only one of the six major powers to stand in the way of an agreement between Israel and the Common Market about the importation of fruits and vegetables.

"What do the people in France think?" she asks. "Peace is more important to us than victory. One more victory won't give Israel what she lacks. Every soldier who falls in combat is an unwritten poem, an unfinished piece of music, a thought unborn, a world disappeared. But a peace that means the destruction of our state, the physical liquidation of our people, never!"

Abba Eban, the minister of foreign affairs in whose house we were spending the evening, punctuated her remarks as though adding emphasis by saying, "No thanks!"

These were the "old guard" of the Israeli State, and one cannot recall them without a mixture of tenderness, admiration, and irritation. They constituted a kind of Sanhedrin which, in the last resort, understands the choices that have to be made. At odds with the political majority, Ben-Gurion, who is now eighty-six years old, and divides his time between writing the second volume of his memoirs and working three hours a day on the kibbutz in the Negev where he lives, is consulted on key issues and decisions. Ten years ago they referred to Golda as "getting on in years." Today she is ageless, she personifies the will to live of a people with a solid appetite for survival.

In her kitchen, which doubles as a living room, her hospitality reveals itself in the inexhaustible supply of coffee which she serves to her guests from the huge coffeepot permanently on the stove. Chain-smoking, she presses both coffee and little cakes on her friends with the same insistence with which she urges them to act. "For the adolescents of this new race of Jews, she had been the earth mother of the Old Testament," wrote Lapierre and Collins in their book *O Jerusalem.*

The mother of her people, that is it in a nutshell. She has their bluntness and their affection. To those who see and hear her talk, she gives the feeling that she is bearing a thousand-year-old child, a child so healthy that she is bursting with pride over it, and yet one so fragile that she would use the last ounce of strength at her disposal to protect it. In that ardent mouth, the word "peace" rings clear and true. "Israel's situation hasn't really changed since we won the Six-Day War," she says. "Nor will it ever change until we work out a fair and durable arrangement with our neighbors in the Middle East."

But that is as much as she will tell us about her precise intentions, about what she means when she refers to borders that are "safe and recognized." All we know is that she remains that "young girl who would not walk across the village square in a white dress," because of the people on the far side she knew would stare at her with reproach, and that she will not rest until she is certain that the girls of her country can wear whatever they like.

SATURDAY, MARCH 18

Dinner with Yigal Allon, the victor of the war for independence, in his kibbutz on the banks of Lake Galilee. At present, Allon is vice premier, and minister of education. As a possible successor to Golda Meir, he is considered on a par with Moshe Dayan just slightly behind Pinhas Sapir, the minister of finance who is highly respected by the old guard. Of all the Israeli leaders we have met, he is the only one to deal with specifics rather than generalities when discussing the issue of the Arab-Israeli conflict. The others explain with great firmness that they do not demand annexation of the Arab territories, but simply an adjustment of the borders; that they do not recognize the necessity for a separate Palestinian State, but consent to a special status for Trans-Jordan; they are in favor of direct negotiations, but have no objections to negotiating through an acceptable intermediary. For visitors like ourselves, who are not asking for any state secrets, their generalities are, to say the least, frustrating.

Yigal Allon's plan: a demilitarized Trans-Jordan, linked to Hussein's kingdom by Jericho; Israeli military posts along the Jordanian frontier; a new border to be drawn between Israel and Jordan, some points of which would be sensitive politically, but not many; Jordanian sovereignty over the holy Moslem places, accessible to the Arabs via an extraterritorial route; separate accords regarding both the Suez and Sharm-el-Sheikh. At first, this plan was rejected both by the doves and the hawks of both camps. Everything suggests, however—including the recent and much-attacked speech by the king of Jordan—that the plan is not far from being implemented.

MONDAY, MARCH 27

Before leaving for Israel, I gave a press conference at the Salle des Agriculteurs, to advise French opinion makers as to our position vis-à-vis the evolving political situation in Czechoslovakia. I stressed the point that the French Socialist Party felt a solidarity with all those anywhere in the world who were the victims of arbitrary rule or injustice, torture or exile. I cited the cases of Angela Davis, the Jews in Soviet Russia, the democrats of Spain and Greece; I made mention of the massive purges in Indonesia, the tragedy of the Bengalis. I could have gone on at great lengths on the subject. But since I had also cited the case of "the Palestinians in search of a country," the minute I landed in Tel-Aviv I was greeted by an avalanche of abuse on the part of the Israeli press. It ranged from irony ("Mr. Mitterand is easily moved to shed tears") to irritation ("Mr. Mitterand should learn to stay away from things that are no concern of his"), with a bit of nostalgia thrown in for good measure ("How the French Socialist Party has changed!").

Golda Meir, Abba Eban, and Ben-Aharon, leader of the powerful Histadrut Union, are all used to these excesses on the part of the Israeli press, and tactfully refrain from even commenting on the charges. Still, since I was interviewed from morning to evening on the radio and television, I finally did answer that as far as the French Socialist Party was concerned, the fact that we recognized the existence of a Palestinian problem did not imply that we denied the right of Israel to exist as a nation, a right proclaimed by the United Nations some twenty-five years ago (Soviet Russia had in fact been the first country to establish diplomatic relations with the new state) and which was no longer a matter for discussion. I added that the right to exist presupposed that Israel had the means with which to survive.

The next morning, two local press agencies took my declaration, cut it into shreds, keeping only what they wanted to, and deleted from it any reference to "the Palestinian problem." What was I to do, deny my denial? I decided to abandon what was clearly an unfair combat.

Then, when I returned to Paris, without having altered my position on the Middle East, I was violently attacked by pro-Arab journalists, who demanded that I explain my new positions on the matter. Rather than expound once again on the subject in all its ramifications, to rectify, correct, and protest my attackers' attacks, I preferred to let the serious political commentators ferret out the wheat from the chaff and limited myself to recalling the Socialist Party's position on the subject.

What a mistake that was! I was accused in some quarters of approving Yigal Allon's plan, while in others it was claimed that I now espoused the view of the Israeli extremists from A to z. The official spokesman for the Paris branch of the World Christian Conference for Palestine denounced my having "bought the most hard-line Zionist positions," and my having "supported the expansionist policies of the Israeli leaders."

The Algerian daily *El Moudjahid* called me a "social-Zionist,"
attacked me for having been a partisan for "all-out war in Al-
geria," said that my basic policy was "a philosophy of aggres-
sion," and that my aim was ultimately to "resurrect the colonial
mentality of the nineteenth century."

What could I say? What could I do? For a moment I thought I
ought to reiterate my basic position in order to clear the air for all
parties. Yes, I had indeed said this; no, I had not taken that position. But then I thought better of it. Here as elsewhere, in the
times we are going through, "yes" and "no" are currencies that
have been seriously devalued.

TUESDAY, MARCH 28

Last year, as I was reading Annie Kriegel's *Bread and Roses*, in
which she lays the groundwork for a history of socialism, the
chapter entitled "Léon Blum as Viewed by the Communists" took
me completely aback. I opened the book again this morning to
help me prepare an article I am writing in celebration of Blum's
centenary, and in leafing through it I can't help feeling the same
shock as when I read it for the first time. What an incredible
anthology. "Blum, the political wire-puller with parliamentary
inclinations, bosom friend of the major well-heeled cosmopo-
lites . . ." (Marty); "Blum, traitor of the working class, of the
people and of France itself . . ." (Bonte); "in Blum there is Millerand's aversion for socialism, Pilsudski's cruelty, Mussolini's fe-
rocity, and a hatred of the Soviet Union like that of Trotsky. The
working class cannot fail to pillory this moral and political monster. It cannot fail to reject with horror and disgust Blum-the-
bourgeois, Blum-the-noninterventionist, Blum-the-do-nothing,
Blum-the-policeman, Blum-the-warmonger . . ." (Thorez).

And these kernels, gleaned throughout the fifth volume of
Maurice Thorez's *Complete Works:* "Blum-the-baleful; the crafty
politician; disgusting Tartuffe; hideous, a hypocrite of such pro-
portions that those who have no choice but to approach him from

time to time cannot do so without revulsion; political scoundrel; his political twists and turns, his snakelike hissing are loathsome; Blum-the-jackal; the rogue; purveyor of prisons and convict camps; the hardened criminal of treason; aider and abetter of the police; Blum-the-informer; professional liar."

I shall simply note, not to excuse them but to explain, that these imprecations date from the early part of the war, that is 1940, when the once proud Popular Front had degenerated into all-out hatred. Still, I consider myself lucky to be living at a time when the Communist leaders are so gentle and indulgent by comparison. Just think of the progress we've made! No accusations of scoundrel, of reptilian conduct; no jackal, no informer, no Tartuffe, no cries of "murderer"! Should we thank heaven that the present Communist leader has been given us as our partner? Let today's pessimists, who are worried and concerned about the arguments between Socialists and Communists, be reassured: we've seen worse.

SATURDAY, APRIL 29

The French consul general was ranting and raving in the automobile that was taking us to our lodgings. "Those ridiculous English," he stormed. "All it would take to put an end to this nonsense are a couple of machine guns."

I had just landed at Accra as the official representative of Guy Mollet's government at the ceremonies marking Ghana's independence. It was 1957. The sleek black Chrysler crossed the square where, a few years earlier, the riots had broken out. The consul, a ruddy-faced Alsatian, called upon me to witness that stupidity. "Two machine guns for an empire! Two machine guns was all they needed! I tell you, that would have sufficed, those stupid English!" Seated in front next to the liveried chauffeur, the young African interpreter who had greeted me at the airport, named Kwame Nkruma, listened without comment. He was probably meditating on the way in which, on this festive and glorious occasion, the

French guests invited by the "savior" perceived the meaning of history. I didn't say a word. With open annoyance, the consul swallowed his wrath.

The various delegations from around the world resembled a theatrical company on tour, with only one play in its repertory. The main roles were played by Richard Nixon, then vice president of the United States; the chairman of the Supreme Tribunal of the USSR, whose name I forgot the moment I made note of it; Prince Faisal, prime minister of Saudi Arabia and brother of the king, whom, as we met, he was planning to depose; and Habib Bourguiba, who went around extending invitations to all assembled to his forthcoming independence celebration in Tunis.

We spent hours together waiting for the ceremonies to begin. Friendships were formed, rivalries were born without any regard for the existing alliances or conflicts that reigned between the countries concerned. Pat Nixon, a fixed smile on her thin face, showered attentions on one and all. Except for the four personages mentioned above, protocol was dictated solely by alphabetical order, country by country. Thus after a while I knew all there was to know about my neighbors to left and right, Ethiopia and Greece.

The independence of Ghana was proclaimed twice. First, at Parliament. Seated stiffly and primly on her throne of gilded wood, Marina, duchess of Kent, represented the queen of England who either could not or did not care to appear in person. The president of the Assembly, wearing a white wig and a long red robe and shoes with buckles—as did his colleagues—pronounced the sacramental phrases. I observed Nkruma, lost in the throng, standing there motionless. He did not speak during the occasion. Everything unfolded as though it were England deciding and bestowing. Butler, who it was rumored would succeed Harold Macmillan as the next prime minister, yawned with boredom. We were back in England, at a session of Parliament! Once the ceremonies were over, the colorful crowd applauded, stretched, and began to congratulate one another in the thick, moist heat swarming with buzzing flies.

Another spectacle was about to begin that had not been mentioned in the official program. On the square adjacent to the palace a tubular scaffolding had been erected around an arena. In the center was a tall, narrow podium, which was reached by a wooden ladder. The bleachers were jam-packed, and a crowd was trying to press its way into the arena. Drawn by it, I followed and with some considerable difficulty managed to squeeze my way in. There, another ceremony was taking place: Africa, in all its frenzy, was moving, shouting, singing. In the shimmer of colors, I noted that blue seemed to dominate. But the merry-making was not what I had expected it to be.

The men who were now climbing up the ladder one by one were the same ones I had seen an hour ago grouped around Nkruma. They were the new dignitaries, the leaders and ministers of the revolutionary organization, the Convention People's Party. They had taken off their togas and donned the striped tunic worn by Her Majesty's prisoners in Ghana. Their hands were bound in chains, their feet in ball-and-chains. They were chanting, and as they reached the podium they danced and gyrated to the sound of warriors' tam-tams. Then they raised their hands above their heads, and silence ensued. Nkruma spoke for a few moments. The crowd responded with a deafening roar.

That afternoon I asked Nkruma about the meaning of that scene. Was it a challenge? An expiatory rite? He smiled and said nothing. Philippe Decraene, writing in Le Monde, noted: "When he emerged from prison, where he had spent fourteen months on orders of the British authorities, Nkruma had soaked his feet seven times in the blood of a sheep offered as a sacrifice to wash away the impurities of prisons." This time, they had not sacrificed the sheep, but had washed away a very deep, very ancient misery.

On the last evening of our visit there was a ball. I went to the Governor's Palace, where the duchess of Kent headed the receiving line. The heads of delegations bowed to her as they arrived. She kept each one for a moment or two, and although none was forgotten, each had the feeling that she had singled him out. After some brief exchange about the weather or the pleasures of travel, a court usher hastened the proceedings by pointing with a haughty finger toward the door through which we were to go.

The duchess was to open the ball with Nkruma. She arrived, sheathed in a gown studded with gold thread and pearls which forced her to stand very straight, and took up her place in the center of the ballroom. Nkruma, who, resplendent in his white spencer, had listlessly seconded Marina in her diplomatic functions prior to the ball, made his way to her through the throng of uniforms, coat-and-tails, tuxedos, and the line of glazed torsos. He had changed costume once again, and was now wearing the *kente* ("a precious toga, made by the careful collage of long, narrow lengths of woven cotton," as Philippe Decraene noted in his newspaper piece), which left the right side of the torso bare. He grabbed the gold-and-pearl package and began to dance. "It's *he* who's the king," whispered the French ambassador, whom the French Foreign Office had given me as a companion for the events.

Kwame Nkruma—with his broad forehead, his serene facial features, and his strong athletic body—emanated a sense of unequaled strength. The memory of how he looked that day has remained engraved on my mind, despite what I later learned about the wear and tear on him, with all that implied. He died only a few weeks ago of cancer, in Bucharest, where I have just arrived on an official visit. A long way from his native Africa, which has lost, through the death of this failed messiah, one of its founding fathers.

TUESDAY, MAY 16

I don't like to write while I'm traveling. The only reason I finished my article on Nkruma was to help out a friend, Claude Estier, who was waiting for it before closing out his issue of *L'Unité*. I usually take notes at random on little pieces of paper which I lose more often than not. I tend to mistrust my initial impressions, that "lyrical illusion" which inevitably leads me straight into pathos. What a waste! A good cognac has to be distilled twice. My maternal grandfather, who did not drink cognac, was nonetheless famous for his infallible nose, which could at one sniff tell you not only the vintage but the hillside whence it came.

The last thing I'd want would be to picture my readers making the same wry face in reading me that my grandfather made as he tossed the contents of his cognac glass away after having performed. Not that it won't happen. I don't know how Jacques Chardonne used to write. Slowly, and very carefully, I suspect. For me, he remains the model writer of his generation. Out of parochialism, perhaps. I was born only a few miles from his house, and I have taken many a walk along the sandy bluffs he wrote about ("For me," he notes in his *Letters to Roger Nimier*, "countryside means the Charente region, and more specifically a sandy bluff . . .") where during his vacations he used to walk with his friend and neighbor, Jacques Delamain, listening to the bird songs. There better than anywhere else does the advice he offered, *sotto voce*, become clear and take on meaning: "One can say everything in a few words. The only sin would be to linger over things that turn out the way you expect."

As it was, I spent April 30 to May 4 in Rumania. Gaston Defferre and Robert Pontillon went with me. We were told not to miss the May Day spectacle, with its traditional parades, typical of Communist countries. But our informants were behind the times. This year the government had decreed that there would be no official ceremonies, no parades, no quasi-military mobilization of the masses: May Day would really become what it was intended to be, a day of rest and relaxation for the workers. From the estate which had once belonged to the Brancovan family, then the Hohenzollerns (it was here that King Michael signed his act of abdication), where our hosts had brought us upon our arrival, we could hear the beat of a local band playing popular songs well into the evening. After midnight, only the sound of the hoot owl broke the silence.

The following day, we visited Bucharest, which was virtually deserted. On the façades of the public buildings, framing the portraits of the regime's nine leaders, all aligned from left to right in strict hierarchical order (Ceaucescu, Maurer, Bodnaras, Manescu, Visil, etc.) red pennants were draped. Throughout the city signs were posted proclaiming LONG LIVE MAY FIRST. The balconies were adorned with garlands of foliage and flowers. The few passersby crossed the broad thoroughfares without hurrying; on both sides of long, wide avenues grew elm and plane and linden trees, which gave the city its noble appearance. Children were playing on the sidewalks. Our automobile, preceded by a squad of police, was the only disturbing element in the whole scene.

That morning we had been received by the General Secretary of the Rumanian Communist Party, Nicolas Ceaucescu, together with various other Party leaders: Voitek, president of the National Assembly; Manea Manescu, a member of the Politburo; Cornel Burtica and Stefan Andrei, members of the Central Committee. We talked for a good four hours, seated around a rectangular table in a well-lit but bare room of the former palace. Ceaucescu, a former worker in the leather industry, who at seventeen (he is now fifty-four) was the youngest political prisoner in Rumania, speaks like a peasant. He literally chews up his words. Before a sound emerges from his mouth, his lips move and sculpt the shape of the sentence to come. His face is dead serious, his features chiseled, and his head is sunk into his shoulders. You feel that he is crouching, attentive, vigilant, leaving nothing to chance, the mortal enemy of political careers in this part of the world. On rare occasions he laughs, and when he does you have the feeling of a whole other person, who enjoys life, lurking behind that austere façade.

The other members of the Rumanian delegation have scarcely opened their mouth, limiting their contributions to approving with a furtive smile what their leader says. I began by commenting on what seemed to us Westerners as a rather unusual diplomatic policy on the part of Rumania, both in its initiatives and its freedom. After his election, Nixon chose Bucharest for his initial visit to a Communist country. Rumania had chosen not to follow the Moscow line in Russia's disputes with either Yugoslavia or China. It condemned Czechoslovakian "normalization." It maintains diplomatic relations with Albania, yet keeps an open line to the Common Market. It invites Golda Meir to visit the country.

"What's so surprising about that?" Ceaucescu wants to know. "Russia has nothing to fear from us. We're loyal allies. As for the rest, we shape our policies to our national needs. The world is changing very rapidly. There are no longer any super-powers. The growth of the Common Market, the increasing influence and strength of Japan, the return of China as an international power, the revolutions in Latin America, the economic bonds of the two Germanies have created so many poles of attraction. In the West, American domination is either disputed or refused. In the East, there are no supranational institutions anywhere, not even within COMECON, contrary to the tendencies of Western Europe. This situation offers great opportunities for small or middle-sized countries. No one can any longer pretend to act or decide in their name. Brezhnev was the first to recognize this, even before Nixon and Chou En-lai. But all three were wise to see it and understand its implications."

Ceaucescu had just returned from a trip to Africa, with a long stopover in Cairo. This past week he had inaugurated, with Marshal Tito, the dam at the Gates of Iron in the Danube. He is interested in establishing the basis for a new stability in the Mediterranean, and a new organization of Balkan nations. Scarcely a capital in the world has not had a visit from him. "Madrid, Athens, and Pretoria," he shot at me, as though to overcome any objection.

That eclecticism on the part of the Rumanians is at odds with the rigor that continues to dictate their internal politics. To be sure, the time of Anna Pauker and the Stalinist excesses is ended. But in Bucharest, they hew pretty closely to the Soviet model. As though orthodoxy were the price one had to pay for independence. Independence! That was the crux of the matter, after all. What an odd situation for this young nation to be in, a nation made up of old disparate provinces and which, on the frontier of a vast empire, proclaims to all who would hear its right to dispose of its own destiny.

TUESDAY, MAY 30

I have interrupted this account of my Rumanian trip on two occasions, and I regret it. But every week I travel to the provinces, where I visit Socialist federations and hold public meetings. On Saturday or Sunday I go to the Nièvre where I preside over the General Assembly of the county at least six times a year. In Paris,

Wednesdays and Thursdays are taken up with discussions of the Party secretariat and the Executive Committee. Moreover, rare is the week when at least one evening is not taken up with district meetings or local workers' commissions. Not that I'm complaining. But when to this rather full calendar is added a parliamentary debate (as was the case recently), the writing of an article (I write three or four a month for French and foreign newspapers), the preparation of a book (somewhat against my better judgment I have undertaken two), the final planning for a television debate (I face Michel Debré on June 13, "on equal terms," using film clips to back up our statements, a new experience for me)—yes, I have to confess, there are times when I feel out of breath. It is a mistake to spread oneself so thin, as I am well aware. As the saying goes, tomorrow I'm going to organize my life.

The world of action uses up the material you toss into it as fast as you provide it. The quiet earth yields abundant harvests. Oh, for the useful pleasure of taking long walks in the woods, where to breathe is to think. I walk in the forest. The birds that sing so boldly near the house do not venture this far. They remain, like dogs, within range of human voices and prefer not to fly too far from places where people dwell. I measure the progress of the ferns which, suddenly uncoiled, spread out their carpet of bright green. I feel my feet meeting the softness of the path I travel. Silence and space cure me of the illness of cities. Brief foray into an almost forgotten kingdom! A few Sundays ago I parked my car at the side of the road, two kilometers from Pierre-Ecrite, in the Morvan, which used to be the last stop on the old Paris-Lyon route. I cut through the fields and woods until I reached Alligny, at the bottom of the valley, a little less than two hours later. I stayed there long enough to drink a glass of water at the inn just below the village church, before retracing my steps. The golden light that shot through the dark sky in full glory majestically crowned the peaks of the hill, where the beech groves still managed to resist the increasing incursion of the pine trees. On several occasions I was so tired I had to stop, like a tree: for those who know how to stop, roots grow quickly. But it was growing late.

Writing for L'Unité refreshes me, even if two-thirds of my efforts end up in the waste basket. I don't try to use its columns to comment on current events, which the staff journalists cover very well. Current events simply serve me as points of departure. And yet there was no dearth of them over the past few months. Without trying to sort them out, I was sorely tempted to write about Nixon in Moscow, the Burundi massacres, the new developments in the Vietnam War, the *Joint français*, the milk strike. Each subject had its own lesson, each added one more piece to the jigsaw puzzle of this world which lives by, and is interesting because of, its contradictions. But I left my readers suspended somewhere in the middle of my trip to Rumania. I was so impressed, in Bucharest, with the way that country's leaders went out of their way to emphasize their independence. One day in Moldavia, not far from the Russian border, I came to the realization that it was perhaps the most important concern they had.

The Putna monastery houses the tomb of Stephen the Great, governor of Moldavia near the end of the fifteenth century. The head of the delegation who was acting as our guide pointed to the little lamp flickering over the tomb and said to us: "That lamp has always been there. Its flame, however weak, has never gone out. It is a challenge to time and to the madness of mankind. Putna is our Jerusalem, or, if you prefer, our Mecca, in any case our patriotic school. These oak leaves sculpted into the marble symbolize the resistance of our people. Ever since the Roman conquest we get along as best we can, always in the shadow of one empire or another. Don't forget, we had to protect ourselves from the ambitions of Turkey, the Austro-Hungarian empire, and Czarist Russia. It goes without saying that there were times when we had to swallow our pride, pay tribute, lend our soldiers, but we have never accepted any unwarranted interference in our domestic affairs. Stephen the Great is our national hero because for the forty-seven years of his reign he managed, by diplomacy or war, to expel all foreigners from our territory. Our children learn in school that on his deathbed, Stephen called his son Bogdan to his side and said, 'If force does not suffice, grant the victor whatever he wants, provided he agrees to leave.' Through the centuries we have always heeded that advice, which is still the wellspring of our politics. We have wended our way with great care through history, to avoid being wiped out."

During the lunch that ensued, served by the nuns of the

Suceviţa monastery, spirits were high. We toasted everyone we could think of, especially the Mother Superior, who was presiding over the meal. "Within the socio-political context of the present times, the Mother Superior is to be commended for the excellence of her cuisine," said the local political leader with a straight face, before breaking into a hearty laugh that immediately permeated the whole table.

In Rumania, the level of patriotism has a definite Gaullist ring to it: the scale on which it is felt and judged is eternal. Will nothing ever change? They use the same terms that were used by the French in 1848. Nations are still so young, Rumania foremost among them. And yet they seem so old to me. How can I explain this basic difference I feel so strongly? People, like individuals, do not easily give up what they have acquired at such a high price, the price of sacrifice.

SATURDAY, JUNE 3

As a schoolboy, I was terrible at math. The math teacher, Mr. Trinques, had given up on me after only two semesters, abandoning me to what he called my daydreams. I nonetheless remember the four basic operations, though I can't guarantee the latter two. Geometry still holds its fair share of secrets for me. For instance, I'm far from sure I interpreted correctly this definition: "A straight line is the shortest distance between two points."

These thoughts are prompted by my reading of a proposal from a ministerial commission on education suggesting a new program for school children from twelve to fourteen. Having reread it several times I confess to not understanding a single word. . . .

Paul Fort, a true poet who has unjustly been neglected by literary history but who, if there is any justice in the world, will be restored to his rightful place one day, had another way of putting it: "The shortest distance from one point to another," he said, "is the happiness of a single day." Poetry and mathematics have been sisters since time immemorial. Have they quarreled?

TUESDAY, JUNE 20

Lunch with Sicco Mansholt. There he is, solid as a rock yet light on his feet, a weather-beaten sailor or farmer, used to open spaces. Almost immediately we begin discussing a subject close to us both, one which I regret not having raised the other evening during my television debate with Michel Debré, namely the fate of our long-neglected friends—the air, water, the plants and animals of this earth—which in recent months have been the subject of such intense controversy. In the past few weeks half a dozen French magazines and newspapers have either had special issues on the subject or devoted long and learned articles to ecology. On my table I also have a number of books, either just out or soon forthcoming, all questioning the direction in which the world seems to be heading. One, by John Kenneth Galbraith, maintains, for example, that "the measure of economic success is not our productivity but what we do to render life more tolerable and pleasant." I am also looking forward to reading the newly published report from MIT—which I understand has to be the basis for any serious discussion of the matter—which, in the light of the increasing pollution problem to which our planet is prey, fed into its computers the comparative statistics relative to demographics, food resources, energy reserves, and raw materials.

But let me come back to my luncheon companion. Sicco Mansholt (short, with a limp, he is one of those useless relics which contemporary society has conveniently relegated to the dustbin of history) has fortunately entered the fray in his own inimitable way, head first, by denouncing the gross national product as a measure of anything meaningful. "Teaching, public health, tourism, the places where people live, open spaces, the quality of our air, are all as important to our well-being as economic growth in the classic sense of the term," he declared to *Le Nouvel Observateur* recently. At any rate, we are in accord on one basic point: it will be impossible to maintain our rate of economic growth without profoundly modifying the structures of our society. That thought reminds me of the Socialist Party motto: Change life. Tomorrow? No, now! And I think of Saint Augustine's question: "If the future and the past really exist, where are they?"

The fact is, present events point up the urgency of the question. Just as Prime Minister Michel Debré is preparing to explode an atomic bomb in the skies of the South Pacific—a bomb they refer to as "clean"—John W. Gofman, a physicist and codiscoverer of uranium 233 and its fission, writes that "a nuclear reactor of the type currently in use producing a thousand megawatts of electrical power also produces each year as much radioactive waste material as would a thousand Hiroshima bombs." That doesn't seem to bother the French Government which, at the demand of Australia and New Zealand, will soon find itself in the position of defendant at the United Nations. The strontium 90 set free by the explosion will continue to affect the bones and blood for dozens of years to come, as will the carbon 14, the only difference being that the latter will reap its grim harvest for thousands of years. "Simply becoming aware of that threat," Sicco Mansholt remarks, "forms the basis for future policy."

TUESDAY, JULY 4

I'm sorry not to have seen Jean-François Revel recently. I would like to have laid out to him our current plans and policies the way I used to at the time of the counter-government of which he was one of the moving forces. The report he wrote for me in 1967 on cultural policy still remains the best document on the subject I have ever read, and remains just as pertinent today as it was then. I had come to know him through his books, and was quite taken by his style—which I still admire as much today as I did then—a style solid and slightly ponderous, which moved with the steady pace of a Burgundian, diametrically opposed to what was fashionable or stylish as he went about composing work after meaningful work. If I had been more far-sighted, I should have been concerned about the passionate side of his nature, which impels him to want to prove that he is right even after he has reached the point where he begins to be wrong. But his attacks on the subject called de Gaulle or Gaullism were so on target that I began to think his judgments right all the time. If I tend to view his opinions more harshly since he has turned his arsenal against me, it does not diminish one iota the regret I feel for a friendship somehow lost (probably my fault) as soon as it ceased to exchange concern for indulgence.

And yet Jean-François Revel is someone I care about. Enough to tell him how his last article in *L'Express* upset me. His thesis can be summed up in one sentence: "When, with respect to the Common Program, we are told that it wipes out the Congress of Tours, that is indeed true, but in this sense alone: that fifty-two years afterwards, the partisans of Léon Blum have joined forces with the Communists Cachin and Frossard, as republican socialism has aligned itself with bureaucratic centralism." In other words, according to Revel, socialism has capitulated to communism. If the author wanted the pleasure of hurting me with a cruel word, he has succeeded. But I am assuming that even when he makes outlandish charges, he is still sincere.

The arguments he uses to back up his charges prove it, for they are totally ridiculous. It would require a great deal of good faith on the part of an impartial judge to conduct a trial based on such allegations.

The first of these arguments relates to the dissolution—by double détente—called for by the Common Program. As we know, the Communist Party hoped that the breach of contract between the government and the National Assembly at the opening of the legislative session would be followed automatically by the dissolution of Parliament. In which case universal suffrage would have settled any serious conflict between the signatories of the majority pact. The Socialist Party, on the contrary, deemed that it was unacceptable to give any of the parties constituting the ruling majority the right to choose the time and place of legislative elections. That would have made one-upmanship and demagogy even more tempting, as well as creating a climate of permanent instability.

On the other hand, by giving the president of the Republic the possibility either to name a new prime minister representative of the same majority or to find another majority in the same Assembly, not only would the Left avoid the blackmail-dissolution and the dissolution by surprise, but would also demonstrate that it was serious when it declared that it was willing to submit to the notion of democratic alternation. You will understand the validity of the Socialist position if you take the present political situation in Germany and transpose it to France: in Germany, all it would take for a shift of power from the hands of the Socialists to the Christian Democrats would be for the Liberal Party to change camps.

General de Gaulle showed less patience and less concern for legal formalities than the Left proposes when he dissolved the Assembly which had given Georges Pompidou a vote of no confidence in 1962, or the Assembly which hesitated to follow him in 1968.

I would appreciate it if Jean-François Revel would give me an example of some regime, assuming it is democratic, where one can prevent a party from leaving the majority if it so desires. And if there is no longer a majority within any national assembly, what regime, assuming it is a parliamentary one, can prevent the people from going back to the voting booth? The Communist Party, by aligning itself with the Socialist position on this issue, enabled the Common Program to guarantee political alternation, increase stability, and preserve the powers of the chief of state in an area which is his. What then is this dispute all about?

Among other things, my opponent should have taken the precaution of reading, or rereading, the program of the Socialist Party adopted last March 12 at Suresnes and published on May 15 as *To Change Life*—a program that Mr. Revel had in earlier times found to be excellent. If he had done so he would have found that the program calls for nationalizing the banks; natural resources such as coal, oil, and gas; the defense and space industries; the companies that hold concessions along our national highways; our waterworks, airlines, and maritime companies; our nuclear, electronic, and aeronautic industries. With the exception of the computer companies and waterworks, he would have found that rundown the very one that he himself had proposed to his constituents when he was a Socialist Party candidate for the National Assembly five years ago from the district of Neuilly-Puteaux. Within the framework of those industries where real competition is not feasible on a national scale, he would have noted that the Socialist Party program cites Pechiney-Ugine-Kulhmann and Saint-Gobain. If he had been good enough to read on, he would have noted on page 72 that certain sectors, including iron and steel mills as well as smelters, the textile industry, and materials involved in telecommunications, are put into a special category because of their special responsibility to the public. Finally, he would have noted that for those industries which depend in large measure on collective financing, such as pharmaceuticals, "a public service will be created starting with the nationalization of certain companies." In short, of the nine industrial groups which the Common Program includes in its nationalization plan, the Socialist Party agreed to eight (the ninth was the chemical complex, Rhône-Poulenc). Similarly, in the list of sectors which "have a special responsibility to the public," the Common Program includes only one that the Socialist program does not: the French Petroleum Company. Actually, nationalization of the banks suffices to ensure that the state will be a majority stockholder in the FPC!

I am not forgetting that above and beyond the question of which and how many groups should be nationalized, Revel places the debate on the level of the principle itself, asking: "Is nationalization a good way to socialize the economy?" I will answer him in the same way I would apropos of foreign policy. When you really think about it, are those two companies—Rhône-Poulenc and the French Petroleum Company—worth changing camps over?

TUESDAY, JULY 18

. . . The Fifth Republic is, according to the 1958 Constitution, a parliamentary republic. During the preparatory proceedings, General de Gaulle went out of his way to stress this point when he was asked to appear before the Advisory Committee, presided over by Paul Reynaud, to clarify his thoughts. That he was at the time—already backed by the armed forces, if necessary—trying to curry favor with the various political parties, does not alter the basic facts of the texts which the French people overwhelmingly approved. Limiting myself to the essentials of the debate opened by the departure of Jacques Chaban-Delmas, I would simply note that the head of government, responding to the whistle of his master, the president of the Republic, Charles de Gaulle, yielded his post—less than a month after having received an overwhelming vote of confidence from the National Assembly—to a new fair-haired choice, who takes over the reins of government with sole responsibility to the chief of state and without bothering to keep Parliament informed about what he is doing.

There are two kinds of Western democracies: one is the parliamentary system under which the government is responsible to the Parliament; the other is the presidential system, under which the government is named by the head of state and is responsible only to him, but where a Parliament, which cannot be dissolved, exercises the legislative functions without appeal. The institutional policies of General de Gaulle, followed by Georges Pompidou, are neither parliamentary nor presidential. They derive from a third system, widely used in Latin America and many countries of Africa: personal power. Our president is a bat-president. Under the guise of a parliamentary system in keeping with the French tradition, he appears like the debonair protector of the nation's partisan passions—"see my wings!"—while by virtue of a presidential authority vested in him through the people's vote, he responds, or seems to respond, to the demands for stability and political continuity—"long live the rats!" Actually, Georges Pompidou behaves like a potentate who rules by pure whim, the head of a clan who takes care only of his clan members. No one in Europe—aside from Greece, Spain, and Portugal—is as free to act without restraint as he. No one, therefore, is as responsible for the consequences of his acts as he. If he takes it upon himself to punish Chaban-Delmas for his income-tax oversights, he should be reminded that the fiscal assessment was invented when he was prime minister. If he wants to erase all trace of scandal, he should be reminded that this regime, in which the line of demarcation between private and public domains was erased, was of his doing. That the bluff of the "new society" is his.

✗ The Common Program put forth by the Left is reasonable when it proposes to correct the Constitution whereas it allows legal pretexts to the president for committing abuses. In case the present majority loses in next year's elections, it will no longer be possible to juggle national representation. I do not ask for other powers in this area than those that exist. I ask that the means to use them be restored. If I were—thank God I am not—a member of the majority in the present government, and if in spite of that affiliation I had not lost my sense of dignity, I would have received the news of the prime minister's dismissal as an unpardonable offense. As a member of the opposition, I couldn't care less whether the prime minister's name is Messmer rather than Chaban-Delmas. Having been elected by the people, I have a right to know the reasons why, and what this act was meant to accomplish. . . .

TUESDAY, JULY 25

A visit from Jiri Pelikan at the Cité Malesherbes toward the end of June made me aware of the imminence of the new political trials brewing in Czechoslovakia. Our friend, who arrived from Rome where he lives in exile, had in his possession the list of intended victims, together with the legal complaints lodged against them, most of which were trumped-up charges meant to confuse them. I immediately took the steps—which I am sadly compelled to term customary—to make certain that Prague is fully aware of the effects an all-out campaign of repression, by means of the men who would testify on behalf of the State, would have worldwide. It would truly put an end to the hope for a lovely spring. Not that I had any illusions as to the efficacy of my arguments. An earlier appeal—which had been made publicly—had simply resulted in the Czech Communist Party organ, *Rude Pravo*, vilifying me with a sorry list of insults and invective. That will not keep me from beginning all over again, and from saying and writing as often and as loudly as necessary, that above and beyond the concerns of the trials themselves, the Prague actions have a symbolic value. To combat and destroy capitalism, the dialectic of the historian and the courage of the militant will remain powerless so long as they show themselves incapable of coming up with a viable and desirable type of alternative civilization. In my view, the Czech leaders are, in the area of international communism, heading backwards.

In France, the Right sees this drama only as an excuse for making waves. It doesn't make any effort to call to account Michel Debré for the declarations he made a few weeks after the Prague coup. No, it aims its barbs at me. Let it be known, therefore, that I do not hold the French Communist Party responsible for what happens in Czechoslovakia any more than I hold Mr. Pompidou responsible for the tortures inflicted on the Portuguese political prisoners by his friend Mr. Caetano. But let the Right also know that I shall believe in the possibility of freedom in the world the day I see political and ideological solidarities give way before the truth.

MONDAY, SEPTEMBER 4

The letter from His Excellency Mr. Abrasimov reached me in my house in the Landes countryside two days before its publication. I immediately informed my honorable correspondent that we were in agreement on one point: the inadvisability of the trip to Moscow that we discussed in the course of a lunch to which he was kind enough to invite me last January.

If I understand Mr. Abrasimov correctly, whoever has the gall to believe the rumors according to which foreign troops, specifically Russian, entered Czechoslovakia in 1968 without the consent of the Czech leaders, reveals himself to be anti-Soviet. Anti-Soviet too is he who believes—always on the basis of false information—that the Jews of the USSR who wish to emigrate to Israel are prevented in any way from doing so. Mr. Abrasimov is at one and the same time ambassador, historian, and member of the Central Committee of the Communist Party. What he says comes from the horse's mouth.

TUESDAY, SEPTEMBER 5

This summer, with the exception of a few stormy days in the middle of August, the Bay of Biscay has achieved a magical, timeless quality. Before sunset, there is a miraculous hour when the light has the color and softness of honey. The birds, who are beginning their southerly migrations slightly early, stop in our clearing, which for a brief moment becomes a forest of straight takeoffs into the sky, branches of wings. An extraordinary perfection, quivering, uncertain, and somehow poignant. From which stems the confusion that happiness gives.

In the course of this same summer, in Argentina sixteen political prisoners held at the Trelew Naval Base were murdered by their guards. In Brazil, a bullet in the back of the neck of several union leaders settled, if only temporarily, the problem of higher salaries demanded by the rank and file. Torture is also a commonplace occurrence. The techniques used by the torturers hardly evolves. Bathtub, electrodes applied to tender parts, kicks in the stomach, burned eyelids. The Shah of Iran has lost track of the number of his citizens he has been obliged to hang or shoot. Bokassa, in Central Africa, cuts one ear, two ears, one hand, two hands, slits a throat. Who steals an egg steals a cow: each according to his own barometer. In Chad, Tombalbaye had until recently arrested only members of the opposition. Now he is arresting members of his own government. In Tibesti, people are shot at in the streets. The prisons are filling up, overflowing. In Prague, people are being put on trial so that there can be new hope in the country. In Savannah, Georgia, a black is lynched. In Moscow, Jews are made to pay special taxes. A single American bomb dropped on a North Vietnamese village kills more people than the odious attack by the Palestinians in Munich. And that is but a partial list of man's inhumanity to man on this shrunken planet. But the worst is not spoken of.

That was one summer on the planet Earth.

WEDNESDAY, SEPTEMBER 13

Amnesty International has just published its annual report on the political trials and prisoners around the world. The document devoted to Brazil reveals that in that country there are 12,000 political prisoners, 15,000 exiles, and 500 people who have been tortured to death. Amnesty International is an organization with close ties to both the UN and UNESCO. Its report was disseminated throughout all the countries of Europe, with one exception: France. Minister of the Interior Raymond Marcellin had all the copies of the report stopped at the border, "so they could be examined more closely." What is the government, and its majority, so afraid of, that same government which never hesitates to accuse the Left about its complacency with regard to political repression in the countries of the Eastern bloc?

MONDAY, SEPTEMBER 18

During the television program on Channel 2 last Friday, the journalists who questioned me had only one thought in their minds: What would happen to our freedoms if the Left won the election? They had perhaps read our Common Program, but it was clear that despite the democratic guarantees it contains they had not found in it the answer which they probably weren't looking for. Ready to give the Socialists the benefit of the doubt, they denounced our pact with the Communists as the sure omen that our freedoms would not survive if we won. Perhaps they were playing the devil's advocate, in order to push me up against the wall. And yet I understand, the more they attacked me and called on me to come clean, that the word "freedom" did not mean the same thing to us, that the discussion was going nowhere because we were spinning our wheels. Beyond the question of polemics, these journalists, who I know very well are independent-minded, reflected without knowing it and without meaning to, the notion that the Right has of public liberties.

The Right sites the golden age in a mythical past, a perfect model of a finite world toward which humanity is moving. When it arrives, it will have come full circle: the end will have rejoined the beginning. The Right considers that everything has been given Man, who has never stopped dissipating that extraordinary heritage, freedom, for example, with a capital F, the earthly projection of a lost paradise. The Left, on the contrary, believes in the future and constructs in the future the ideal society. It knows today, since Rousseau and in contradiction to him, that man is not born free, even if he is everywhere, or virtually everywhere, in chains.

For a Socialist, freedom is something you make up over and over again every day of your life. In 1789, the advent of political democracy was called "revolution." It was a revolution, indeed, in that for the first time it recognized individual rights: the right to speak and write freely, to come and go as you please. But the principle, inscribed in gold letters across the façade of public buildings, little by little lost its meaning. Freedom of expression, for Camille Desmoulins, was the possibility to sell on the streets of Paris, for whatever price he could get, a pamphlet. Today, it would be the right to speak on television. Or to publish a newspaper without passing through the strictures of advertising. But the bourgeoisie, once the spokesman of popular aspirations and now the stockholder on whose capital industrial society is founded, holds the purse strings and controls the major channels of communication, be they audio or visual. Camille Desmoulins will await the next revolution. Meanwhile, he will have to remain silent, or speak in whispers.

The decent man of the Right speaks of freedom as though it were an axiom of public right, and not as though it were a living, daily reality. He makes a good speech, goes home, and sleeps in peace. One suspects that he will be very surprised the day when freedom, marching beneath his window, will be singing a truly revolutionary song.

SUNDAY, OCTOBER 8

Twenty-five years of Parliament: a milestone, a major milestone of my life has been reached. Since my friends insisted, we're going to celebrate at Château-Chinon. Anyone who wants to, can come. There is no guest list, no priorities, no protocol. I'm staying in the Vieux-Morvan Hotel, Room 15, and eating at my usual table. I say hello to all sorts of people, some from my past, some from my present, who together erase the passage of time that only a look in the mirror restores. I started the day with a slight chip on my shoulder. I don't like feelings expressed in words, and am moved by symbols as though I needed, more than ever, to perceive a reflection, however slight, of the hidden face of things. Perhaps that is why I feel so at one with the Morvan, a deep land whose flanks bear the waters of a hundred streams.

Mikis Theodorakis, who is present, leads us into the secret region where silence becomes music. Soon there are three thousand of us listening to a song that comes from somewhere far beyond us. The journalists keep asking me: Why? Why? I'm in no mood to improvise a balance sheet. I tell them: Mikis will tell you more eloquently than I could. Up on the stage, facing his musicians, he has his back to us.

A poem. A woman's voice. Copper and bronze. On the steps of the house blinded by sunlight, blood flows, death transfigured. Somewhere in Spain, they are killing García Lorca. Nothing moves. Yes, that spot of blood on the stone, perhaps it is the source of a river that will carve out its banks to the ends of the earth. The little throng at Château-Chinon holds its breath. It senses that it is taking part in one of those all too rare moments when you can touch the truth. As for me, I recognize my oldest, most deep-rooted *raisons d'être*, and my reasons for fighting. Freedom, back-lighted against the white wall of a Greece asleep, is a rendezvous not to be missed.

MONDAY, OCTOBER 23

I have a confession to make: I do like the towering skyscrapers of the Défense suburb of Paris, and don't dislike the one that graces Montparnasse. A difficult confession, to judge by a perusal of the last two issues of L'Unité.

The first time I saw New York it was from the air. How dazzling! We had taken a night flight, and dawn had not yet chased the early morning mists. Manhattan, gray and golden in its geometric outline, had a rounded softness to it. I thought of Botticelli. I've returned to New York five or six times. Only once by ship, a voyage I recall with mixed feelings: I'm not a very good sailor. Coming by plane, I've always had the same shock, the same feeling that I was entering the future through some window. Whenever I'm asked what my favorite cities are, I put New York in the same category as Venice, Ghent, Florence, Jerusalem. . . . Not because of its skyscrapers, but because I was given it like that, as it is.

Tall cities, flat cities: there's no accounting for the way in which love will strike. I feel comfortable with my contradictions. Peking is on the same level as the plains that surround it, as are London and Marrakech. I wouldn't have it any other way. In any city, I feel an emperor, or architect—which comes down to the same thing—I make decisions, settle disputes, arbitrate, I condemn, and in that I resemble my fellow citizens: each makes up his or her own rules based on individual taste and preference. But I temper that intolerance by the constancy of my infidelity: I love the city I'm in—assuming I like it to start with—once and for all.

Is that because I live in Paris? I love the ever-changing aspect of Paris. At least when my taste accepts the changes, which is not always the case. I'm worried about the proposal to tear down the Gare d'Orsay. Completely redoing the rue Barbet-de-Jouy grieves me. The Avenue Paul-Doumer makes me sick. The monumental projects being discussed for the Rond-Point of the Champs-Elysées are hideous. Official French architecture is floundering in ugliness, in mediocre ugliness. Any project emanating from the Architectural Institute is the sign of duds and duffers. I shall be the first to applaud the minister who starts by blowing up the Ecole des Beaux Arts, with only a tinge of regret for those who live and teach there.

The argument about skyscrapers reminds me of an impassioned discussion I had one night in November 1967 at Pierre Salinger's house in Beverly Hills. We were discussing urbanism, and held opposing viewpoints—sharply opposing, I might add, as one might suspect knowing the bitterness partisans of horizontal architecture feel about proponents of the vertical, and vice-versa. Each was complaining about the problems of his own environment. San Franciscans were deploring the way in which buildings on their tight little rock were all piled up—San Francisco is the most geographically circumscribed of all major American cities—and the resulting need to build upward in order to find adequate space. They held that the steady increase in crime in San Francisco—women no longer went out after nine o'clock at night, they maintained—and the breakdown in human relations, the inevitable end-of-day fatigue and listlessness, were a direct result of this urban crowding. The people of Los Angeles, on the other hand, described the terrible boredom of their immense city, not only devoid of visible landmarks but also virtually without borders. It would take a car more than a day just to drive around its circumference. Some of the avenues are fifteen and twenty miles long. Anyone out walking is considered suspect, or mad, and any policeman worth his salt would feel obliged to stop him and ask for his I.D. Despite its vastness, Los Angeles has built only a smattering of skyscrapers, mostly because of the fear of earthquakes. It is a city of low-lying houses, often private, separated by gardens, stretching from the Pacific Ocean to the Rocky Mountains, roughly half the size of Belgium. People in the same neighborhood generally don't know one another. Actually, there aren't any "neighborhoods" in the real sense of the term. No one is anyone else's neighbor. People lock their doors at night, since theft is a

major fear. They are wary of their own shadows. Eight million
solitary inhabitants tend their flowers and their psychoses. San
Francisco or Los Angeles?

Paris has not yet reached that stage. The Montparnasse Tower is
not a threat to French civilization. If someone had made off with
the towers of Notre Dame, I would have considered it a small loss.
If I had my way, I'd have them torn down! Mr. Pompidou would
like them built higher? How hard it is to agree on anything! All
that matters, really, is that art feel itself free to create and build.

Art, yes, but what about the promoters and speculators? The
overall architectural plan of the Défense respected the perspective
of the Tuileries Gardens and the Arch of Triumph. What has too
often ruined a fine project—and, far worse, an admirable site—are
the arrangements made under the table. Beauty is an art of life.
Money, alas, doesn't give a damn about either art or life.

WEDNESDAY, OCTOBER 25

In Vietnam, the killing goes on, and will continue to the last minute. Let's give the diplomats plenty of time to reflect. It has been
going on so long that a day more or less doesn't matter to them.
Around a green baize table, nothing is more variable than the
price of death. But to write the word "peace" apropos of Indochina—which an error of destiny, a French destiny, toppled into
disaster—is just too much! I think back to that moment, twenty-
seven years ago, when anything was possible. Leclerc* wanted
peace and accepted the notion of Indochina's independence.
Thierry d'Argenlieu† dreamt of the old empire and opted for war.
General de Gaulle, who had to decide between them, chose d'Ar-
genlieu, the empire, and war. Leclerc related his doubts and his
sadness to one of the ministers at the time, Gaston Defferre. In

*French general and World War II hero, who headed the French Army in Indo-
china in 1945.
†A French admiral, one of de Gaulle's inner military circle, who was high commissioner in Indochina from 1945-1947.

Algiers, at the Summer Palace, where we all were living then, not long before the automobile accident that took his life at Colomb-Béchar, I heard him voice his regrets that the heads of government had not heeded his advice. One of my friends, Jean d'Arcy, who was in charge of squiring Ho Chi Minh around during the weeks preceding the fatal conference at Fontainebleau—they didn't know quite what to do with the Indochinese leader to keep him busy—heard the same laments from General Leclerc. One gesture was all it would have taken to set the situation right. This gesture—that neither de Gaulle nor Bidault nor Vincent Auriol nor Jack Kennedy nor Lyndon Johnson was able to make—ended up, ironically, being made by Richard Nixon. Does that surprise me? The more I think about it, the more I believe that there is no paradox in history.

TUESDAY, NOVEMBER 28

While our minds are on other things—wars, crime, elections, famous loves—Zorro is coming. Zorro is already here. Contrary to legend, his manners are so discreet and his step so stealthy that no one even turns his head when Zorro walks down the street. What is he doing? He is buying. Everything. Anything. At the rate he is going, he will soon have bought up the entire collection of enterprises that go by the name of France. But he has other ambitions besides settling in the suburbs. France is small potatoes for the man I'm referring to. One day, Zorro will rule the world.

Do you think I'm writing a children's story, or the lyrics of a popular song? The Zorro to whom I'm referring is the arrival on the scene of a phenomenon as important in history as the birth of nations: the advent of the multinationals. Thirteen of them are among the fifty top economic entities of the world. If you extrapolate from the tendency we have seen happening from 1960–1968, some sixty companies, three quarters of which are American-controlled, will by 1985 control all the channels of power. Each of the sixty will have a business volume greater than the gross national product of a country like ours. Taken together, they will dwarf even the GNP of the United States itself.

One can foresee the time—without resorting to the speculations of science fiction—when a holding company controlling credit, research, production and monetary exchanges on five continents will have at its disposal both the reality and authority of a world government that politicians—always at least one period behind the times—will not yet have worked out. Let me correct the verb I used above: This is not something one can "foresee"; it is a certainty, at least so long as the economic system practiced by most of the industrially advanced countries continues to be capitalism. Let me make myself clear: I do not view capitalism as a monster greedy for human flesh. It appeases an appetite, which leads it—simply for lack of what it requires to satisfy its needs—to devour itself. But before it reaches that stage, it will have devoured everything else.

The inner logic of the system condemns each company to gain control of the economic environment within which it operates. The sheer magnitude of the capital investment, the high degree of risk involved because of the time lag between the decision to go ahead with a specific product and its success in the marketplace, and the constant necessity to expend ever-increasing sums in research and development—all these factors lead companies to adopt strategies not only of continued growth but of expansion on a global scale. Paradoxically, the very fluidity of these companies, which by their multinational nature do not have specific legal status internationally, enables them to escape the various legal constraints that often bind their smaller competitors, whose markets are restricted, and thus to penetrate favorable markets anywhere in the world where money is to be made.

With the help of virtually inexhaustible sources of financing, the multinationals can also get around local credit restrictions, transfer their capital freely from country to country, either on speculative ventures or to protect themselves against possible speculations, and avoid certain costs or taxes by formulating within the group clever pricing policies. In short, they no longer have a political partner in their own league. As for the workers in the multinational corporations, their unions can't find whom to talk to or deal with: top management is always located in some distant place, out of reach, while local management does not have the power to make real decisions. Traditional concepts of profit, price, and capital no longer take into account the development and the motivations of capitalism once it has reached this stage of elusive concentration. With its direct and ready access to the capital markets, the forced passivity of its stockholders, its mechanism for self-financing, and the sheer magnitude of its liquidity, the multinational firm is already above and beyond the framework of classical economic thinking.

While waiting to assume the hegemony to which they aspire, they meanwhile serve as the instrument for American penetration of the viable commercial sectors of European economy. Out of 150 leading corporations, less than 15 include European directors. Of 125 billion dollars invested in the world, 60 percent comes from the United States. We know full well how the relationships of economic inequality are transformed into relationships of political power.

It is important that during the past few days this situation has been the subject of public debate and controversy in France. A long document on the subject by Paul Mock was presented at the Economic and Social Council, and a press conference was held by the major unions, both of which brought the subject to the forefront of political debate, the repercussions of which will long be with us. We Socialists should waste no time in clarifying our position in the matter, for we alone, who question not just policies but the system itself, can offer an answer.

WEDNESDAY, DECEMBER 13

I began to write *The Rose in the Fist* on August 1, the day I began my vacation in the Landes. The Common Program had just been published, and I felt the need to explain it, to clarify my own position. Not only to reply to the critics—often unfair and extreme—of the government majority, but also to clarify a text that was too elliptical on some points, incomplete on others, and the full scope of which I felt might not be apparent to many readers who were unaware of the historical and political context out of which it came. It did not take me long to find out how large was the task I had set for myself. To comment and annotate the Common Program in all its aspects and parts represented a mammoth job that I had no hope to complete in time to make my observations useful, that is prior to the elections. I did not have in my country house enough of a research library for such an encyclopedic undertaking, and I knew that if I returned to Paris the immediate demands on my time and energy would not leave me enough free hours to complete it there, either.

The Common Program was drawn up by work committees who gathered, sorted, drew on literally thousands of documents, and consulted the best experts available. To follow its evolution would have meant my dealing pell-mell with foreign policy, social policy, economics, law, education, urbanism—everything that touches people's lives. Chances were that I would add little more, and perhaps considerably less, than could be found in the brochures and pamphlets published for the Socialist Party and the Communist Party. I therefore decided to confine myself not to the essentials—for how was one to choose among them?—but to the subject that concerned most people: the fate of our freedoms.

If the Left comes to power, say our opponents—and this concern is shared by a fair number of people who are prepared to vote for us—it may well manage to distribute more equitably the national wealth, reduce injustice, correct social inequalities, but it will not escape its destiny, which is to lay France open to the possibility of a Prague-like "coup" on the one hand and, on the other, to yield to its demons which, as we all know, are statism and management. Socialists and Left radicals are spared the first grievance, that concern being laid squarely on the doorstep of the Communists. But since it is required to insinuate in certain circles that the Socialists, fascinated by the Communists (the rabbit and the cobra), will put up no resistance to the ambitions that the latter harbor, it ultimately comes to the same thing. As for statism, or state control, Socialists and Communists are put into the same sack, and the radical counterweight, in the eyes of our opponents, does not appear to be sufficient to prevent peasants from being shipped off to collective farms and our shopkeepers to the factories.

There is an element of dark legend in these accusations, which either irritates or amuses, as the case may be. At the time of the Second Empire, official posters of the period already spoke of these *partageux** in the same way, and painted the future in terrifying colors. But there is also the feeling of insecurity caused by the widespread abuses of the Stalinist era which cannot be explained away as figments of one's imagination. In short, the French Left has to prove that it has returned to the sources, to its *own* sources, that it is the daughter of the revolutions where one swore "freedom or death" and kept one's oath.

I therefore limited my study to the political and economic freedoms as they were spelled out in the Common Program. The present majority leaders talk until they're hoarse about the freedom of expression, but they use radio and television as only the totalitarian regimes dare do. They constantly make exceptions to the law, multiply repressive jurisdictions, reestablish administrative internment, introduce into our laws the formidable notion of collective responsibility, and flout the clauses of the social contract that link the state to its citizens, that is to the Constitution. Let us not confuse license and liberty.

A text can often be best judged by various turns of phrase or apparently incidental passages. The careful reader will see that whenever the Common Program was faced with difficult political or moral choices, it inevitably opted for dignity and the responsibility of the human being: abolition of the death penalty; giving women control over their own personal destiny, i.e., contraception and abortion; divorce by mutual consent; the right to vote at age 18, and so on.

I am not trying to act as attorney for the defense. All you have to do is take a long hard look at our present society to understand that on top of its iniquities it adds the sin of lying. In the name of political democracy, a man, a special interest group, a class, impose their power and—what mockery!—the economy they refer to as liberal organizes what amounts to a dictatorship of the privileged class. Once it has reached the stage of monopoly, of the giant corporations and of multinationals, it has effectively killed

---

* Partisans of the equal distribution of wealth and property.

competition and free enterprise. I am fairly itching to denounce imposture wherever I find it. Hence this book. But when I state that freedom is on the Left, and the Left must return freedom to all Frenchmen, I am not asking to be taken at my word. The Common Program is a contract that we are making with the country. There are thirty million voters who are witnesses to that contract and who will if necessary pass judgment on it in the near future.

Since last Monday I have been correcting proofs which the printer snatches away as soon as I have finished reading them: tomorrow it will be done. All I can see now are the faults and failings of that text, the near misses, the unfortunate turns of phrase I would like to repair. But they are no longer mine; they have been taken from me forever. Writing, like any act, does not forgive.

WEDNESDAY, DECEMBER 27

I harbor a thousand friendly memories of the United States. I can picture the lovely, pleasant evening that my friends from Indianapolis, the D's, must have just spent with their family, scattered to the four corners of the globe but which gathers to celebrate each Christmas Eve together. They are unpretentious. They use words sparingly, especially those that might betray their feelings. I should have written them. But I shall wait. What can I say to an American, however close, however dear? Above the outskirts of Hanoi, American B-52s wend their way through the night skies. Star, rain of fire, death, silence, they celebrate in their own way the birth of the savior they call the bread of life.

1973

MONDAY, JANUARY 22

And now Cabral. I have just learned of his death, murdered on his own doorstep in Conakry. Sékou Touré accuses Portugal of the assassination. Caetano claims Portugal had nothing to do with it. I don't have enough information to go on to make a fair judgment. All I know is that Cabral is dead, as are so many others before him who fought for the same cause. Who killed Félix Moumié? He had dined in Geneva with an agent of the French secret police. A short time later he was seized with terrible stomach pains, thanks to some subtle poison that had been introduced in his food, and a few hours later he was dead. The inquest produced no results. A victim, but naturally no assassin. Who killed General Delgado, whose decomposed body was found in a crevice not far from the Portuguese border? Who killed Eduardo Mondlane, one of the rebel leaders from Mozambique, who was blown to pieces in Dar-es-Salaam by a bomb planted in a parcel he received?

Amilcar Cabral was my friend. Although he was banned from France for his politics, doubtless at the request of the Portuguese Government, I had invited him to spend a few days with me over this coming Easter holiday. He was delighted to accept, for he loved France deeply, and spoke French fluently. During my recent voyage to Guinea, we had been virtually inseparable, and he had confided in me all his hopes and plans. His companions, he told me then, already occupied two thirds of the Bissau region of Portuguese Guinea, where elections had been held and an Assembly was already functioning, with a provisional executive soon to be named. Portuguese troops no longer dared to venture into the liberated zones. The liberation movement had already opened schools in the back country, as well as country hospitals, and built a basic administrative structure. One had to hear Amilcar Cabral. The gentleness of his words fit perfectly with the subtlety of a free style of thinking which had a single focus: freedom, its conquest.

In him Portugal loses the adversary who was most sensitive to, and formed by, its values. Stupidity aimed well, which lends to this crime an added element of horror.

WEDNESDAY, JANUARY 24

Lyndon Johnson is buried at the precise moment when Richard Nixon affixes his signature to the peace treaty with Vietnam: history as symbol. The photograph of Henry Kissinger and Le Duc Tho shaking hands on the sidewalk of Avenue Kléber in Paris, each smiling broadly, acts as counterpoint and shows the capacity of a world where, suddenly, the long martyrdom of a people appears as nothing more than a bit of vapor on a window. Long live peace! And yet how many generations will it take to forget that if you go back to the Geneva accords signed by the then Premier Pierre Mendès France nineteen years ago, that war in which so many men and principles perished, was truly fought in vain. Everything there was to say was said in 1954. The rest—words, promises, projects, challenges, bombs, and death—all the rest is excess.

SUNDAY, MAY 27

This evening, the taxi driver taking me home looked up at the sky and said, "Careful, it's going to rain tomorrow." I asked him how he knew. "I'm Portuguese. In my country we know that May is crazy." At the Place de Trocadéro, I walked out onto the terrace. The Montparnasse Tower was alight in the setting sun, its windows reflecting the burnished light back onto Paris. Not a cloud in the sky, not a single sign of bad weather to come. I thought back for a moment on my own months of May, on those people and situations I remembered because of that month. The phony war, which on a May 10 ceased to be a laughing matter. The death of my father on a May 5. Slow to arrive, the night bore him away just before the first light of day. A May 28, at Courville, on the road to Chartres, when a friend of mine fell asleep at the wheel and, going sixty miles an hour, wrapped his car around a linden tree. Not to mention politics and its craziness on a May 13. There were also marvelous moments, exquisite pleasures, many happinesses that only a May could bring. Your head buried in the grass to smell the fresh grass, and breathe in the life rising up from the reawakened earth. The tulips are still in bloom, though nearing their end, while the iris still stand proud and purple benefiting from the April showers. The stock, which have taken root between two stones in the wall, make a far more eloquent case for the existence of God than do all the priests of Notre Dame. The May of Rome and the May of Amsterdam mingle their red ochres. One does not need the presence of the boats on canals to suffer a case of wanderlust. The city is a sea, with its islands and currents. A Volkswagen at the door, and there we are! Christopher Columbus, ready to set sail!

The title of Ira Levin's most recent book gives me the word I was looking for. If May is crazy, it is crazy for life. An unbearable happiness.

SUNDAY, JUNE 10

Each blade of grass I'm walking through on my way up the Solutré rock is a flower. My steps trace a rainbow path, where blue and mauve are the dominant colors. These days of Pentecost, just before the summer solstice, are truly the high point of the year. Soon, lying on my back under a cherry tree, I will watch the slow arc of the sun. It is as though time had stopped. How apt, that thought, here in Lamartine country. Milly is less than three miles away, on the other side of the Gransart peak. I'll stop there this evening, on my way to Cluny, just as I always do at this time of year. In front of the tall iron gate which leads up to "the dark and rustic roof that only the mountain shelters in its shadow," we will exchange the ritual remarks over the ivy, which in this instance is wisteria, and the three steps which are really five. Someone will recite "Here is the rustic bench where my father sat," and "Life has scattered, like seeds of grain in the air, mother and children who once dwelt happy here." I repeat this confession: I have a tender spot for Lamartine that has resisted all efforts to dislodge it, despite the sentimentality of his poorer poems (among so many that are admirable) to his fantasies as an historian. I consider "The Lake" (yes, I said "The Lake"!), several pages from *The Stonecutter of Saint-Point*, a number of characters "the Girondins," countless aspects of *The Layman's Guide to Literature*, and certain of his speeches to the National Assembly of the Second Republic as among the best political and literary works to come out of his century.

The eclipse he has suffered upsets me. From the top of the Solutré peak, when there are no mists rising from the Saône River, you can make out the line of the Jura range and, at times, beyond the soaring summits of the Alps, the square face of Mont Blanc, more imagined than visible. But today the light is too dense, and one can barely see beyond the Bresse mountain peak. The peculiar aspect of today's light brings the term "black light" to mind, not as chemists would use the term but as Giono does in his *Ennemonde and Other Characters*, which is perhaps his masterpiece. In it he tells how, in the Camargue, when you come down out of the hills sometimes the landscape suddenly vanishes, as though burnt, black with light.

I remain a long time, sitting and watching this view that I've been contemplating now for some twenty-eight years. From this vantage point, I can best view everything that comes or goes, and especially that which does not move at all.

TUESDAY, JULY 10

I wrote a letter to Prime Minister Messmer, urging him not to go to Tokyo, saying that it did not serve our national interest or ambitions to do so. They will not listen to me. But I shall have said what I thought. Here is the text of my letter:

Dear Mr. Prime Minister:

I am introducing today a written question at National Assembly, requesting that Parliament be informed, in an extraordinary session, of the development of the monetary crisis, so that it can learn what the government's position is on the matter and hear the opinion of the people's representatives. While I apologize for this unusual procedure, I nonetheless think it worthwhile for me to write you this letter, the purpose of which is to stress how important it is, as I am sure you are well aware, to clarify the situation as soon as possible.

In the course of the last parliamentary session, I expressed to your government on two different occasions the concerns the Socialists and Left Radicals feel about the American offensive against both the economic and monetary mechanisms of the European Economic Community, and the inability of the latter to defend itself. During the debate on the economy, Mr. Giscard d'Estaing limited his answer by saying that in focusing on the Nixon Round I was departing from the basic subject agreed to, then went on to deal with growth, expansion, foreign trade, prices and employment, as though French views on these subjects were not wholly dependent on the economic situation worldwide. Minister of Foreign Affairs Jobert cast a new light on the matter during the debate on foreign policy, and showed that he viewed most seriously the situation created by the decision on the part of the United States to impose on the Tokyo talks on international trade the dictates of its own national and imperial interests. But, either because he lacked further hard evidence or because he may have yielded to the usual temptations of diplomacy—which often lose sight of priorities—Mr. Jobert explained to the National Assembly the tactics France had at its disposal within the preestablished framework of Western relations, without going any further or outlining the strategic themes without which it would be unreal to hope that present tendencies might be reversed.

Your declaration yesterday to the Financial and Economic Press Association did not clarify matters, or, to be more precise, only confirmed my impression that the government had not yet fully assessed the situation, unless of course it had decided not to make its knowledge public. "The real question," you said yesterday, "is to find out how far the Americans intend to let this situation evolve." But my response to that, Mr. Prime Minister, is that the answer to that question has been known since the day in 1971 when Mr. Nixon decided unilaterally to break the agreement on which worldwide stability was based. We know, the world knows, "how far the Americans intend to let this situation evolve." They have already devalued the dollar twice. Do you believe that the stabilization of the dollar Monday on European money markets, at exchange rates roughly equivalent to those of last Friday, is actually very different from a third devaluation, this one official? We know, the world knows, that the United States has no intention of reverting to a convertibility that would make immediate and extraordinary demands on its gold reserves. We all know that it has no intention of modifying its present policy of foreign investment, which is one of the underlying causes of the present difficulties; that in order to reestablish its balance of payments it first has to reestablish its balance of trade, and that in order to reestablish its balance of trade nothing is easier than keeping the dollar weak. What point is there in begging the government of the United States to strengthen its own currency? If it has not done so, it is because of a deliberate decision and not the result of chance, negligence, or impotence. It doubtless deems it more opportune and urgent to provoke constant imbalance in the foreign money markets, especially those of the Common Market, and, on the eve of the Nixon Round, to take advantage of the absence of international regulations to advance its pawns on a chessboard it already controls. This tactic enables it to capture new markets while at the same time giving its domestic production the chance to regain its former health. Thus a weak dollar is a means like any other to adopt protectionist measures. To expect the United States to accept fixed parities, even if they were flexible, before the end of the trade battle in which it is involved, is to be either blind or totally unrealistic. The only point at which one could imagine it might decide to stop the hemorrhage is when the double danger caused by continuing inflation on the one hand and the problems posed by the necessary imports of oil and raw materials on the other, threatens its domestic economy. At the same time, the risks that the members of the Common Market run (and their interdependency is clearly open to question, judging by the unilateral instability of both the pound sterling and the lira) is clearly evident, if they have to look forward to an even greater economic cooperative effort in order to withstand the shocks that may be forthcoming from the American economy.

You declared to the press that "if the monetary crisis deepens, the risks for the French economy are certainly not negligible." The wilful use of understatement will not keep French citizens from understanding very quickly that it is not a matter of "if," that the crisis is worsening, that the French economy will be affected by it, and that the French Government has a duty to react other than to hope that the Americans "will not let the situation deteriorate any further." It would be foolish to take at face value the opinion expressed by the American ambassador that the devaluation of the dollar at its present level is sufficient to redress the problem of the American balance of payments. The spokesman for the American Treasury Department in Basle, at the conclusion of the meeting of the governors of the central banks, expressed the state of mind more clearly when he maintained, "No measure, imminent or long-range, is contemplated that would lead us to change our attitude."

Mr. Prime Minister, despite the differences that divide us in a number of areas, I am convinced that neither your own character nor your conception of France's role in this matter will allow you to let the situation remain at this pass. But the government has not properly assessed the full importance of the stakes involved, on which our future depends. The commercial success of the Common Market is as evident as is its failure on the monetary front, a failure linked to the absence of any real political policy. In order to combat this success on the trade front, the United States must increase its pressure on the particular point already proven to be weak, namely the monetary area of Europe. If one also takes into account the apparently insatiable appetite of the multinationals, which gobble up everything in their path, even at the price of speculation, unemployment, and poverty, how can anyone, faced with that rising tide, that conjunction of dangers, fail to be upset by the apparent passivity of our government leaders? What we are dealing with is nothing more or less than our national independence, as well as the survival of the European Community, which we have freely brought into existence. It is clear that the United States is going into the Nixon Round with the clear intention of breaking up the Common Market, starting with its agricultural interests. Perhaps in this endeavor they will find ready partners among some of our European colleagues who are not overwhelmingly committed to perpetuating a system they themselves deem inadequate.

Be that as it may, any new measure, presumably protective, which instead of going to the heart of the matter prolongs its ambiguity, will serve only to strengthen the resolution of the United States to persist in its present direction. Among the stop-gap measures of which we are aware, the reactivation of the Swap agreements between the Federal Reserve Board and the European Central Banks will doubtless only help the Americans strengthen their currency. But is that what they want? So we keep coming back over and over again to the policy underlying the monetary moves. What is Nixon's policy? We can guess it easily. What is ours? It remains invisible, or at least undeclared.

I would not like to resume in any easy formula or by a wholly negative act the essential attitude to take. But I write you to say quite openly and bluntly: We must not go to Tokyo. Your minister of economy and finance has gone on record as saying that France reserved the right to make its position known as soon as the Nixon Round talks begin. Won't that be too late? It would be better to let the United States know that we have no intention of participating in negotiations which make no sense to us. To do so would be to make our opinion clear to everyone, especially to the American people themselves who above and beyond their political leaders— and often despite them—remain aware of and sensitive to their great historical mission. The time has also come to turn to our own partners in the European Community in an effort to make them close ranks, and to have France once again assume the role that, over the past twenty-five years, has several times been hers, namely to come up with imaginative proposals and possible solutions to the problems confronting us, to act as a catalyst for the collective energies of the European countries to which we are joined.

Such are the thoughts I wanted to submit for your consideration, Mr. Prime Minister, while waiting for the full-scale debate the situation calls for at the National Assembly. I trust that they will be

understood as the contribution of one citizen among many toward
the defense of our people, who today are threatened from without
by a formidable coalition of public and private interests.

The government has nothing to fear from total candor, that form
of courage no one disputes you, but the most difficult.

Yours very truly.

THURSDAY, AUGUST 23

An invitation to the festivities marking the anniversary of the
Liberation of Paris reached me this morning. I shall politely decline, as I do every year. I have long ago ceased taking part in
official ceremonies. I cannot picture myself greeting and shaking
hands, and listening to speeches as though there were some tie of
the past stronger than the realities of the present. I shall be sorry
not to see some of my old comrades-in-arms. But I shall be happy
to feel myself free of any obligations with regard to a history I
lived through, and that I know well enough so as to no longer be
willing to accept any counterfeit versions. So I shall stay home.
Over dinner, my oldest son, Christophe, asked me about the first
meeting between de Gaulle and the people of Paris, at the time of
the Liberation. Here is what I told him.

De Gaulle arrived at the Hôtel de Ville, "cold, preoccupied with
this new world he was trying to figure out, which he generally
did," as Georges Bidault relates, "much more by closing his eyes
in order to meditate than by opening his eyes in order to learn."
The top leaders of the Resistance within France were there to
greet him with pomp and circumstance in the second-story salon.
He listened, ill at ease, to Georges Marranne talk about the Resistance, Georges Bidault about the Republic, and his answer was
brief, to say the least. Then an incident occurred which de Gaulle
related in his *Memoirs*. "As I was preparing to leave," writes de
Gaulle, "Georges Bidault called, 'General! We ask that you solemnly proclaim the existence of the Republic to the people assembled in the square outside.' To which I replied, 'The Republic
never ceased to exist. Free France, France fighting under the Oc-

cupation, the French Committee for National Liberation, all in turn incarnated the Republic. Vichy was, and always shall remain, null and void. I am the president of the Republic. Why need I go and proclaim it?' "

I did not personally hear that exchange, which took place in the office of the Prefect for the Seine, Marcel Flouret, but several eye witnesses told me of it. I noted nonetheless that the new master of France was ill at ease, especially when others managed to slip into the popular mold. During these emotion-filled hours, he neither said nor conveyed anything, and remained totally uncommunicative. In the midst of this feverish circle, all those unknown noisy people who surrounded him and pressured him in one way or another, he tried to isolate himself, raising his head toward the ceiling, shook it from left to right as though trying to sort out the obtrusive suggestions being wafted up to him. Then, wishing to greet the throngs of Parisians waiting in the square below, he climbed onto a windowsill (there is no balcony at the Hôtel de Ville), waved his arms, and held up his fingers in the familiar V for victory sign, while the crowd, never strong when it came to identifying faces, shouted "Long live Leclerc!" Behind him officials were crowding the window, and the pushing and shoving was such that de Gaulle almost lost his balance. He turned around and said, "For the love of God, watch out!" Two of us, Colonel de Chevigné and I, were holding his legs to keep him from falling. We took advantage of the occasion to introduce ourselves again.

The following day the official arrival of de Gaulle took place, a solemn entrance into this kingdom which was offering itself to him as it had never done since the reign of Henry of Navarre. I participated as best I could in the extraordinary procession that took him from the Arch of Triumph to the Cathedral of Notre Dame. In spite of the seeming spontaneity of the moment, a protocol more careful than ever about the prerogatives of the chief executive placed the provisional secretary-generals, of whom I was one, a few yards closer to the tomb of the Unknown Soldier than were the members of the National Council of the Resistance, but still too far to be overly close to the handful of real VIPs, who themselves were kept a suitable distance from the hero of the occasion. De Gaulle made a quick tour, shaking several hands, his head high, his eyes seemingly fixed on the horizon but in reality looking within. That was as much as I could see. Caught up in the human river that one of the biggest floods in our history had caused to overflow its banks, I disappeared in one of the many eddies of the current. Thus was I excluded from the photographic record of the only public event I have really wanted to be in. It is not every day that you see, in bright sunlight, France incarnate in its high hopes for the future parading down the Champs-Elysées toward its future. In order to get a better view of the extraordinary spectacle, I left the parade and took up a position overlooking it on the fifth floor of 44 Champs-Elysées. I was watching it from the window when suddenly firing broke out. It seemed to come from every direction at once. Wherever the crowd had room, it flattened itself against the pavement. Elsewhere the mass of people seemed to freeze and stand stock-still. It looked like a field of wheat during a summer storm, where part of the stalks are flattened while elsewhere they remain upright. Groups of armed commandos formed almost immediately and disappeared into the doorways and to the roofs of the buildings from which the gunfire seemed to have come, and soon reappeared leading a few ill-kempt unfortunates whose expressions of terrified innocence seemed to betray their guilt.

Was one of those captured yellow-skinned? The rumor grew and grew until it reached the Tuileries Gardens: "Apparently the ones who opened fire were Japanese." Last year, one of my former comrades-in-arms asked me, in all seriousness, "Where in hell did those Japanese come from, anyway?" But the bullets, whether of exotic origin or not, were real bullets. They killed or wounded several dozen French citizens who had forgotten that death had not signed any truce. Fearless and undaunted, General de Gaulle, whose height loomed above the crowd, continued walking down the Champs-Elysées without wavering so much as an inch from his predestined route. In fact, he had profited from the confusion to save the State from yet another danger. Having noticed that André Le Troquer, high commissioner of the liberated regions and, therefore, a member of the new administration, was walking on his left, while Georges Bidault, president of the National Council of the Resistance, was walking on his right, with a peremptory gesture he reversed their places. At Notre Dame, during the Te Deum, there was another burst of gunfire. Standing, de

Gaulle was a perfect target. But again he did not move a muscle. Probably the shooting was not meant to kill him. Or was it an act of provocation? Staged by whom? And to what end? No answer was given to these questions, nor to my knowledge was any ever sought.

WEDNESDAY, SEPTEMBER 12

Shortly before midnight, I learned of Salvador Allende's suicide. This morning, I have followed the latest events on the radio and through the newspapers. The bulletins issued by the rebels who prepared the coup have to be considered suspect. But it is clear that they are in control of the capital and major cities. This carefully prepared coup, which we have felt coming for several months, was nonetheless belied by Chile's own history. There had only been two military coups in a hundred and fifty years, one of which collapsed after only a few days. The other, which in 1891 had toppled President Balmaceda from power, seemed to be the exception which only reaffirmed the democratic traditions of the country. The Moneda Gallery, which leads to the presidential office in Lima, is lined by the busts of earlier chiefs of state. Salvador Allende showed them to me during the visit I made to Chile with Gaston Defferre and Claude Estier in 1971. I remember that he paused in front of the bust of José Balmaceda. "He was a Conservative," he said, "elected by the Right of the time, the same Right that is still with us today. But he was a Conservative who firmly believed in the rule of law. He killed himself. All Chileans respect his memory. His heroic act has become part of our national heritage. I think that by taking his own life, Balmaceda saved what was basic to our democratic traditions."

A few hours before our departure, Allende invited us to return for another visit. Gaston Defferre and Claude Estier remember that moment as clearly and vividly as I do. Standing behind his chair, with his elbows leaning on the back of it, Allende spoke to us at some length. His tone, utterly serious, his precise description of the obstacles he was facing, the affronts he had received, that feeling of isolation because of the United States embargo against

Chile, his impassioned appeal for understanding, for friendship among all democratic countries, for human solidarity, all made a profound impression on us. We were in the presence of the man who incarnated that unusual experiment, a revolution that had evolved legally. The deep concern he voiced in no way diminished his resolve. On the fragile scale of humanity, what does that faith in man's reason and in the ineluctable march of societies toward progress weigh, now that on the other side of the scale there is Allende's death? Tomorrow millions of people around the world will ask themselves that same question even more impatiently, and with even greater anger.

A reporter says to me, "Doesn't this prove that a Socialist experiment of this sort is not viable?" I reply, "Doesn't this prove that the Right and all its incarnates—the power of money and the dictatorship of a class—refuses to recognize any law except its own, a law which is unwritten but irrevocable?" Salvador Allende was elected president of Chile in accordance with the constitution of the land. The popular majority which nominated him was confirmed by a vote of Parliament. He formed his Popular Unity Government with a mixture of Socialists, Communists, radicals, Social-Democrats, and members of the Christian Left who had nominated and supported him. I do not know the name of a single member of the opposition parties, a single Catholic priest, a single journalist who has been either persecuted or put in prison because of political beliefs. The commander-in-chief of the Army, General Schneider, was assassinated shortly after the election of the new president. The murder was attributed to "far-Left extremists." But the truth soon became apparent: The extreme Right wanted to take advantage of this crime to rally the army to its side. Organize a putsch. General Viaux, instigator of the attack and sentenced as such, was liberated two and a half years later. In recent days he has been reported in a country near Chile, and by now he is probably back in the country. A plot fomented by the CIA together with the American multinational ITT was exposed in the nick of time. A regiment marched on the presidential palace, opened fire, killing some innocent bystanders and several sentinels before giving themselves up. Allende's aide-de-camp was machine-gunned to death at home. Allende himself became an open target.

The Chilean Parliament voted unanimously for the nationalization of the copper industry. The United States froze the market. In this country which has historically been an importer of foodstuffs, and where huge farms and ranches are commonplace (one family owned more than 1,500,000 acres of land), the Social-Democratic Government of Allende's predecessor, Eduardo Frei, had passed a law expropriating all lands whose arable land exceeded 250 irrigated acres. Allende applied the law: he was blamed for organizing famine.

At Santiago, literally beneath Allende's windows, I bought one evening copy of the largest daily newspaper, El Mercurio, which was owned by Chile's largest banker. Its headline that day was: SALVADOR ALLENDE, LIAR. There were no legal proceedings against the paper for defaming the head of state. Freedom of the press! Two out of three radio and television stations were owned by the opposition parties, who used them to incite the population to violence. One had been shut down for several months, but this past week Allende had authorized it to start broadcasting again.

I write these lines in haste. There is so much to say about Salvador Allende. A young minister of health in the Popular Front Government of 1938, a member of Parliament, president of the Senate, three times candidate for the presidency before winning the election, he could be proud of his successful career. But he was also the first person to join Fidel Castro and Che Guevara in the great struggle that he in turn symbolizes, for he now counts among the heroes of the revolutionary movements that foreshadow a new day in Latin America.

Later, I shall discuss what might have been in relationship to what actually was. I shall draw up a list of gains and losses. But on this day of mourning, I think that if there are other riches besides gold and insolence, the world is poorer today than it was just a day ago.

TUESDAY, SEPTEMBER 25

The television reporter Etienne Mougeotte asked me this morning on camera what I thought of General Maurin's declaration: "The army is not in the service of capitalism," and added: "Does that strike you as reassuring?" I explained that it was not up to me to be reassured and that I believed in General Maurin's sincerity. The temptation of a military coup d'état faced by a tottering regime always exists, and that is true anywhere in the world. Neither the United States nor Soviet Russia is free from the possibility of a military takeover. A succession of political setbacks in foreign policy, and therefore a threat to the integrity of the empire or sphere of influence, the weariness that derives from corruption, political scandal or simply insecurity of the people and their goods—however modest they may be—can tear the fabric of even the most firmly established societies. If I were asked what I really thought, or to rely on my intuition—which, under the circumstances would be imprudent for someone who is careful not to make political prophecies—I would venture to say that both countries in question are open to that possibility.

But that was not what Mr. Mougeotte was referring to. The parallel he was drawing, however implicitly, was between the end of Allende's Chile and the issue raised by the publisher of the French Conservative newspaper, Le Figaro, among others, and aimed directly and exquisitely at the head of a possible future Socialist government in France. The debate was by the Socialist magazine Frontières, and picked up by General Maurin: Is or is not the French army in the service of capitalism? On this point, I haven't the slightest doubt. The army, or more precisely most of the officers—for that is who the question is aimed at—have no sense of allegiance toward capitalism as an economic entity based on the domination of the social class which controls the means of production. They do not serve money, which they do not have themselves and to which they do not aspire. The young man who chooses a military career has aspirations foreign to the world around him, whose supreme law, rules, and regulations, whose ultimate end is and remains money. I do not see him becoming incensed because the nation might seek to regain control of its mineral rights or its oil or gas reserves, or because it chose to nationalize its armaments industries rather than leave them in the hands of a few private individuals. August Pinochet himself and his entourage of little Caesars would think twice before turning the Chilean copper mines back to their former North American owners. The duty and interest of the Left are one and the same: explain that the policies it proposes are in fact aimed at preserving France from enemy occupation, I mean from the rape, already well under way, of our natural resources by the multinationals. Which of our generals would scale the ramparts in defense of ITT? Even if anyone did, few soldiers would follow. This week's *Canard Enchaîné* * reveals that many younger French officers are heartsick over many of our military policies: the research carried out in our military laboratories and utilized by Dassault;** the creation of unofficial sales offices for arms and armaments, for which the French high command too often serves as intermediary. "Between the military missions and the members of the French foreign service throughout the world, literally thousands of French officers are participating in this arms traffic." A traffic that results in billions of francs of profit for the bankers and industrialists involved, notes *Le Canard Enchaîné*.

To be sure, the officers promoted to the highest ranks remain faithful to the bourgeoisie from which they come. But those who hold political power today would be wrong to assume the continued and automatic fidelity of that military group to the present system if it continues in the direction it is going. Blind obedience is no longer the way of the world, and those who look with open eyes may well react differently than earlier generations might have. In other words, the army is beginning to distinguish between a coup d'état and a stock-exchange coup. The Socialists' task is to hasten that awareness by constantly explaining and exposing, and to demystify the criteria of a society which has had the audacity to sanctify, in the name of property, the lion's share. But capitalism cannot be reduced to that. If the question is raised about the army's attitude in the face of a possible change of regime, it is because other values besides profit are at stake. To limit our criticisms of the present system to economics would be to reduce our capacity to convince. Socialism demands a morality. Any plan for a society which would turn its back on a plan for

* The satirical weekly whose political articles are especially pointed.
** The largest French aircraft company, makers of the Mirage jet fighter.

civilization would lead nowhere. Love and beauty, freedom and knowledge, have to be constantly reinvented.

In an article in the French weekly *Le Nouvel Observateur*, Gilles Martinet notes in fact that "almost a third of the younger officers are ready to listen to a Socialist language which will be one of pride, rigor, and courage." Those young men must know that with us they have nothing to lose of what constitutes their true reason for living.

WEDNESDAY, SEPTEMBER 26

I remember. Pablo Neruda is speaking. He is on the second floor of the Paris embassy, in his private quarters. Standing, he is as tall and as solid as a tower. His weary eyes narrow until they are half closed. His voice pronounces French syllable by syllable. If he is unsure of the right word, his tone questions it, changes the word for a synonym, and the flood of the sentence carries away the silt that will make the poem. Now he is dead. His house, his life, sacked and pillaged. "Already his eyes are dead with still water and with doves." I reread his *Residence on Earth*. He laments: "There are times when I grow weary of being a man." He voices hope: "When the rice withdraws from the earth its grains, when the wheat hardens and lifts its face to a thousand hands, he comes running to where the man and woman embrace to touch the innumerable sea of continuity." He rails: "Generals of treason, look at my dead house, look at shattered Spain, but from each house a burning metal shall rise instead of flowers, but from each breach of Spain, Spain shall rise, but from each dead child there will rise a rifle with eyes, but from each crime will be born bullets which will one day find your heart."

Tonight, Pablo, there are millions of us who listen to you.

SATURDAY, OCTOBER 6

"Now I wait for them, I spend all my time waiting for them." Isabelle tells me that in a toneless, almost neutral voice. They have taken her children away from her, a boy of seven, a girl of four. "They" are the French judiciary. A minor matter, when blood is flowing in Santiago, when fighting rages in the Sinai. Are we so sure it's "minor"? A thread links all men in that profound region where their true history unfolds. Like the sound that vibrates infinitely in time and space, so the suffering of a single human being encircles the earth.

But to have maimed a mother in this way, she must have been guilty of some heinous crime. Which is indeed the case. Did she kill someone? Does she drink? Take drugs? Is she a whore? Does she steal? Is she guilty of child abuse? No. She is guilty of turning her back on wealth or, to use her own expression, the one that produced such an unfortunate effect on the judges that they included it among the grounds on which they based their decision, to wit: "She intends to live outside the Establishment." To be sure, there are other charges. A divorce (agreed to by mutual consent) in which she was named the guilty party but which awarded her the custody of the children. A lover. Indian dresses that were ankle-length. A mind set and a way of thinking that came from the events of May 1968. On the other hand, her erstwhile husband who had once shared her life and tastes has returned to the Establishment. Shaved his beard, tossed his blue jeans in the garbage. Resumed his former station in life, which on the material scale is fairly high: a beautifully furnished apartment in one of the best sections of Paris. To which I could add, "etcetera, etcetera." Everything to reassure the tribunal, which made no bones about it in rendering its verdict: "The arrangement whereby the husband has an apartment communicating via an interior staircase with the apartment above occupied by his father and mother, and the hiring of a child nurse, constitute the commitment to the kind of stable life that children need, together with all the amenities attendant thereto . . ."; whereas the mother "has opted for a lifestyle diametrically opposed to that of her parents," and that "however authentic or praiseworthy the court may find that disinterested lifestyle as it applies to oneself . . . it remains that this admittedly indifferent attitude regarding material problems must be viewed differently when small children are concerned, and the court is inclined to believe that such an attitude can and must lead to traumatic conditions of life." Case dismissed. The mother shall have her children taken away from her.

Don't think for a moment, from the above description, that Isabelle is penniless or ready for public welfare. She has a job, and is not poor by any standards; there was a great deal of happiness in her household before the court intervened. Too bad for her. She does not like the society in which she lives, and society has punished her. Tit for tat. Henceforth she will exercise her right to visit her children "freely," or in case of disagreement "the first and third Sunday of every month." In such terms does Justice express itself. This mother will visit her children. The interchangeable child nurse will lend them to her from time to time for several hours at a stretch. She will not wake them up with a kiss, nor kiss them goodnight. She will not prepare their meals, nor fetch them at school. She will not see them growing up. She will wait. The days and nights will be long. At least she will have plenty of time to reflect on the foolish philosophy of those who dream of "living outside the Establishment."

Isabelle is nothing but pain and revolt. She stands there before me motionless, filled with that absence which is tearing her apart and which, I can see, is actually destroying her.

By pure coincidence, I receive a letter this morning from another young lady from the same city as Isabelle. A saleslady in a shop, she wrote me that her divorce (in which both parties accepted equal responsibility) caused her to lose both her boys. The father has the ability to bring them up in relative wealth, which she cannot do. I ask the opinion of lawyer friends and judges, who confirm my worst fears. In this area, the judiciary adds one more bead to its necklace of wrongs, if I may express myself thus. When it comes to wives separated from their husbands, they have less money than the man, or none at all. The very idea should traumatize our children horribly! This tendency—to award the children to the husband—seems to be growing, especially in several provincial courts where the judges belong to the upper middle class and adopt its norms. And what is more, any vestige of May '68 cannot go unpunished. Let it serve as a warning to the girls not to try it again. My opinion is not hard to guess: Let us do something about it, and do it quickly, or the curtain will fall on something called "the right to love."

WEDNESDAY, OCTOBER 10

I am trying to get a clear and unbiased fix on this new outbreak of war in the Middle East. Regarding the Middle East, the Common Program is a good guide, which unfortunately stops at the very point where the paths become confused (the majority is stuck there too).

On the question of Israel's right to exist, no apparent problem. The 1948 vote by the United Nations remains binding in international law, and I cannot forget that Soviet Russia was the first country to send an ambassador to Tel-Aviv. But what about Israel's right to obtain the means to exist? Here things immediately become more complicated. First of all, what is a fixed frontier? We know that since 1967 it is not the border guaranteed by the UN and the major powers. I must also point out that if, last Saturday, the Egyptian and Syrian armies had launched their attack from the Gaza Strip and the Golan Heights rather than from the Suez Canal, they would already have reached the heart of Israel. How can one trace safe borders and distinguish them from those that are not?

In concert, nations around the world have called on Israel to give back the territory (English text) or territories (French text) won during the Six-Day War. Territory or territories? A fine distinction, that shows to what extent dictionaries have become part of world strategy. Alas! Wars are not paid for with words.

TUESDAY, OCTOBER 16

I have nothing against Henry Kissinger. In fact, he interests me enormously, this Jewish immigrant who came to America as though he were setting out to conquer it. A language all his own, too, and what a pleasure that is in this cold, mechanical world. His style is also inimitable: Kissinger lives like Kissinger. All of which I view as qualities in this second-in-command of the most powerful empire in the world. And yet his Nobel Prize bothers me. First of all, I find it unfair. Speaking from a strictly logical viewpoint, it is Nixon who should have won it. The Vietnam peace is Nixon's to the same extent the Vietnam War was his. The merits of the president in the matter are one and indivisible. Or rather they should have awarded the prize by default to the Pentagon. Credit where credit is due: When you've grown accustomed to killing and you one day are forced to stop it, the change is drastic. Enough to move the Nobel Prize judges to tears. While on the subject, I would like to make a few suggestions to the Nobel Prize jury to make amends for past oversights: Suharto, who has stopped massacring the Communists in Indonesia, or at least has drastically cut down on his kill rate; Papadopoulos, who has put away his instruments of torture and reopened the islands that had been serving as his political prisons to tourism; Idi Amin in Uganda, who since the first of the year has not broken the skull of a single minister. I could go on at length, but I am sure my readers get the point: I don't want to alienate half the world.

I nonetheless noted in the press that sixteen Norwegian Socialists, all members of Parliament, were sufficiently surprised by the choice of the Nobel Prize jury that they sent the members the following telegram: "Why Kissinger rather than Helder Camera?" I shall have more to say about Camera, who is the Archbishop of Recife in Brazil, a towering figure in our time whose work among the poor there is almost legendary. But I'm afraid my Norwegian friends are missing a very important but basic point: Wherever the blood of the poor flows, there is neither truce nor peace.

FRIDAY, NOVEMBER 2

Benoîte and I are both gardeners. With Paul, her husband and my friend, she is spending two days here at Latche, as a respite. I have to confess that my last year's flowers have been a humbling experience. No problem with the dahlias, cosmos, daisies, and zinnias, who need only friendship to prosper, but my dwarf asters became so dwarfed that they disappeared from view; my black currants failed to bear; I'd prefer not to talk about my nasturtiums, which were devoured by the aphids; and as for my fig tree, it bore only one leaf, which I plucked the morning of August 15. As for Benoîte's two gardens—one in Provence, the other in Brittany—both are total triumphs! In my defense, I could try to blame the sun and rain, which last summer alternated in a manner that I can only describe as anarchical, affecting all sorts of plans and projects. But my neighbor just across the clearing, whose flowers are blooming so brightly, leaves me no choice but to give up the pretense that the mists of the Bay of Biscay drowned only my flower beds and nobody else's.

Since we are both prudent gardeners, we went down to the Landes in anticipation of the forthcoming feast day of Saint Catherine. Better to plant before winter sets in. By the time the sap begins to move in early spring, the mysterious ways of nature have already done their work, linking the root to the earth itself, nourishing the seed awake. If you put off planting till the end of February, you run the risk of being either too early or too late. It's not along the major boulevards of Paris that something in the sky, a gentle rustle of wind on your skin, a quality of silence different from that of the preceding days, will alert you to the fact that nature is about to reverse its course.

Benoîte, who is both my helpmate and rival, is modest about her success. Trowel in hand, she looks for all the world like some unpaid helper that a kind-hearted employer took on out of the goodness of his heart. But by the end of the morning I would have to be blind not to realize that of the various rights guaranteed me under the Constitution, I had lost the one that said I could plant anything I liked anywhere I liked. Nonetheless, I obey. First of all, I need her. Second, it would be unwise to pose too early the problem of woman's role in modern society. Finally, she's always right.

What knowledge she possesses! She knows every seed catalogue, which she whips open without hesitation to the right page every time; she examines, ponders, compares, hesitates over—leaving me totally out of the picture—and makes up her mind. She goes so far as to note in her rounded handwriting the various kinds and varieties of the flowers she's decided on, with, across from them, the unit price and the price per dozen in a vertical column. It looks like a poem. I can already picture as her pen moves on the Japanese anemones, white, so white around the green pistil, so very green, itself circled by a yellow ring, so yellow, or sometimes mauve, pale pink with a black heart; the gaillardias, like so many little purple and gold suns; the delphiniums, whose stalk will bend gracefully under the slight weight of the delicate blooms; the day-lilies, more sensitive than a photographic plate; and above all the blue president's clematis ("It's the variety's official name," Benoîte shrugs, "nothing I can do about it") which lives on love far more than water.

During the afternoon, high-level meeting. High on her agenda: the abysmal productivity of my fruit trees. This year I harvested a handful of apples and pears. As for my cherries, peaches, plums, and nectarines, not a single one. We reach agreement: the difficulty is in localizing the enemy. The local railroad lineman, who is interested in what we are doing, blames the westerly winds, which he claims are salty, coming as they do from the ocean. In his view, I planted the orchard (some twenty trees in all) in the worst possible location, right where the evil winds whistle in from the sea through the gap in the hills. The owner of the local nursery advises patience and reserves his judgment, adding that my trees are too young and that, before they'll begin to bear, I'll have to wait till the roots have reached the ground water. Felix, the Spaniard, leans to parasites and counsels insecticide. My neighbor, who is both farmer and carpenter, has only one word: bullfinches. We incline toward his opinion, although the nurseryman points out that bullfinches only like the flowers of the peach and plum tree, which leaves at least half the problem unsolved. I've seen these pretty thieves swoop down in their bright red vests and pounce on the buds. Following which they rub their fat round beaks to clean off the gum, then burst into songs of satisfaction. I know where they live, behind the house at the edge of the woods. They make their nests out of little branches, which they line with moss and lichen. They're friendly birds, enjoying sitting on the windowsill and, from their profile position, look at what's going on inside. The only thing that upsets them are dogs, which clearly belong to another world.

The mayor, who happens by, gives his own diagnosis of the problem, agreeing with some points, disagreeing with others. When his speech is over, I understand much more clearly than before how happy I should be, how lucky I should consider myself, how privileged a person I am to have obtained the little from my orchard that I did, and how silly I was to have complained at all. For in the unlikely event that a bud survives the wind, the frost, the parasites, the bullfinches ("and," adds the mayor, "the fertilizers") and, miracle of miracles, reaches full bloom, only a fool or madman would celebrate prior to biting into the fruit itself. Far faster to get there will be the blackbird and starling. Have you ever listened to the blackbird sing in that silence that marks the fragile line between the end of night and the start of day? When the soloist hits the first notes, a whole concerto of flutes responds. The blackbirds of the area are celebrating dawn. But when later in the summer the garden is in full bloom, they will be more discreet when in the first light of day they swoop down upon the varied delicacies it has to offer. At the slightest sound they take off into the thick woods nearby, from where they can survey the interrupted banquet area, to which they will return as soon as the all-clear signal sounds. The starlings, less ardent music lovers than the blackbirds, are possessed of a singular gift. Like their distant cousin the myna bird, they are excellent mimics. You think, for example, that you are hearing the innocent oriole, or else the high-pitched whistle of the tea kettle on the stove, when all the while the starling is having fun. I can always recognize it with its dark plumage tinged with purple, in winter spotted with white. Always on the lookout for a good deal, an inveterate nomad with sedentary habits, the starlings travel in noisy groups which sweep away all in their path.

Against the advice of the other members of this high-level council, I haven't the heart to solve the problem by shooting the birds, or, far worse, setting traps for them. Benoîte, who in the course of any discussion on any subject invariably opts for the pacifists, approves my decision. Which leaves the cruel dilemma unresolved: birds, or fruit? In an effort to solve it, someone suggests setting up scarecrows. There is the old-style model, the one that looks like a phony vagabond with his broom-head topped by an old hat, arms crossed, shirt flapping in the wind, to be posted wherever there is any danger that birds might steal your seeds. More modern are the rolls of plastic you find in these parts, leftovers from the local factories that manufacture yogurt containers famous around the world. When you unfold them they are useful either as ornaments or for garden fencing. Because of the holes they don't tear in the wind, and since they shine in the sunlight the birds are frightened by them, or at least have not yet figured out quite what they are. There are also nets you can wrap around the boughs, which make your orchard look for all the world like some gigantic display for a hairdresser's salon. Attacking birds discover that their beaks are too short to reach the coveted buds, and finally settle for wild berries instead. After having examined all the pros and cons of the problem, we make up our minds to spend the winter thinking about it.

So does the day pass. But we still haven't prepared our compost. Benoîte goes about it with all the skill of a master chef preparing some secret sauce (and those who have tasted her cooking know that the analogy is well taken). Not only will the plants feed on elements richer than the normal sandy soil, but the compost will also retain the necessary degree of humidity to get the onions and rootlets started. Planting is a ceremony. Benoîte sets out, and I water. One to three quarts for each plant. The water from the house smells of iron, and less than a hundred yards from here, the water from the studio smells of sulphur. In one spot blackberries grow wild, and a short distance away not at all. On one side of the hill the pine trees flourish, while on the other they

refuse to grow. The thick carpet of ferns that covers the underbrush along the dunes stops at the edge of the water, while a tall,
sickly grass invades the neighboring parcel. Try and figure it all
out! Experience alone will teach you to understand the nature of
water and the operation of the winds. Bent over a seed, Benoîte's
smooth face is ten thousand years old.

When we go inside, Paul, his brow furrowed with thought,
brings me back to the intertwined torments of literature and politics. "I remember your writing somewhere," he said to me, "that
the words *baragot* and *baragouin* have the same root. Wrong. The
latter comes from the Celtic, and the word derives historically
from the words *bara* meaning bread, and *gwin* meaning wine,
which the Breton soldiers during the Franco-Prussian War kept
asking the Army of Mans for in 1871. No one had the faintest
notion what they wanted. Fact is, things haven't changed very
much."

WEDNESDAY, NOVEMBER 14

This past week has been a heavy one for me. Sunday I was in
London to attend an emergency meeting of the Socialist International called by Bruno Pittermann in order to hear Golda Meir
and to compare opinions on the Middle East situation. Monday
long hours at the House of Representatives, in a session that went
on well into the night (I'm not a night person) on foreign policy,
for which I was our party's spokesman. The next morning, Tuesday, a major press conference, which I find fatiguing because of
the tension created by the necessity to weigh every word, for one
wrong one, or one word taken wrongly, can result in all sorts of
unfortunate and undesired polemics. Today I have to spend the
morning writing an article for *L'Unité*, and this afternoon preside
at an executive committee meeting of the Socialist Party. In short,
I need to catch my breath. In these pages I've earlier mentioned
my meetings in 1961 with the Chinese leaders in Peking, and with

Chairman Mao in Hangchow. Those meetings began at nine in the morning, broke off for lunch, reconvened at three in the afternoon and went on until dinner, without ever once being interrupted by a phone call. If an urgent message had to be transmitted to any of the Chinese leaders, the scope and magnitude of whose problems are no less than those of other leaders, who seem more frantic, discreet messengers would tip-toe in and place folded sheets of paper into a basket. The only disturbance in the course of the working day was the tea ceremony and the perfumed napkins that tradition demanded. If for no other reason, one might well dream of becoming Chinese! Of all the French political figures I've known, Robert Schuman was the only one whose desk was always clear and who always seemed to have plenty of time to spare. I'm not there yet. But I do know that I work best when I leave action and work at the door. To each his own drug. Mine is silence. As one might expect, I love it and fear it. But without it I lose that subtle sense which allows one to communicate with the essence of things. Perceptions wear thin very quickly. Three months in Paris and I can no longer tell the odors of the forest apart. That is an alarm signal for me. When I am no longer able to recognize the workings of nature, I am on the verge of forgetting what makes men tick.

THURSDAY, NOVEMBER 15

All Saints Day, in Latche, while I was reading Bourniquel's *The Lake*, a neighbor who was hunting called to me to hurry outside. A group of cranes was flying overhead, against the background of a sky more blue than gray, more gray than blue, a sky so pure and fragile it raised a lump in your throat. On the other side of the clearing other hunters raised their heads and we could hear their cries. Up there, every ten seconds, the lead crane would be replaced by another, taking its place at the rear of the formation. A never-ending relay, accompanied by a great flapping of wings, added a further intensity to the migration without altering the perfection of the design. Do you say of cranes as you do of crows that they caw? In any case, rough birdcalls filled the air.

In times past this sight would not have had such a strong effect on me. But we so quickly forget the great game of life that the migration of these long-legged birds aroused in me the obscure memory of the species, the memory of signs and symbols.

WEDNESDAY, DECEMBER 5

Venice is dying. Will it soon be said that Venice is dead? All that remains of Byzantium are the traces of horses, and the desert winds reign where Babylon once stood. Why pity Venice? After all, birth means death. But I feel that death-struggle as a fundamental defeat.

Nothing is more disturbing than beauty. Of what is it the sign, and to what else does it relate? What world does it reveal, to which only the soul has access? Whatever affects you most profoundly—be it the asymmetric relationship of one part to the other, the line of a roof, the curve of an arch, the precise measure of a column; when the juxtaposition of two walls, one the weary color of ocher, or the scald of purple, next to a washed-out blue forces you to stop and drains you of all substance; when every house is a palace and every palace a ship, when every stone is pride, every church an ornament, every island Bucentaurus; whether the city be reminiscence, theater where the actor is dream, idea of God, baroque ceremony—the beauty of Venice proves first of all that man exists.

Therein lies the scandal. The wear and tear of time and stupidity here join forces. Venice is sinking into a lagoon that is drying up and becoming polluted; the factories built at its gates are sucking in the underground water, spewing back acids, pouring smoke and detritus; domestic heating befouls the air and water, eats away at both wood and stone. Even in the slightest storms, the sea pours through the three openings into the lagoon and floods the low-lying districts. Over a ten-year period, the Piazza San Marco has disappeared forty-eight times beneath the flood waters, and the 1966 flood almost carried everything away with it. As it was, it left behind a layer of sickening sludge six feet deep, and befouled no end of frescoes and paintings. But if we can do little about the wear and tear of time, the stupidity of men, at least of the Venetians, has always given way to their will to live. Geographers know that the level of the seas varies according to the cooling or warming phases of the polar caps, and that the level of the Adriatic has been rising slightly more than a millimeter a year since the middle of the nineteenth century, while under the weight of the alluvial deposits brought in by the eight torrential rivers that pour into the lagoon, the level of the lagoon is lowered each year by two to two and a half millimeters. Added together, these phenomena leave the city at the mercy of the *acqua alta*, that great tide at the north end of the Adriatic which occurs when the moon, sun, rainfall and sirocco wind are in proper relationship one to the other. There are other times when the *acqua alta* is replaced by the *secca*, that time of very low tide which empties the canals, interrupts communications, brings the water level down to the sludge. The activity of the rivers, which change their beds in accordance with the rise and fall of the tides, accelerates that silting effect, all the more so because, coming from the other direction, the currents of the ocean bring sand deposits with them. Dunes emerge, small islands topped with the shells of crustaceans form, cut off the normal currents, and modify the offshore bars. And that has been going on for thirteen hundred years. In earlier days, the Venetians dredged the channels, changed the direction of the rivers or canalized their beds, sacrificed the areas that were choked with mud, constructed breakwaters that reinforced the offshore bars and enabled them to control the entrance of the sea the way doctors control a patient's breathing. Thus "the most prodigious urban event on the face of the earth," as Le Corbusier describes it, continued to exist over the centuries. Now, however, this miracle of equilibrium is threatened more than ever. To the already existing natural pressures are added the aggressions of the industrial era. A stone's throw from old Venice a new Venice has risen, filled with petrochemical and metallurgical factories, plus a number of other industrial enterprises, all of which attract natives of old Venice in search of work. In the past fifteen years, the City of the Doges has lost a staggering 40 percent of its population. Each year, twenty thousand tons of sulphuric acid pour out of these factories and attack the stones, the paintings, and pilings of the Old City. Because of the heavy maritime traffic in and out of the industrial area, the access channels have had to be deepened, which in turn has led the banks to slide and impeded the circulation of the lagoon's canals. The constant passage, day in and day out, of the big merchant vessels and of thousands of motor boats shakes and loosens the foundations. As a result of all these unsettling factors, the normal movement of the waters no longer protects the ebb and flow on which Venice's health depends. Braunstein and Delort write that each year Venice is losing 6 percent of its marble work, 5 percent of its frescoes, 5 percent of its furniture and sacred decorative art, 3 percent of its canvas paintings, 2 percent of its paintings on wood, not to mention the buildings themselves.

Experts who were called in for consultation right after the 1966 catastrophe argued at great length about the remedies needed to be taken before they finally agreed on an emergency plan: the construction of aqueducts, the suspension of pumping waters from the water table, the transformation of the factories (or, more drastically, moving them away entirely), the substitution of gas for oil for both domestic and industrial consumption, creation of a network of sewers, and the protection and replacement of the pilings. The Italian Government passed a special law allotting 300 billion lira to finance the five-year plan, and borrowed the money from two English banks. UNESCO decided to support the Italian effort, and its Director General René Maheu was named to the board of the International Committee to Save Venice, created for that purpose and headed by René Huyghe of the Académie Française. National committees were set up in a number of foreign countries. Money raised in France was used to restore the Church of the Salute. From Germany, Great Britain, the United States, came two billion lira. So was Venice saved? No, it was not! The decrees implementing that special law have still not been passed by the Italian Government. The 300 billion lira borrowed for that purpose have been used for other things, and dissipated. Given the level of inflation over the intervening years, it would take two or three times the original amount to accomplish the same work. Lord only knows what became of the two billion lira raised from abroad (which, by the way, the Italian Government did not exempt from taxation). Part of the plan includes the construction of concrete buildings within old Venice which will rise twelve to twenty feet above the traditional buildings (and if we're to judge by the modernization of the Goldoni Theatre, which was a shocking display of poor taste, we can scarcely be reassured as to the intentions of the Italian architects). Finally, the plan calls for reducing accesses to the sea to two hundred yards in width, whereas a reduction to one hundred would in itself constitute a dangerous breach. No one will be surprised by the reasons for this gross negligence. We are all well aware that the Christian Democratic Party has other things on its mind besides the health of the most beautiful city in the world. It is impossible to serve two masters at the same time, and it would appear that the Italian leaders have made up their mind that they must at any cost—and what a cost it is!—not upset the status quo. Let Venice perish rather than risk upsetting the silent partners, those who keep them in power by controlling the vote. The factories neighboring Marghera and Mestre belong to powerful industrialists. Two of the companies are part of multinationals. Who would dare refuse them necessary legal permits to carry on their business? Who would dare tell them to stop breaking the law, cease their past abuses? There is no more terrible example of the contradictions of capitalism, which is incapable of resisting the temptation of immediate gain, even if it means destroying a priceless treasure.

FRIDAY, DECEMBER 7

On a short stop-over on his way to Moscow, Cuba's Assistant Prime Minister, Carlos Rafael Rodríquez, comes over for lunch.

The subject turns to Chile. He tells us about the wonderful day in June he spent at Allende's house, together with the same generals who in September would kill him. That day everyone was in a good mood and chatting aimiably. In the midst of all this friendly urbanity, one person stood out especially by the cordiality of his remarks and his good-natured appearance. His name was Pinochet. In the president's drawing room, there was an easy chair in which Allende liked to relax. As coffee was being served, one of the guests seemed to be going to sit in it. Carlos Rafael recalls that it was one of the military figures, but not which one. Allende stopped him and said pleasantly, "Not in that one, my friend. For you to occupy that place for even one minute would be one minute too much!" Which made everyone laugh heartily. Those friendly generals who embraced the Allende ministers with great slaps on the back bespeaking intimacy were considered by everyone in Santiago to be loyal to the regime. Which leads me to ask: how were the others?

TUESDAY, DECEMBER 18

In his ground-floor office at the Cité Malesherbes in Paris, Claude Estier was listening on his static-ridden transistor to a radio interview with Prime Minister Pierre Messmer. It was shortly before 8:00 p.m. when I entered Estier's office to ask if he would drive me home, as he often did. On the radio, the prime minister was talking in a blustering tone and in a manner I can only describe as regimental, as though his two interviewers were simple soldiers and he was the colonel in command. Pierre Messmer likes to remind us that the period of his life he remembers most fondly was his time in the Foreign Legion. Seeing him, even hearing him, makes it eminently clear why. He walks with his good conscience thrust out, as one refers to someone's chest. Mr. Muscle in a way. And, indeed, the interview he was giving could fairly be described as "muscled." When the interview moved to the subject of bugging devices, Estier's car was caught in traffic in those narrow sidestreets that lead out onto the main boulevards, and we caught only snatches of the conversation. But at a red light the reception improved and we made out the following: "Let me tell you one thing. When it comes to bugging, Mitterrand is a champion. I won't say he holds the world record, but he was a champion." The rest was lost in a shower of static. I remained stupefied. When I got home, several friends called to reaffirm that I had heard correctly, and the newspapers the following day dispelled any remaining doubts on the subject. That afternoon, the authoritative *Le Monde* carried the story in these words, quoting the prime minister: "I have taken a more than casual interest in the matter, now that my position allows me to look into it. . . . When Mitterrand was interior minister there was more bugging going on than there is today, and I don't mind saying that he [Mr. Mitterrand] had no compunction about listening in on what the politicians were saying."

If I had a bent for irony, I would point out that the prime minister—now that his position allows him to look into it—seems far better informed about the bugging devices of 1954 than he does about those of 1973. But I feel too outraged to indulge in tirades. I've thought about the matter long and hard. It is a serious matter, it is difficult to write that a head of government is a liar. I have a great deal of respect for the position that Mr. Messmer holds. And I have always been careful never to attack him personally. First, that's not my style. Second, I have no reason to do so. I knew Messmer back when he was an overseas functionary under the Fourth Republic (in fact, he reported to me), then later when he was an associate of Gaston Defferre, and I found him to be a loyal and courageous man. I am therefore choosing my words carefully in order to find some that will be more measured than those I am tempted to write because of what he has done. One injustice does not deserve another. Perhaps he simply forgot to verify the gossip whispered in his ear, or perhaps he lost his composure and got carried away in the course of the interview. It's sad to see him riding roughshod over the opposition as soon as his own majority attacks him, and I am sad rather than irritated when I see this man losing the sense of what he should be doing. I say all this fully realizing that leading this majority, which seems crisis prone to say the least, cannot exactly be a bowl of cherries, and must be wearing on even the most solid nerves. I find it very hard to believe. But it is up to Mr. Messmer and nobody else to reestablish the truth.

I can jog his memory. I could start by challenging him to back up what he has said with solid proof. But I also ask that he open up the files of the Ministry of the Interior. There he will find a memorandum dated July 1, 1954—in other words only a few days after the formation of the Mendès France Government and my arrival as minister of the interior—from the minister of foreign affairs thanking me for the decisions I had taken regarding electronic bugging devices and asking me to forward him a copy of my written instructions on the matter so that he could pass them on to the security forces that reported to him. He will also find the letter that I sent to Mr. Mendès France himself the following day, July 2, as well as the instructions I had sent both to the prefect of police and the director of national security, expressly forbidding the use of any political electronic surveillance.

Mr. Messmer takes pride in the number of bugs currently in use, "the lowest number," he claims, "since 1946." Less than 500, he adds. Here again I can refer to hard numbers: In 1954, there were between 25 and 30 bugs in operation, all without exception planted with the knowledge and consent of the judiciary on persons suspected of actions harmful to the State either domestically or on the foreign front. I am ready and willing to publish the names of the high functionaries who were in charge of overseeing the execution of my decisions and who have informed me, despite the fact that they are still on active duty and therefore subject to prosecution by the powers that be, that they will testify in my behalf.

This matter has only begun. I declared before the National Assembly that if Mr. Messmer gave me his word of honor, I would be willing to believe his explanations and clarifications. Otherwise, I would have to conclude that the prime minister has two "words," one for the public, the other for private circles, and that his "word of honor" is reserved for the latter. I would be happy to learn I was wrong. This debate transcends ordinary polemic.

What Mr. Messmer said on the radio last Monday evening will remind those whose memories are good that such signs, between the two wars, were the harbingers of the storms which came within an inch of sweeping away what we call our civilization.

1974

TUESDAY, JANUARY 1

During the night the buds of the white camellia opened. I picked my first flower of the year. It is there, on my table, perfectly designed, rust-free. I like this unpretentious, stiff flower, severe there between its glazed leaves, a flower that leaves to others both languors and odors. The fog, which has been heavy the past three days, hugging the ground, has not lifted. You can sense the sun above it. I could follow it yesterday as it moved across the sky at the end of the day, a red disk in a Japanese landscape. A long walk with the dogs warmed us up. Titus, the basset hound, smelled all sorts of trails that only he could distinguish, and as soon as he had sniffed one he would bolt away, his tail raised like a periscope, barking as he does only at such moments, that is, when he is exercising his profession of hunting dog. When on some occasions he was invaded with doubt, which happened when he came to a crossroads where the traces of hare, hart, or deer mixed, he returned to consult with me, one ear awry. Titus is an open book, revealing his every mood, sharing his doubts. Grown soft by the comforts of his urban life, he at first steers clear of the thorny bushes. But how can one resist life's natural passion? Happiness, as long as it lasts, is forgetting oneself. When back home, Titus will flop down in front of the fire, turn his thorn-torn tummy to the blaze, and fall asleep to dream epic dreams of mighty conquests. The other dog, Dick, a good-sized setter, gamboled through the ferns in the underbrush. What a graceful stride he has. He can do five miles as though it were a hundred-yard dash, and conquer in a few strides the tall dunes filled with clumps of gorse and canebrake. And when he reappears, just when you thought he was miles away, it is simply to check on your whereabouts before dashing off again, as fresh as when he first set off. For the sheer pleasure of it, we wandered off the path, following a steep trail that led us to a hunter's treetop shelter, that was used for hunting ring-doves. It was coming on to dusk. If we didn't want to lose our way, it was time to start back while we could still see some familiar landmarks. A water tower rising out of the mists served as our North Star. We returned home, comrades linked by friendship yet nonetheless separated, the way one is when the mind moves in time to the rhythm of your feet, before galloping off on its own once again.

WEDNESDAY, JANUARY 2

Georges Pompidou intrigues me. I sense that he is exasperated at the notion of an ordinary destiny. His ambitions are higher than the chair upon which, it must be said, he sat without lowering himself. But everything he touches crumbles. Either he has clumsy fingers or the walls that he inherited, believing they were of granite, are really made of sand. Of the two hypotheses, I opt for the latter. But no one knows it, except he and I and a handful of other people. De Gaulle made up, for the use of the French people, an imaginary world. In the forest of Brocéliande, Merlin the Magician is king. Where is Brocéliande today? The people are asking for expressways through it. The president of France, who is not at his best when speaking extemporaneously, touched me in the course of his televised New Year's address, because of the trace of emotion I thought I detected at the end of his speech. It has been eleven years now that he has been holding the reins of that phantom team generally referred to as the government of the Fifth Republic. He, who put his pride on the line, is becoming irritated and concerned by the number of obstacles, the twists and turns in the path leading to nowhere. What remains of that career which, on the personal level, can only be termed meteoric until his election as president in 1969? Not much sand left in his political hourglass. Perhaps that is why there was something touching about his speech the other evening. Most of the commentators seemed especially aware of the tartness of the tone. And they were not wrong, either. Beneath the mask of unanimous platitudes, Georges Pompidou was really only wishing one out of every two French people a happy New Year: the one who votes properly, who prospers under the present administration, who is decorated indiscriminately. I would have liked to hear him talk of "order" in other terms. It is not a word reserved solely for the generals. Pascal wrote something on the subject. So did Aristotle. It would not be seemly for Mr. Pompidou to reply: "Sorry, never heard of them."

TUESDAY, JANUARY 22

Following my televised speech this past Monday night, the commentaries ranged from infrared to ultraviolet. I read them, I listen to them, and I try to learn from them. Praise is pleasant, but teaches me nothing I don't already know. Criticism stings me, but forces me to think. I used to be easily hurt, to the quick really, by sarcasm. When I was right I suffered from the injustice of the attacks. When I was wrong, my pride was hurt. Don't be misled into thinking that my equanimity is the result of wear and tear. I feel more agile than ever, even if my legs are not quite as limber as they used to be. If my peace of mind is greater than it once was, it is because I am better prepared. For example, I rarely quote a figure unless I have meticulously checked it out, not once but in several sources. I mull and examine my facts and figures to the point of driving my colleagues to distraction. In fact, they have learned to live with my phone calls at any hour of the day or night, and with my irritation if ever they forget to document their sources. I owe a great deal both to their competence and their friendship. What they owe me in return, I hope, is to have learned to be more accurate, and tougher on themselves, if that is possible.

Thus I was taken aback when I opened the newspapers the day after my talk. One paper attacked me for having miscalculated the pretax price of crude oil in relation to what the consumer pays at the pump, and also for underestimating the cost of a suburban commuter driving back and forth in a compact car to work in the city every day. Another launched a broadside at me for my estimate of the oil companies' profits. I had said: "The major oil companies stand to make an added profit from this price increase of gasoline of five and a half billion francs." Roughly a billion dollars, five hundred million pounds sterling. They were not questioning the five and a half billion, but they refused to term it "profit," claiming it was an "accounting increment." As for Alexandre Sanguinetti, the Minister of War Veterans, he went whole hog, maintaining that everything I said was wrong. Perhaps he was taking his inspiration from the famous trial lawyer who, when questioned by the judge on what article he was basing his allegations, responded, "Why, Your Honor, on the entire penal code!"

I therefore went back to verify my documentation. The notes and files are once again spread out in front of me on my table. I sifted through them from A to z, and to my embarrassment did discover that one of my figures—the price of crude oil—had indeed been erroneous. Which in no way changed the basic point I had been making, that the price of crude prior to the oil crisis had been very low indeed. The eleven other figures or percentages that I had quoted from memory were exact, including the cost of commuting from the suburbs.

I am not bringing all this up for the simple pleasure of proving myself right eleven-twelfths of the time (one error is one too many), but to ponder for a moment, publicly, the question of why it is that a person of the Left is so violently attacked the minute he

ventures into the sacred wood, I mean into that special area t̶
approved economists have reserved unto themselves. It is diffic̶
to flout the laws engraved on stone according to which one shou__
remain within one's circumscribed area of interest or expertise—in
this instance social concerns to the Left, economic matters to the
Right, the twain never to meet. As if socialism, and Marxism in
particular, had not introduced scientific reasoning into economics.

Those who demand that I take a stand or place myself politically outside the framework of the Common Program are talking
to the wrong person. If the Left is voted into office, it will be so
because a majority of French citizens will have felt the need for a
radical change in the direction this country is going. In this respect, the argument whereby Left and Right are direct opposites is
based on a misunderstanding: One side is speaking of structure,
while the other is thinking contingency. The Left, whose initial
task will be to break the chains of social inequality and thus give
the masses the share of national wealth which the ruling class
siphons off for itself, will integrate, both functionally and out of
necessity, its economic policies into the objectives that it has set
for itself and that it has laid out in black and white for the voters
to see and study. As if the factors of production, exchange rates,
and consumption refuse to conform to the fantasies of illusion: let
no one try to preach that truism to us. But is it an illusion to work
toward the creation of a society in which trust—the prime mover
of any prosperous economy—will spring from the people rather
than be handed down from on high?

Another point. Listening to Valéry Giscard d'Estaing argue this
afternoon for a floating rather than fixed franc, after having argued the opposite a month ago and for almost five years, I had to
feel that the Right must have reached the end of its techniques,
that one more step would bring it straight to the edge of the
ultimate contradiction. By taking control of the financial sector
and the major elements of production, by betting on the intelligence of the people, by looking ahead and planning for the future creatively and imaginatively, by counting on the cooperation
of the workers to participate fully in the national recovery, the
Left will be better equipped and better prepared than the mind-
less Conservative Party bureaucrats have led people to believe.

WEDNESDAY, JANUARY 30

The room in which we are waiting for Anwar el-Sadat is plainly
furnished. On a chest stands the photograph of a laughing couple,
the president's daughter and her husband, who were married with
great pomp and circumstance a few weeks ago. I look around in
vain for a portrait of Nasser. The master of the house arrives
without formality, except for the inevitable popping of the photographers' flash bulbs. After the round of introductions, we sit
down, Sadat to my right, on a settee which, except for the striped
fabric, resembles those on which I have recently sat next to Palme,
Ceaucescu, Tito, and Golda Meir. In chairs opposite us, forming a
square in accordance with the same geometry that prevails wherever we go and whomever we meet, sit my two companions and
Mohammed Heikal. The character of Egypt's president is somewhat misleading. The image that we in the West have been given
of him tends toward the caricature: the willowy figure, with a
small mustache, of a modern dancer. Instead, we are struck by the
harmony of his face, whose features are finely chiseled, whose
eyes seem not to miss a trick. His khaki uniform is devoid of
decorations. Although he was born in the Delta, he looks like one
of those peasants of Upper Egypt that you come across near the
borders of Nubia. He chooses his words carefully, and his tone
translates the movement and rhythm of his thoughts. Throughout
the talk, which was to last for two hours, he never raised his voice
or deviated from the courteous tone he adopted as soon as we
opened the discussion. And yet we both go back a long way, and
did not always enjoy the present cordiality. Since 1956 and the
Suez War, the French Socialists had severed all relations with the
Arab countries. We remember and we forget. We forget and we
remember. Is there any other way to live? I did not need to justify
my position or explain my personal responsibility as a member of
the Guy Mollet Government in those days. Sadat made one passing reference to it. "I believe this is the second time we have met,"
was all he said. I did not need to remind him that the French
Socialist Party belonged to the same international organization as

did Golda Meir's and Moshe Dayan's Mapai Party, nor that I was a longtime personal friend of Golda's. Everyone was well aware of that fact. Still, I felt compelled to point it out, so that no one could misinterpret the reason for our visit. Does the fact that one recognizes Israel's right to exist as a nation, and that one works toward that goal, mean that, automatically, one is an enemy of the Arabs?

"We have no desire to destroy Israel, and we want peace," Sadat answered. The previous evening, Vice President Fawzi and Minister of Foreign Affairs Fahmi told us much the same thing with equal conviction. "But Israel must give up the territories occupied in 1967 and recognize the reality of a Palestinian homeland," Sadat added. I raised the objection that if he espoused premises and principles that were diametrically opposed to those espoused by the Israelis, there was every possibility that the two factions would get sucked into a war. I also reminded him that Mr. Jobert, interpreting Resolution 242 in the strictest sense of its terms, had maintained publicly, from the tribunal of the Palais Bourbon, that it meant "minor rectifications of the borders," which clearly meant eventual adjustments of the present situation both in Jerusalem and on the Golan Heights. "There is not a single Arab leader who would find that arrangement acceptable," Sadat replied. "Solidarity is our law. Besides, that is a false problem. Time is on the side of the Arabs. The conquest of South America took more than a century. What is left of it? The same could be said for colonialism. Israel has more to gain from peace than from war, her security first and foremost. In the era of the guided missile, it is not a few millimeters on some ordnance survey map that matter, but the guarantee that the Arabs will offer regarding a new equilibrium in that part of the world. I am not afraid of the words 'peace' and 'reconciliation.' I uttered them solemnly in 1971 and I was totally sincere. Wasn't that a tacit admission that Israel did indeed exist? But the leaders of that country, blinded by the illusion of their own omnipotence, chose not to believe me. If the Arabs are more united than ever, the stubbornness of Israel is certainly a contributing factor."

We spoke further about the oil crisis; the relations between our two countries, which on the surface were friendly but in reality were at best lukewarm; of Europe's conspicuous absence on the Egyptian scene (which, Sadat said, he regretted); of the necessity for a common policy of all the countries bordering on the Mediterranean. But at every twist and turn of the conversation, he somehow always came back to the subject that obsesses him: peace in the Middle East. We only spoke of the Americans in passing, although in Cairo rumor has it that they will soon be returning to Egypt in a major way. I asked him about that. "The revolution has transformed Egypt," he said. "But we are a country of 37 million people, growing at the rate of a million every year, and that, plus the necessity to maintain the country on a war footing, costs a great deal of money. The time has come to put our house in shape economically, to increase productivity, to invest and upgrade our industry and agriculture." From which one could draw one's own conclusions, but it was clearly not a contradiction.

THURSDAY, JANUARY 31

Official meetings such as the one I had yesterday with Sadat are too circumscribed by conventions and formalities to get to the heart of the matter. Thus one should not expect from such a meeting more than it can provide. What does count more significantly are the subtle signs that lend the words and attitudes a new resonance, that cast new light on old problems, no matter how many times they have been discussed and debated before. Nothing replaces direct diplomacy, as the example of Henry Kissinger eloquently demonstrates. In face-to-face meetings there enters into play the game of intuition and exchanges that no other means—be it speeches, exchanges of diplomatic notes, high-level conferences, diplomatic conversations—can provide. In ours Sadat told us very little more about his plans or policies than we already knew from our usual sources of information, and that was as it should be. Yet, as we left him, we had the feeling that we did have a clearer view of things. Was it the charisma of a man who had been touched by the grace of history after it had ignored him for so long, despite the fact that for twenty years he had been intimately involved in the major events of his country? Or had we simply been surprised—and therefore seduced—to discover a man more complex and more thoughtful than the image presented by the media had prepared us for? Or was the importance, and the intensity, of the Middle East such that it also intensified the relationships that came out of such a meeting? We came away from that meeting with a sum-total of hypotheses and forecasts that far transcended anything that a strict analysis of the exchanges could provide, and we also felt, both by what he actually said and the way he said it, that he was in effect announcing a decision he had made.

From all the evidence available, a choice had been made, and that evidence, immediately discernible in the area of foreign policy, was becoming apparent on the domestic front. But if it was clear that the way the average Egyptian citizen had been living for generations was indeed drawing to a close, the interpretation of events since the Yom Kippur War varied according to those Egyptians with whom the matter was raised. Some claimed that Sadat, anxious to obtain American aid in order to put Egypt back on its feet economically, was ready to pay a high price for that aid, namely, to follow the Kissinger line in the area of foreign policy. These same sources added that by so doing Sadat felt he could kill two birds with one stone, for he would profit from this change in the country's direction to gain favor with the Egyptian middle class and thereby broaden the bases of his authority, which in fact were currently under attack from some factions in the revolutionary circles. To support their contention, they cited a long list of isolated instances, none of which appeared important in and of itself but which, taken collectively, clearly indicated a trend: his cool relations with some former revolutionary comrades; the obvious de-emphasis of the once ubiquitous Nasser cult; the elimination of some appropriations for certain social programs; his reconciliation with King Faisal of Saudi Arabia; and the addition to his inner political circle of certain advisers who once had been classified as opponents of his regime.

Others, who used the same information as the basis for their conclusions, judged that it was unfair to accuse Sadat of turning his back on the revolution. On the contrary, they said, to understand his present policies one had to realize that he was not looking to shift the country's direction radically but simply to give it time to catch its breath. For that, he needed to gather around him and his policies in these difficult times as many people and political factions as possible. In other words, he was at present working toward a kind of national union, the soul and inspiration for which remained the revolution. And after all, they added, was that not really the ultimate aim of any successful revolution, to reunite the entire nation?

The supporters of the first thesis stressed the elimination of the members of the Council of the Revolution, with the exception of Shafei, from the inner circle of the government; Ali Sabri was in prison, and Khaled Mohieddin had been stripped of all his functions. They also pointed out that despite the return to government, after five years of prison and with the signs of torture still visible on his face, of a man like Ismail Sabri Abdallah, the former—and remarkable—leader of the Egyptian Communist Party, there was still apparently the constant threat hanging over the intellectuals and militants of the Left, who sometimes were allowed to voice their opinions freely in the narrow circles who read their little magazines, and were sometimes arrested and thrown into prison by the Egyptian police.

Those who took the second view used these same arguments to prove their own point, maintaining that Sadat was employing a subtle but sure strategy aimed at normalizing the political life of Egypt, for, they said, with the exception of Ali Sabri and a few followers, and several Moslem brothers who were still in prison, repression throughout Egypt had to all intents and purposes ceased. They also cited the fact that Sadat had announced that he was allowing the ashes of King Farouk and his sister to be brought back to Egypt to be interred beside the tombs of their Mameluke ancestors, showed how deep were the roots of the revolution and how little it feared the shadow of the monarchy. They added that Sadat clearly was very much in charge of the situation, that it was he who was calling the shots, and, having demonstrated his aptitude for leadership, it was finally possible to move the revolution away from the Nasserian dream toward the practical problems that Egypt was facing in today's world.

Sadat's behavior during the Yom Kippur War, and the sudden withdrawal which had followed it, only heightened the dispute.

That Sadat sincerely wanted peace, no one denied. But that he harbored any real hope of settling, around some conference table, a conflict posed in irreconcilable terms, seemed so unreasonable that some Sadat-watchers thought they detected in that stance a new competence which would allow the Egyptian leader to freeze, through a military truce, the most hawklike members of the country, and to wait, without compromising himself—even if the wait were a long one—for the fruit to ripen among the Syrians and Jordanians.

What did Mohammed Hassanein Heikal think of all this? Heikal was the man who had arranged our visit with Sadat. Hunched over in his chair, he had listened impassively, only nodding or shaking his head from time to time. His only interruption, in the course of our interview with the president, had been when Sadat had suggested that he intended to withdraw from public life at the end of his term, three years hence. Heikal had shaken his head and said: "Egypt will still need you."

SUNDAY, FEBRUARY 3

We in the Western world have only a vague idea of the dimensions of the *Al Ahram* empire, which could also be called the Heikal empire, since for the past seventeen years Heikal has been closely identified with his newspaper. He has a million daily readers, his paper is published in seven different Arab countries, he owns the most modern printing plant in the world, installed in the basement of a skyscraper worthy of New York's Fifth Avenue. He also owns magazines and weekly papers, a center for political study and think-tanks, sponsors seminars, and directs a vast import-export network. Each Friday, his weekly editorial appears, and is discussed, dissected, and commented on throughout the Arab world. The Friday edition of the paper has a fifty percent larger circulation because of that editorial. As it happened, the previous week's editorial had been typically explosive. For a long time he had been predicting the slow but steady shift of the Sadat regime toward other social concerns, the return to power of the bourgeoisie, and the decline of the revolution. A close friend of Nasser—perhaps his closest—he had on several occasions distanced himself from Nasser's successor, without however breaking with him at any time. He had espoused the merger of Egypt and Libya, deplored its failure to happen and sided with Qaddafi in the affair. During the war with Israel he had openly condemned Egypt for calling on Henry Kissinger while Egyptian soldiers were falling on the field of battle, victims of American weapons. But now he was denouncing that policy and those who backed it. In earlier times considered as a moderate and pro-American, because he had acted as a restraint on some of Nasser's more radical plans and policies, he was now launching an all-out attack on imperialism and warning his country against the forthcoming encroachment of the U.S. State Department in the Middle East. The Thursday before this major policy editorial appeared, we were with Heikal at the offices of *Al Ahram*, surrounded by twenty or so intellectuals and political leaders for one of those nonstop, limpid, friendly, impassioned discussions which, in Arab countries, are one of the laws of hospitality. Here, Heikal barely contributed to the discussions. But without saying so, it was clear that everyone was addressing themselves to this man whose bearing, authority, impassivity, and clothes suggested an investment banker, while his keen, attentive eye, the half smile that flitted across his lips, suggested that his self-assurance was coupled with a taste for risk-taking. He seemed to all of us more solid than ever.

And yet the following day, on our arrival at the Paris airport, the wire services informed us that Heikal had been fired and that one of the Amin brothers, whom Nasser had sentenced to life imprisonment many years before, had been named director of *Al Ahram*. Yesterday that disgrace was followed by another, when Nasser's son-in-law was relieved of his duties as director of the Center for Strategic Studies.

Sadat, Heikal—the near future of Egypt is contained in those two names. I can still picture them, huddled together in the bourgeois living room of a Cairo villa, chatting in a peaceful, friendly way, just the way I saw them only a few days ago.

TUESDAY, FEBRUARY 5

The Socialist Party is holding a panel discussion this afternoon on the subject of oil. Asked to give the closing address, I talked extemporaneously about the contradiction, which I trust is temporary, between the need to produce, and therefore to discover new sources of energy, and the necessity to protect the environment which our contemporary world is stupidly and madly destroying in its search for profit. I showed a bit of irritation about the bucolic dream which presupposes a return to a simpler way of life. There were a number of proponents of that viewpoint present, which led me to wave my red flag and play the devil's advocate with them. The result? Although I am wholeheartedly on the side of the environmentalists, they now look upon me with suspicion. It is not the first time that character trait has got me into trouble, but what can I do? Conformity is anathema to me. And the prouder it is, the more I perceive how wretched it really is, especially when those who practice it should know better. "Venerable wise men," noted Chekhov one day as he was leaving Tolstoy's, "are more despotic than generals." That day they had been discussing a fundamental problem: Was riding a bicycle in contradiction with Christian ideals? Chekhov loved and admired Tolstoy, but he was concerned about Tolstoy's ideas regarding progress. "For seventeen years my thinking was dominated by Tolstoyan philosophy," he wrote to the editor of *New Times*, Alexis Souverin, "but something within me says 'no.' Reason and a sense of justice tell me that there is more love in electricity and steam than there is in chastity and the refusal to eat meat. . . ." I sometimes feel like saying something along the same lines: "There is more love in a nuclear power station, etc. etc. . . ." But I control myself and say nothing. Each word is like a stone cast upon the water: The circles emanating from the point of contact grow and continue forever. Which reminds me, this morning I was going through the various documents in a file which sets forth the risks involved in the government's plan to build 200 nuclear power stations between now and the year 2000. What is one to make of the deep-rooted fear people feel about this plan, which compels them to rally and protest against their construction? My first reaction is to think that the people's reaction is a healthy one, after all the ravages that the industrial age has wrought. In France, these major decisions which affect the lives of people and the future of the country are never the subject of public discussion or political debate. Our leaders keep such secrets to themselves, as though they were the sole judges. To oblige them to submit their plans to Parliament, to locally elected officials, to delegates from various environmental protection agencies, would be a step in the right direction. That would at the same time enable us to distinguish the real from the imaginary and, by being made privy to the facts, react more rationally and positively to the proposed nuclear program. With only our ignorance to guide us, who can blame us for being terrified to the point of psychosis? We do know that technology is close to coping with the problems posed by possible radiation from the nuclear reactors, and the dangers of radiation released through either radioactive gas or liquid; and we know that security measures have eliminated the most dangerous effects of accidents: explosions due to excess pressure or to contact between water and sodium, fires, and sabotage. Two basic questions still remain unresolved: how to cool the reactors, and how to get rid of nuclear wastes. Water pumped from a river, or the sea, to cool the nuclear core must be pumped back out, but when it returns to its source it is so hot that it kills all fauna and most flora. A sudden warming of the water temperature of a lake or river is enough to kill it. The four nuclear plants planned for the Bugey region would, once in service, cause the waters of the Rhône River to rise some thirty degrees for a few deadly days each year. As for the problem of nuclear wastes, we have already ceased to bury them on the ocean floor, for it is conceded that the material in which they are enclosed—be it concrete, lead, or iron— are not necessarily one hundred percent watertight. So they are currently being stocked at a spot near Cherbourg, a site promoted to the rank of "national depository." But it is worth noting that while the nuclear power stations themselves have been built to resist the impact of something as powerful as a Boeing 707, the depot near Cherbourg—which as a matter of fact is incapable of handling the wastes emanating from the existing nuclear plants—has not been built to any such rigid specifications.

Will scientific research dedicated to solving the potential pollution problems that face us evolve fast enough to precede the construction of the planned nuclear network? I have heard Mr. Messmer's warning: "No nuclear power plant, no electricity." But is electricity worth the death of our waters? I do not want to open myself to the accusation of playing politics with something that happens to be in reach. But how can I avoid it? Everything is political. A government which would give top priority to research, and would substitute for the laissez-faire of capitalism a new model for growth in which energy and pollution would both be addressed, is only imaginable under another system. We have to look to the future. The respect of nature is dependent on one's concept of man. My idea—and may I be forgiven for it—continues to opt for reason. Sasha, Tolstoy's youngest daughter (to come back to him for a moment), relates that one hot summer afternoon her father saw a mosquito land on the bald head of one of his disciples, and without further ado the master swatted and killed it. Taken aback, the disciple studied his master and then cried out: "What have you done, Lev Nikolaevitch? You have killed a living creature. Aren't you ashamed of yourself?" "And," added Sasha, "my father was indeed troubled by the incident, which caused a general malaise among everyone present."

Which brings me to my own problem. I am requesting the right to kill the mosquito and at the same time adhere to "nature's charter."

FRIDAY, FEBRUARY 15

The other evening in Vienna, Austrian Prime Minister Kreisky told me the following story, about a tightrope walker named Karl. Karl, a real pro, could spend a whole morning either standing or sitting on his tightrope several meters above the ground. One day his friend Johann challenged him to stay up on his high wire for a whole day. Considerably annoyed, Karl upped the ante and told Johann that not only would he stay there as long as he liked, but he would do so standing on one foot. "And you'll play the violin at the same time?" Johann wanted to know. "Let's make it Mozart," Karl replied.

The following day Karl climbed up on his high wire, balanced himself on one foot, took a violin, and began playing Mozart. For good measure, he kept his perch not for a full day but for a whole week. When finally he climbed down, having won the bet by a huge margin, Johann, far from applauding his friend's efforts, remained silent. "So," said Karl after an embarrassed pause, "what do you think of my feat?" "If you want my honest opinion," said Johann, "your playing wasn't up to Menuhin's."

I thoroughly enjoyed that parable on the perils and pitfalls of power. If the shoe fits . . .

SUNDAY, FEBRUARY 17

I note the following passage, taken from a letter that Voltaire wrote to his niece, Madame Denis: "I liken myself to the person who dreamt he was falling from a church tower and who, finding that he was floating in the air, said: 'If only it will last!' "

I don't know why the image of this high-perched sleeper makes me think of Valéry Giscard d'Estaing.

MONDAY, FEBRUARY 18

From the region of Berry on my father's side, and Saintonge on my mother's, I can only speak and understand French. Born at the precise point where the langue d'oc and the langue d'oïl meet, I do not have a good enough ear to pick up the language of the neighboring region. I regret it all the more as I grow older and realize what I am missing. My maternal grandfather used to tell juicy stories, in perfect *patois,* of the Charente region which regaled the members of our family on many an evening. His reputation as a storyteller meant more to him than any official decoration he ever received. With a bit of help from heredity, I in turn was filled with pride when I learned while reading a biography of Burgaud des Marets, the bard of Saint Onge, that my direct ancestor, Beaupré Lorrain, had not only been the great man's closest friend but that he was also the person who used to recite to the bard both poems and fables. One of my sisters inherited that gift. When I go to visit her at her house in Baronnies, between Dauphiné and Provence, a random visitor would be surprised to hear us both laughing in the accents of an unknown tongue. Recently, in a bookshop, I acquired a sheaf of manuscript pages from the estate of our last local poet, Goulbenéze—or, rather, our penultimate one, for I was overlooking Odette Commandon and her delightful collection, *Cagouille Tales.* I reveled in the stories emanating from the people I think of as my own.

It should be remembered, though, that they were written in a dialect that has a sense of its own limits. But this approach allows me to understand the attraction, the love, for the language that gives a name to things men touch, see, to feelings and ideas. To stick a needle in the cerebellum is a sure way to kill. It is so with a language that people refuse to teach: one kills someone, relentlessly. Let me not be accused of appointing myself *ex-officio* advocate for the destruction of the Brittany radio transmitter. To recommend explosives as an answer to our problems would be short-sighted. "Weapons," noted Dom Helder Camara, "are on the side of the oppressors. It is not surprising that those who place their bets wholly on the side of weapons, lose." But I, a Frenchman from France, testify for my brothers from Brittany that I do not know a bloody thing about their history, assuming they had one, before it became part of France's. Gone, erased, vanished. To the point of doubting whether Anne, twice Queen of France, ever really existed. Is that acceptable?

. . . I feel very strongly that any policy that compartmentalizes the people of a country, refusing to allow them to perpetuate their

past, cannot long endure. To deprive people of their own history is
to invite them to violence.

TUESDAY, MARCH 19

José Toha has entered the Moneda reception room, and all eyes
are turned upon him. And yet, he was keeping a respectful distance from the hero of the day, Fidel Castro, and his host, Salvador Allende, around both of whom a crowd of dignitaries,
ministers, ambassadors, and generals were clamoring obsequi-
ously. Short and rotund, the cardinal of Santiago, Henriquez da
Silva, had held in his chubby hands the large hands of Fidel,
commandant of the revolution, and of President Allende. A few
words whispered into their ears had completed that picture—for
the warily watchful people present—of the Chilean Church rendering unto Caesar what was Caesar's, even if he was the anti-
Caesar and therefore someone to keep a careful eye on. Standing
next to a window, General Pinochet was visibly upset that he had
not yet had the opportunity to get close to the two stars of Latin
American Marxism, and pay his respects. One of them all subtlety and serenity, looking for all the world like some rural general practitioner pleased with the diagnosis he had just made; the
other, in his well-cut khaki uniform, the incarnation of strength,
dominating, as he did, the crowd by a full head. That is, with one
exception: José Toha, the minister of the interior, well over six feet
tall, and so thin that he seemed even taller. Impassive, unself-
conscious, and with a skimpy beard that marked him as one of
O'Higgins' descendants, he also looked like the portrait of Don
Quixote that Picasso had drawn (Régis Debray, when I mentioned
that to him earlier today, said that in his opinion Toha seemed like
someone straight out of the pages of Proust). Chile was in love
with this striking personality whenever it was not busy hating
him. Present at that evening in 1971 that I am relating here, and
witness to the scene where the actors of the drama that was soon
to occur were taking up their stations and their roles, in the glitter

of the Spanish chandeliers and for a preamble that, if you did not
know the events that were to follow, would seem banal, José Toha
stood out that day as someone special. One sensed that among all
those present he was a man possessed. I saw very clearly that
nonchalant brilliance which was reflected inward.

Eduardo Frei, Allende's predecessor as president of Chile, who
would have gone to any lengths to regain that post, a democrat in
the classical mold (that of Pontius Pilate), a blood Christian (the
blood of other people), hated Toha and doggedly went after him.
By a vote of Parliament—in which the opposition had the majority—Toha was relieved of his office as minister of the interior "for
cause"—what a joke!—the alleged cause being that he was deemed
a state security risk! Allende responded by naming his friend minister of defense. Last Friday, news reached us that "José Toha, the
former minister under the Allende regime, committed suicide."
Hate has its logic. The rest is really a matter of detail, I dare say:
There are times and places when the most horrible events become
banal. Need we think of that tall, slender body, who according to
the newspaper reports weighed hardly more than 120 pounds,
who ended his all too brief life hanged by the neck in a hospital
toilet?

For as long as men have lived, human history has been strewn
with the corpses of the just and righteous. It is a well-known fact:
For those who would change the world, the death penalty is the
rule rather than the exception. But the Pinochet junta has been
upping the ante: 30,000 Chilean citizens in prison, five hundred of
whom are known to have been tortured. These are the figures that
reach us from a number of reliable sources—youth organizations
that have just visited Chile, and confirmed by various reports that
are piling up on my desk. Guilty of what? The wealthy bourgeoisie does not want to forgive or forget the fact that its world
was shaken to its roots. No question here of the law of retaliation.
The Popular Unity Movement did not kill anyone. But by threatening the establishment it did something worse.

One would like to see someone shout so loud and long that it
would rend the heavens. "Strange is the Catholicism that humili-
ates Pablo Neruda on his deathbed," Altamirano said to the
correspondent of Le Monde. And strange the Catholicism that rec-

ognizes Pinochet as one of its own. Have you heard the protesta-
tions of His Holiness Pope Paul VI? Yes, for as long as it takes to
heave a single sigh. And besides, he spoke in such whispers that
only God could have heard what His Holiness had to say.

Toha is dead, murdered. Others await his fate, on Dawson Island or at Chacabuco. Among civilized peoples, crime has its nice-
ties: Above all, no noise, please.

I cannot and will not accept that: I ask the French Left, and my
Socialist comrades, to raise their voices in protest. We need millions of witnesses to those in Chile who have been killed. And for
the murderers, we need judges.

SATURDAY, APRIL 6

The most recent paradox of French politics is that Gaullism did
not die with the demise of General de Gaulle but of the blood-
poisoning which, this past Tuesday evening, April 2, killed President Georges Pompidou. That is not the least of fate's ironies.
From close up, Pompidou's policies directly contradicted the
raison d'être of Gaullism. From afar, they will appear as its ultimate
projection. As did all French men and women, I knew that the
head of state did not have long to live and, like them, his death
took me by surprise. Probably it was because I found it distasteful
to read the daily reports on his temperature or to try to interpret
the latest medical reports that were running like wildfire throughout Paris; as I found it repugnant to look at the bloated television
reports, or try to make wild medical guesses about what the
changed look about his eyes meant. Perhaps, too, I unconsciously
preferred to turn my back on death itself, knowing that the Grim
Reaper would one day reach out and pluck me too. In any case, I
was deeply shocked when Roger Caze, the owner of the Brasserie
Lipp at Saint-Germain-des-Prés, where I was dining that night
alone at the back of the restaurant, working on a major speech
that I was scheduled to give two days later at the National Assembly, came over to me and gave me the news. About ten o'clock he

whispered to me, "Word is that the president is dead," and a few minutes later, "The radio has just confirmed it." Others, I am quite sure, had been following the evolution of the president's illness more closely than I, watching that now portly man seated in his presidential chair, and confiding to one another, "He hasn't got long, that much is sure," while he, a prey to the appetites of the living, was being desecrated during the waning days and hours of his life. I cannot help but feel a certain pity for this man, now dead, and forgotten even before he has been buried. What will he be remembered for? Nothing, or so little. The cruelty of fate is not that his death was premature but that he left so little to be remembered for: so much power, no power at all, and history slipping through his fingers. He loved the State, loved himself in the State, but after five years of an undivided presidency, nothing had yet begun. Bad luck? Illness? Character defect? A great deal has been said by many people on all sides about his almost desperate eagerness to remain in office to the very end, despite an illness that was known to be terminal. Did real courage rest in resigning? Or did it rest in staying on? I'll not mince my words. I sense that there was a certain pride manifest in his open display of his disintegration.

Many will find what I am about to say somewhat surprising: Georges Pompidou and I, who fought and battled for ten years, each in the front lines of his own side, who debated each other so many times, never had a private conversation, never even exchanged a word, were it about peace, improved relations, or simply an exchange of amenities. The two Frances simply did not know each other any longer. From dreaming so long and hard about his France and conferring upon it that abstract majesty which today serves as the cast-off clothing for wealthy businessmen and bankers alike who, in the wake of the events of May 1968, were allowed back to their former positions of power, de Gaulle in effect exiled half of the French citizens within their own country. When de Gaulle made up his mind that he wanted to charm one of his opponents he felt could be useful to him politically, he could really turn it on. Which, when you think about it, is the worst form of contempt. Although I was not subjected to it, and for good reason, I saw how he treated those he wanted to suffer this ultimate humiliation. They ended up as ministers in his administration. But de Gaulle was even less tolerant of those who resisted his blandishments. His rule was intolerance. There was on one side the France that loved him—in his eyes the only true France—and on the other, the reverse, the dark side, the Great Void.

After de Gaulle's death, Georges Pompidou could have answered his own greatness by reconciling this people divided by so many jealous factions. I do believe he made an effort in this direction. But he had taken unto himself the leadership of a faction, and was incapable of opening himself up to the totality of France in all its many contradictions. Unless he understood, in the very depths of his being, that he would not have the time to effect such a reconciliation, that it was already too late, and therefore not worth the attempt. That would be my assessment of the situation. The Pompidou of 1962 was someone to be reckoned with. When after three years in the Senate I came back to the Chamber of Deputies, I detected in that orator, who was not at ease when he spoke and had real trouble reading his prepared speeches, an unusual strength, unusual in the arena of politics. The deputies, who made short shrift of amateurs, were having a field day at his expense. I remember calling on my colleagues to temper their judgments. I was responsive to his straightforwardness, the quality and tone of his voice. In the halls of the National Assembly I saw him standing proud and tall in the midst of a crowd of friends. I stopped and watched him more closely. He emanated a kind of weighty power. The defeat he had just suffered in making his speech only served to strengthen his resolve. He had a defiant look about him, which he carried with him throughout his career, as though he always had to prove himself, a student weighted down with honors but always in search of the one that eluded him; functionary, banker, diplomat, politician, a man who was successful in every area and was too used to being first to settle for that position alone. His ability as a speaker improved greatly, until he became a consummate orator. His policies blossomed, based on his desire to place France among the major industrial powers of the century, and when in 1968 de Gaulle seemed to hesitate and lose his bearings, Pompidou took charge. The Markovic affair,* which wounded him doubly, also strengthened his resolve to make himself, in his own way and his own time, part of that history of France which those close to him say intrigued and interested him most since childhood.

Did he win? No, he lost. What a strange adventure, that of a monarch whose roots were deep, who was taught to distinguish, in a many-faceted mirror where intelligence plays, the original image of reality, and who ends his reign in the company of Polignac looking like Charles X.

Yes, I feel sorry for Georges Pompidou, and I am not his enemy. Perhaps he was greater than he was. That shout, during the final act: "In my family the only time we lie down is when we die," has a very special ring to it. Those who knew and loved him tell us that he was a man who enjoyed a good laugh, was creative, a feeling man, a giving man. But private virtues do not suffice to redeem a public life that can only be categorized as passive.

France already has other things on its mind.

SUNDAY, APRIL 7

In no hurry to return to Paris, I left Château-Chinon early in the afternoon. At Lormes, instead of continuing toward Avallon and the superhighway I turned off toward Vézelay. A golden, powdery light made everything look different. As the road dipped and rose throughout the foothills of the Morvan chain, I tried to recognize, on the constantly changing horizon, the familiar landmarks—a church, a road, a farm, or better yet the water towers that stand out against the blue ocean of the distant horizon. Some people may object to my choice of "blue," claiming that up close the colors are green and black. But anyone who has traveled through

* Stefan Markovic, Yugoslav bodyguard of the film star Alain Delon, was found dead October 1, 1968. Like the "Profumo affair" in England, the Markovic affair touched upon sex, drugs, and the underworld. It also had political ramifications: Alain Delon and Georges Pompidou seemed to have moved in that same circle. Pompidou was asked to testify but refused, further obscuring the scandal.

the highlands of Burgundy, where land and sky meet, knows that the image is indeed precise.

It has been some thirty years that I've been a pilgrim, in my own way, to Vézelay. What I am looking for there is not exactly a matter of prayer, although everything is an offering in the agreement between world and men. I could trace from memory a circle joining all the points from which—from the farthest point on—one can see the Madeleine Church. Long before a road sign, somewhere between Voutenay and Sermizelles, I slowed down at the exact spot on National Highway 6 from which, for a brief moment, you can see the church before it is immediately blocked off again. As I descended through Pontaubert I saluted it, as does everyone, standing there on the edge of the hill. From Vauban, I watched the setting sun spread its shadows into the valleys. Beyond Saint-Aubin-des-Chaumes, I passed the last ridges of the Yonne valleys in order to sketch (but with what a clumsy hand!) its portrait. I went past all the gates of the town, by the grassy paths of Asquins. At Maison-Dieu, I followed the forest path which suddenly reveals, there at the end of the street, the village church. "Vézelay, Vézelay, Vézelay, Vézelay . . ." Is there any more beautiful alexandrine in the French language? That poem of Aragon's made me like him more than before.

Today I returned to Vézelay by instinct. The decision I shortly had to face seemed to me easier, almost simple, dictated by this sublime countryside as I sat on a café terrace under the linden trees while, little by little, night began to fall.

TUESDAY, MAY 7

If I were to try to ferret out the real reason for Chaban-Delmas' fall from power—be it in his character or reputation, or in a certain "absence" while on television—I would have to admit that the slightest error weighs heavily in the balance in such matters. But that explanation is superficial. The truth is, the natural heir of de Gaulle's regime is Valéry Giscard d'Estaing. I understood that ten or twelve years ago, when I read the most remarkable book published on the events of May 1968, a short but incisive work by Maurice Mouillaud entitled *The Mystification*. In it Mouillaud demonstrates the strict mechanism, the logic by which the ruling class rallied to the man it detested: It gave the government to the person who gave it—the ruling class—real power. Through his personal style and his verbal gifts, de Gaulle managed to mask throughout his reign this revenge on the part of Vichy France. After he left the political arena, the hollow epic, with all its heroes and adventurers, was over too. The idea was over. Conservative France, made up of presidents of chambers of commerce, leading businessmen, the medical profession, the lawyers and notaries, no longer needed any pretenses or façades. Last Sunday, with the fall of Chaban-Delmas, it settled its accounts for a second time.

Poor man, how could he have forgotten that the roots of the Right in France are as old as our history, that what it yields to Bonapartism—of which Gaullism was only one offshoot, a cyclical bloodletting of a patriotic people—it always takes back, and always with a minimum of delay. By dragging out the Cross of Lorraine, by bringing someone like Malraux into the act, by dredging up the ghosts of a time long past, a time out of time, he consciously created a misconception, and went down with it. But if, as the saying goes, misery loves company, de Gaulle should take heart: the common grave will be filled with many more.

SUNDAY, MAY 12

At this point, just a week before the presidential elections, when France will have to choose not only between two men but two philosophies, two ways of life, the greatest mistake would be to confuse types.

Valéry Giscard d'Estaing, whose major concern seems to be to try to rid himself of his image of moneyman, of computer-accountant, confusing types consists of trying to demonstrate by any means possible that he too has a heart. That he does have one

I have no doubt, but that is not what is asked or expected of him.
Those in France who believe in him politically are not looking for
a king who is also an individualist. On the contrary. They need a
prototype, or better yet, an architect. Giscard's diplomas, his im-
pressive higher education and family background, his distinction,
his intelligence and long association with the world of business,
all make him a guarantor, a protector, a conservator in the strict
sense of the term of an enfeebled society struggling to survive,
and discovers to its utter delight the man who incarnates that
desire. He symbolizes success as the term is defined in that seg-
ment of society. But more would be too much. "The heart" for
example. They don't mind his being superior; but he would be
more appreciated if he were less "different." In these times, at the
beginning of the audio-visual era when everything is reduced to
its simplest form, the individual astonishes, jars, at worst worries
and upsets, in the same sense that an actor in classical Chinese
theater is deemed poor whenever by his tone or mask he lends
a personal interpretation to an established form. Happily for
Giscard, no matter how hard he tries to escape from the character
he has invented for himself over the past several years on the
television screen, the automatic reactions of the viewer bring him
back to reality. His own reactions do as well. Whether he describes himself as he really is, or as he imagines himself to be,
each new touch has the strange effect of drawing his portrait in a
nonobjective way. His manner of talking about himself and his
acts erase whatever he says about them. All of which is his good
fortune.

Clearly, monologue—however difficult it may be technically but
behind which he takes refuge—suits him better than does political
debate, which unmasks his weaknesses. Last Friday, for example,
his anger was not feigned: his eyes widened but immediately
hardened, like a cock ready to do battle. He was undoubtedly
irritated and humiliated by my remarks regarding the errors of his
administration. But the fact is, you cannot claim to be infallible
with impunity: he was obviously suffering. I do not hate my opponents enough to strike again immediately after drawing first
blood. That lack of killer instinct worked to my disadvantage at
this point in the duel. If I were more aggressive, if this element

were not lacking in my makeup, I would have followed up this obvious advantage with a further blow. But his weakness was so apparent that it became a bond in that subtle relationship that occurs between adversaries at the point of a battle when anything goes. I immediately toned down my arguments, withdrew a pace or two, and was unmoved by his rude counter-attack, as he recited the well-prepared litany of my shortcomings, harping on the fact that I was, in his view, "a man of the past." I listened, I watched from the depths of an internal detachment which in retrospect I realize was most unwise: lowering your guard just as the opponent counter-attacks.

Giscard's amazing ability to pull numbers and statistics out of a hat is not only meant to demonstrate his virtuosity but also to intimidate the opposition. In his eyes, what is most important is not whether he is right but whether people believe him. In this respect, the man has a touch of genius. In the course of our televised debate, as I was quoting the cost of an average rent in a subsidized-housing unit in the Paris region, noting that the figure represented two thirds of a worker's income, he looked at me in utter astonishment, shook his head in denial, took a piece of paper from the table, turned it once, then again, as though upset and overwhelmed by the extent of my ignorance . . . then quickly changed the subject. Faced with such absolute assurance on his part, I could have doubted the accuracy or validity of my figures if I had not noticed that the piece of paper he had picked was absolutely blank.

Many people have criticized my slowness, or hesitation—which, they quickly add, is so atypical of me—in responding to Giscard's attacks. I do not wish to defend myself here. But if I were asked for the word to describe how I felt during that debate, it would have to be "peaceful"—and as I am writing these lines, less than two days after the event, while I am still inundated by a flood of commentaries and public opinion polls about who "won," I can honestly say that my state of mind could still be described by that same word.

Perhaps I too have been guilty of betraying confusing types. People wanted me to be a boxer, and I was avoiding a head-to-head fight. For fear of getting hurt? Not at all! I had a worthy opponent, but who could doubt that I had all the training and arms that I needed? I simply had a whole other view of the matter. I have taken part in too many political contests in my life not to have retained a bitter aftertaste of many swashbuckling wins. Although the articles about the debate always referred to it in sporting terms, I do not have the feeling that this campaign was some kind of competition. I admire Giscard's gifts, his speaking ability, the vigor of his ambition. But I appreciate these qualities without being implicated.

For Valéry Giscard d'Estaing, the presidency is a point of arrival; for me it is a point of departure. What I am doing now involves so much more than myself. If he is elected, Giscard will be capable of accomplishing many fine things. If I am elected, I will change the course of things, and therefore the life of my contemporaries. This said, the fate of socialism is not at the mercy of one election.

TUESDAY, MAY 14

For the friends who surround me this morning, and who are already proclaiming victory in the forthcoming election, I draw up a list of our opponents. First of all, the press, both written and spoken, with of course several notable exceptions: *Le Monde, Le Nouvel Observateur, L'Humanité, Témoignage chrétien, Le Provençal, Canard Enchaîné,* and *La Dépêche du Midi.* At the slightest shift in the political tradewinds, the provincial daily papers, which to date have proclaimed themselves neutral, could shift position. The large-circulation papers and magazines use color and sensational headlines to glorify my opponent. The last issue of *Paris-Match* devoted ten pages to Giscard, in full color, filled with smiles, dogs, well-manicured lawns, luxury, peace and quiet, lots of family. To his opponent? They gave me one black-and-white picture, showing me sitting in my kitchen having breakfast, looking tired and haggard, with my thrust-out chin. *Le Parisien libéré* takes its inspiration from the illuminated manuscripts of the Middle Ages,

devoting its first page to a contrasting depiction of the two candidates: the way we are portrayed, and the qualities or defects with
which each of us has been endowed by the newspaper's editors,
leaves no doubt as to its choice: one incarnates heaven, the other
hell. The magnates of the press have all come out wholeheartedly
for Giscard. The millions of copies they distribute daily or weekly
throughout the country do their best to denigrate the Left. . . . The
financial and economic press goes out of its way to dream up a
thousand reasons to terrify its readers with the possibility that I
might be elected, or what would happen if I were. *L'Express* goes at
me hammer and tongs. Through their control of the press, we
have against us the following industries: sugar, wool, paper, cotton, advertising, pharmaceuticals, even military aircraft! Turn your
set to Radio-Télé-Luxembourg, and whom do you see attacking us:
Jean Prouvost, who also owns the Conservative daily *Le Figaro* as
well as *France-Soir* and *Paris-Match*. Try the Europe 1 channel, and
there you'll see Sylvain Floirat doing the same. Floirat is a large
shareholder of that television channel, which many people believe
is "politically objective"! In fact, they mistakenly believe that
most of the other stations are independent of government control.
But the fact is, with the exception of the RTL (Radio-Télévision-
Luxembourg, or RTL), the outlying stations are under the control
of a State-owned company, therefore of the government, a company with the acronym SOFIRAD *(Société Financière de Radiodiffusion).*
SOFIRAD owns 97 percent of the capital of Sud-Radio, 83.84 percent
of Radio Monte-Carlo, 35.26 percent of Europe 1. No need to
comment on Sud-Radio and Radio Monte-Carlo: the percentages
speak for themselves. Europe 1 is only slightly less obvious, for in
addition to the SOFIRAD percentage, four percent of that station is
owned by the Principality of Monaco, and another large percentage, as I have noted, is owned by Sylvain Floirat, a man beholden
to the present regime. Finally, the chief operating officer of
SOFIRAD is Denis Baudoin, former press secretary of President
Georges Pompidou and later head of the Government Information
Office, which is in charge of government propaganda. Those who
were outraged by the wretched trap set for me by Europe 1 (the
invited audience insulted me during my first televised debate with
Giscard d'Estaing) will be less astonished when they read these

lines. As for the RTL, Jean Prouvost, chief administrative officer of
the station and owner of 14 percent of the stock, was on the point
of signing an agreement with three Belgian magnates—Baron Jean
Lambert, Count Jean-Pierre de Laumont, and Baron Edouard Em-
pain, who together owned 37 percent of the station's stock—when
the government made it known that it opposed the transfer
abroad of any of RTL's stock. As a result of that ruling, the Havas
Company, which owned 15 percent, wasted no time in working
out a deal with the Belgians. They formed a Luxembourg company
called Audiophina in order to manage their common property,
that is, 52 percent of the capital. Georges Pompidou refrained
from intervening in an operation of which, in fact, he was the
instigator. To be sure, it is important to distinguish between
the people who control these stations and the journalists who
work there. Professional ethics do exist. I admire this one or that
(to mention their names would be the kiss of death for them) who
still feel honor-bound by the rules of the profession. But those
journalists know as well as I do that their presence is at best
tolerated. Oddly, the fairest area in the present electoral campaign
is the French National Radio and Television (ORTF). The proce-
dures invented to restrain the opposition have actually turned out
to be beneficial. We have learned how to keep a careful count.
Equal air-time must be granted to each party. Alain Poher, who
remembers the 1969 elections, has been intractable on this point,
and Marceau Long is a paragon of patience in making sure the
equal-time rule is rigorously applied.

But big business is not content to finance a press which acts as a
shield. It puts its money wherever it thinks the return will be the
greatest, where it will do the most good, at any price—that's the
proper expression, making sure the candidate of the Left will lose
the election. To that end, nothing is too expensive, no method too
base. A phony newspaper prints up two million copies on the
presses of the daily *Nice-Matin* under the similar name *France-
Matin*. False documents of all kinds abound: Using the French
mails, they are sent to all sorts of professionals throughout the
country, with the sole and express purpose of inspiring terror in
the hearts of those to whom they are addressed. Church services
will be forbidden, factories will be taken over, private property

will be confiscated, managerial positions will be taken away from those who now hold them, treasuries will be emptied. A rich industrialist congratulates himself for having backed the counterfeit documents, and is honored for doing so by his peers. The pamphlets printed by the Independent Republicans—Giscard d'Estaing's party—repeat these same arguments and disseminate these same allegations in a somewhat less blatant tone. The millions of francs currently being handed out by big business are given for one reason alone: to influence the people who vote. François Ceyrac gave the order, and French big business lined up squarely behind him, which is quite natural. Only a few free spirits, including a handful of personal friends, refused to follow. In contrast, my own fund-raising has been modest. What is more, there are many local committees who have gone about their work without any funds whatsoever. For lack of money, I had to turn down Claude Pedriel's request for a series of large-size election posters, while on virtually every streetcorner of the country huge portraits of Giscard hit Frenchmen in the face every day. Ingenious militants try to compensate for our lack of visibility by pasting ironic comments on the handsome posters put up by the minister of finance, and we try to make up for our lack of numbers by the savage intensity of the posters we do have.

It is time to remind everyone that Valéry Giscard d'Estaing has remained, in spite of the example set by Royer, a member of the present administration. That is not the least of our difficulties. To the coalition of those who control the money in France is joined the full power of the present government. Pierre Messmer is prime minister, Chirac is minister of the interior, Poniatowski is minister of foreign affairs, Giscard is minister of economy and finance. Together, those four control the civil service, the hospitals, they dictate the flow of money, which in an election period is no mean factor. They take advantage of their positions to convince the French people once and for all that they *are* the State. Other ministers travel the width and breadth of the provinces, using official transportation, which is a nice little saving in the context of the election budgets. Galley, after first having sent letters ahead to the mayors and members of the city councils that he would be pleased to meet with them during his visit, made a trip to the French Antilles, without of course bothering to point out that the minister of the armed forces was in that event nothing more than an official electoral agent for the abuse of trust which consists of identifying the interests of the Right with those of the nation. In those outlying areas, prefects and sub-prefects feel free to act without restraint. In Guyana, the assistant administrator of Saint-Laurent-du-Maroni distributes election tracts printed on local government printing presses. I have seen some of them: they are pure rubbish! The farthest corners of the overseas territories are thus covered. My delegates organize as best they can some kind of counterattack. I had no delegates on the islands of Wallis and Futuna, and could find none on the spot: as a result, the first round of elections found me with 1.6 percent of the vote! Fortunately, the number of voters there is relatively small. I'm more concerned about the Comoro Islands, that archipelago in the Indian Ocean with a population of about 130,000, and its evolving situation. I learned, for instance, that the head of government, Ahmed Abdallah, who controls the votes, recently landed in Paris, where a government limousine was awaiting him, put at his disposal by the minister of finance, and lunched with Giscard. A hundred thousand votes involved. That whets the appetite. I know Ahmed Abdallah, who was a colleague of mine in the Senate, and we have many friends in common. When I met with him, he told me the blandishments of which he had been the object. In the first round of voting, Giscard had garnered 10,000 votes, Chaban-Delmas 73,000, and I had 27,000. Abdallah told me how sorry he was that he had no choice, this coming Sunday, but to pass on Chaban-Delmas' 73,000 votes to Giscard. In exchange, Giscard had promised him independence for the Comoros on June 15. Who knows, 100,000 overseas voters whose main concern is to free themselves from any ties with France as soon as possible, may well elect the next president of France! As soon as I came back from the meeting I informed Alain Poher of my conversation.

At Djibouti, capital of French Somalia, my delegates are waging a hopeless battle. In the preceding elections, several Issas tribes the government feared might vote for the opposition were prevented from reaching the ballot boxes. Detours were set up along the roads, boats were burned. The result? Ali Aref and the French colonial administration took 30,000 of the 35,000 votes cast. The Comoros, and the territory of the Afars and Issas, account for about one half of one percent of French voters. Since the public opinion polls, only a few days before the elections, show that we're still 50-50, you can see that this one half percent could be decisive. Such is a rapid overview of our weaknesses vis-à-vis a government that clearly does not intend to overlook any of the means at its disposal.

But money and power are not the only givens. A clever campaign makes the potential voter think that the election of a Leftist president would also dangerously undermine the international role that France would otherwise play. Official propaganda cleverly plays every ball and takes it on the rebound. And the balls are coming from every direction. One day it's the new German Chancellor Helmut Schmidt who lets it be known that he, as a solid Social-Democrat, would be very pleased indeed to see the election go to a French Conservative. Then the Soviet ambassador Tchervonenko, who under some ridiculous pretext pays a visit to Giscard d'Estaing, congratulates him on his success to date. The American ambassador is slightly more discreet, but from Washington all sorts of dispatches and newspapers arrive which give pause to our businessmen and middle-class voters. Chinese diplomats openly declare that they hope my opponent wins since, in their eyes, I bear the stigma of being allied with the Communists. The holy union joins orthodoxies, no matter how different and varied, in the hope that nothing will change in France so that nothing will change in Europe so that nothing will change in the world.

With those thoughts I finished my assessment of our present position. One of our colleagues, Georges Fillioud, cried, "Goodness, how pessimistic you are!" If we have a wall before us and only our bare hands to fight with, our strength is immense. With so much power and so many means marshaled against the Left, it is surprising that it has not yet been reduced to nothing. And yet it is the forces of conservatism that are shaking in their boots. All its efforts have done no more than merely keep its head above water. And the tide is rising.

SATURDAY, MAY 18

Over the past forty days I have written, dictated, corrected hundreds of articles and interviews; received countless journalists; been subjected to photographers' flashbulbs from morning till evening; given seven press conferences; appeared on twelve television programs and as many radio broadcasts; debated both my opponents, Valéry Giscard d'Estaing and Jacques Chaban-Delmas, five times; taken part in nine other debates on regional radio and television stations; been the subject of six films, including two full-length documentaries. Since the French National Television only shoots in its studios in Paris, I limited my public appearances to thirty-two. Almost every night I appeared before huge crowds—50,000 in Toulouse; 25,000 in Nice, Grenoble, and Nantes; 15,000 to 20,000 in most other places—and afterward returned home. I spent the rest of my time listening to delegations from organizations and associations of every kind, sent to me, their briefcases and pockets brimming with petitions, resolutions, protests, motions. In between I did my best to maintain my work sessions with my staff, personally checking the posters, pamphlets, and books that were prepared for the election; and kept up my contacts with party leaders in the various departments, as well as with the various political organizations, unions, and other groups working for me throughout the country.

I interrupted that mad race only once, the evening before I was scheduled to debate Giscard on television. I had felt for the first time during the campaign the onset of fatigue and accepted the hospitality of a friend, not far from Ferté-Alais. Despite the pleasure of that short hiatus in my schedule, with its attendant rest, I'm not sure that it was a wise decision. When I remove myself from the field of action I really do leave it far behind, and I have some trouble coming back to it. Yet it was only a warning. I resumed the rhythm demanded by the presidential race, and only interrupted it for a second time last night. And I see now that I could have continued much longer.

The election of a French president, a cross between a competitive high-level examination and a sporting event, requires of the candidates both physical and intellectual stamina. One may recall that in 1965 Charles de Gaulle had at first superbly disdained to lower himself into the political arena: He was discovered, catastrophically fallen from his Olympian heights, seated on the edge of a chair talking with Michel Droit. But the institution has its limits. All it would take to set it spinning is a sneeze. A cold, and here we are with Cleopatra's nose!

SUNDAY, MAY 19

Two men before millions of men, two faces of light and shadow, two glances that cross and no longer meet, two voices that speak of two different worlds, the echo of two presents, a promise of two futures: This France, so deeply divided, what loving care she needs from all of us!

TUESDAY, MAY 21

A daily newspaper comments this morning on the election results and commiserates. "Fate does not love him," it writes of. me, in such a way that it's impossible for me to guess whether the implication is "so much the better" or "what a shame." Charles Hernu, who brought me the pile of newspapers and who does not try to conceal his unhappiness (he shakes my hand, shakes it a second time, then a third, can't seem to make up his mind to let it go), places the newspaper I've just mentioned at the bottom of the pile, hoping I won't see it. When I get to it, Charles heaves a sigh and says, "That's of no importance. What matters is that 13 million French citizens have spoken," which only directs my attention to the incriminated article. I read it and laugh. What do they know about my fate? Is the fate of the Seine to feed Paris or to flow to the ocean?

It's true, I felt in harmony with myself and with history. It's true, I would have liked to dry the tears of those who are fed up with waiting and hoping. Others will tell the story of the battle that came to an end on Sunday, May 19, its evolution, its ups and downs, its heady moments. But our people have other and better things to do than linger over the past.

And so do I.

PART II

THE BEE
AND
THE ARCHITECT

Translated by
HELEN R. LANE and
CONCILIA HAYTER

To IRÈNE and GEORGES DAYAN

"... by the complexity of its wax cells the bee puts more than one architect to shame. But from the outset, what differentiates the worst architect from the most expert bee is that he has built the cell in his head before building it in the hive."

Karl Marx

1975

WEDNESDAY, JANUARY 15

As a child I never played cards and I still don't. If I learned to play
chess when I was about ten years old, it was because my maternal
grandfather, with whom I lived six months out of twelve, lost in
the wilds three kilometers from the nearest hamlet, could get hold
of no other partner. We spent long evenings oblivious of time,
engrossed in our chessmen till the final checkmate sent us to bed
filled with thoughts of glory or revenge. Monopoly already existed. But I hated to waste my time contending for money. I had
no taste for trade and I still haven't. I preferred the game of dice.
The laws of chance have the same strange attraction as philosophy. A throw of the dice could send you to prison or to hell, and
at times, with the goal already in sight, right back to zero, to start
all over. Then again, the dice would dodge the pitfalls as though
they could see them. It thrilled me to watch them decide for me.
Quite frankly, I never expected the small rolling cubes could dis-
appoint my hopes, regardless of what happened to me. My trust
was based on the faith that I had in myself. You might think that
such a disposition would lead me to gambling. On the contrary, I
detest it! I never venture a franc at roulette. I steer clear. Anyway,
I soon gave up dice. The very thought of throwing dice onto the

felt, of depending, however minimally, on those miserable cubes, revolts me. I have become the opposite of a gambler; let this be an eye-opener to my enemies whose favorite word it is when talking about me. This is how my political life goes: I am incapable of making a move until I have marshaled all the resources of my mind; I am incapable of stopping until I have exhausted all the reserves of my will. I leave but a minimum to chance. Am I still gambling? History's perennial stragglers will no doubt think so. Surely a statesman is recognized by his capacity for taking into account unknown territories, once the known have been explored.

Having written these words, I must amend them. The unknown is not quite unknown when I tackle it. Something informs me— call it intuition, that ancient wisdom transmitted from generation to generation since the world began and anchored in some corner of our genetic code. I do not calculate, I feel. The instrument is approximate, especially where time is concerned. If I'm off by twenty years, too bad for me. Change in continuity. Last year this catch phrase made us smile. The one I was, I am; or rather, to quote Walt Whitman, I become. I cannot remember much of the little boy I was save for three or four images which come back again and again like the repeated notes on a worn record. These memories are so bright that everything else fades into darkness. A sunken lane which our family geography had named "the little hill," the adjective somehow conferring on it a singular dignity; a path bordered by apple trees crossing a wheat field; a flat-topped wall I used to lie on gazing up into the sky; the French landscape I contemplated through the window of an attic smelling of corn, which became for me the archetype of French landscape. I'll not describe it except to say that there were oak trees, willows, a river, a valley fading gradually into a blue horizon—a suitable color in the years following World War I—and hills just high enough to deserve their name. I can still hear the murmur of evening chatter. When darkness had fallen, my grandmother would sit, her hands idle on her sewing, gazing out over the garden, in no hurry to get up and light the kerosene lamp overhead. Words rose and fell like a Gregorian chant with intervals that seemed made up of shadows trailing off into a yes or a no which answered no spoken question. Each rode down the path of his own imagination, beyond the boundaries of time and space.

My purpose here, however, is not merely to stir the past at random but to evoke specific events in order to help me encapsulate a truth which otherwise would fly away through memory's wide-open windows. From our country dining room, the boat or dinghy in which we as kids dreamed our lives, to this day in Nevers where I write these lines on a midweek evening against a background of backfiring motors, loudspeakers blaring from the stands of a fair, and the sweet-sour notes of electronic church bells, there have been no breaks save those on the surface. The impetus with which I started still carries me, the same impulse drives me.

Did I ever see myself as king or pope? If the idea did cross my mind, it didn't last more than a summer. I felt that the weight of the whole world, of which I knew only ten villages in one province, rested intolerably on my shoulders. I was in such total, sublime communication with it that I even felt a kind of vocation. I can safely say that I felt more in touch with myself and others at fifteen than I do today at sixty.

MONDAY, MARCH 17

I prefer reading and conversation—those forgotten pleasures—to television. But I'm not a fanatic about it either. Sighing for the past and moaning over the present are not my favorite pastimes. In fact, I think they show an inability to live life as it should be lived, with gusto and love for what is to come. I cannot work up any pity for Alfred de Vigny's lament over the consequences of railways.

> We'll never hear galloping on the road
> The hoofs of horses striking sparks from stones.
> Farewell slow travel, charm of distant sounds,
> The stranger's laugh, the axle's slow protest.

These lines, taken from *La Maison du berger*, (The Shepherd's House) were perhaps written at La Maine-Giraud, Vigny's house in the Charente close to my childhood home. They bring back the memory of my grandparents' horse which used to bring us from Petit Barsac to spend our holidays at our house at Touvent. The twentieth century was still young; it was around 1925. From these holiday journeys behind the rump of an old horse that the first rise in the road exhausted, I retain a store of rich sensations. But this does not stop me from enjoying trains and planes and every variety of speed while awaiting the day of rocket travel. "Science traces round the earth a sad and rectilinear path . . . the equator is redued to too tight a ring," moans Vigny.

Why carp at science? It produces only what we ask of it. By the time the earth becomes too small, man will have conquered other worlds. To what use will he put them? Sometimes I hope and other times I tremble. But I insist on the difference between the instrument and the hand that guides it. Calumny has been poured on Eve, that innocent initiator of knowledge. Were it to do over I would bite into that apple myself.

What a long way round to get to my point! In Paris I avoid both radio and television. But as soon as I am in a car, I turn on the radio.

WEDNESDAY, MARCH 19

Everything concerning Berlioz involves a lot of noise (including his appearance on French banknotes along with Pascal, Racine, and Voltaire, pressed into service by some strange whim of the Banque de France). Catherine Guérard in *Elle* tramples on this "worthless redhead." Claude Manceron replies in *France-Soir* that by and large he prefers his music to Fauré's "cooings" and Debussy's "arabesques," and considers him France's greatest composer. I don't share the delicate ear of my two friends and won't commit myself. Do I dare confess to Manceron that Hector's sonorities get me in the solar plexus but don't reach my heart or my guts? And though the solar plexus may have been the seat of the soul for the Greeks, it moved to another home a long time ago.

SUNDAY, MARCH 23

I left Angoulême in 1934 to go to the University of Paris with two aims in mind. One was to go to the Vel' d'hiv', temple of indoor cycle racing, to see the "Tour de France", when teams of two— called "squirrels" by the sports writers—vied for places, prizes, victory and glory by pedaling nonstop six days and six nights round the "Ring of Grenelle" before a fanatical public: upper crust in the boxes, plebeian in the stands, all moved by the same enthusiasm. The din they raised still echoes in my ears. The names of the twinned cyclists Broccardo-Guimbretière, Wambst-Lacquehay, Wals-Pijnenburg seemed as prestigious as those ancient heroes, Hector and Achilles, Orestes and Pilades. Unhappy Vel' d'hiv'! A sinister aura was to surround its name nine years later when the Germans rounded up the Jews in it. Nonetheless, the old *habitués* were saddened when it was torn down after the war and the present hideous buildings erected.

My other aim was to meet the writers I admired (even if, for various reasons, they have not all stood up to the test of time). My ambition went no further than seeing and hearing them—with no thought of meeting them. So I went to the "Mutualité," a large hall, where Gide, Malraux, Benda, held anti-Fascist meetings; to the "Union pour la Vérité" which Bernanos frequented, and to the Collège de France to hear Valéry lecture.

One of those who intrigued me most was Julien Benda. He looked like a big angora cat; his personality and manner aroused neither sympathy nor warmth, but his intellectual rigor, his lack of play-acting or bias, his refusal to proselytize except through exactness of thought and speech, fascinated us. Like so many students of my generation I had read *The Treason of the Scholars,* that epoch-making book which ten years after publication was still the basis of many violent discussions. In it Julien Benda demolished all those who served the myths and fashions of the moment to the detriment of those values he considered universal: the individual, truth, justice. He crossed swords with Bergson, browbeat the professors of the Sorbonne, and though himself a Leftist, denounced dialectical materialism. For him the logic of contradiction was only "an intentional rejection of reason" ("The nature of reason is to immobilize the things with which it deals, at least while dealing with them; whereas pure becoming, which by its essence excludes any identification with itself, can become the object of mystical adhesion but not of rational activity"). He berated the scholars for their lack of values or involvement. Their role, he wrote, is "to oppose those who claim to see in man nothing but his material needs and their satisfaction." He accused them of betraying this function when they invoked the sanctity of the writer or the relativity of good and evil, or when they were subservient to the State or the established order ("The State, when order is assured, has no need of Truth"). He upbraided them when they allowed themselves to become enmeshed in ideologies which make truth depend on circumstance. He condemned Maistre, Bonald, Maurras, whom he accused of having preached the dogma of the immutability of social classes. He also attacked communism, whose "ideology rejects the idea of abstract justice, identical to itself, above space and time," and aimed this barb in its direction: "I imagine that the tribes Nebuchadnezzar dragged along the roads of Chaldea by a ring through the nose; the hapless man tied to a millstone by a medieval lord who has abducted his wife and children; the youth chained for life to a galley bench by Colbert, were all well aware that justice—eternal and fixed—was violated; and in no way thought that their fate was just, given the economic conditions of their time."

I do not agree with many of Benda's theories (André Lwoff in his preface to the new edition of *The Treason of the Scholars* deplores his unfair tendency to consign to the flames, pell-mell, anyone he does not like: Proust, Valéry, Alain, Mallarmé, Bachelard . . .). But his ideas generate a clean and healthy air, pleasant to breathe. At any rate they help me to shore up the breakwater which protects socialism, our socialism, from the massive flood of preconceived ideas. If I apply today the methods recommended by our philosopher in 1927, I am able to perceive more clearly the buoys which mark the dangerous channels. Every day, several times a day, I look in their direction. It is a good exercise and keeps my eyesight fit for its purpose, which is to discern. For example, in Portugal when Alvaro Cunhal declared peremptorily, "There will be no bourgeois democracy." That is all very well, but bourgeois or proletarian, democracy does have certain laws called freedom of speech, pluralism of parties, universal suffrage. They don't suffice? I quite agree. But surely they are necessary. And I prefer the Socialists' "Socialism, yes, dictatorship, no!" to Cunhal's remark.

In the foreword to his book Benda tells the story of Tolstoy who while in the army, seeing a fellow officer strike a man who had broken rank, said, "Aren't you ashamed to treat a fellow man in this way? Haven't you read the gospels?" To which the other replied, "Haven't you read the Army Rules and Regulations?"

Those are indeed the alternatives.

TUESDAY, APRIL 15

The historian Henri Guillemin writes with a passionate pen. He also likes to blast preconceived ideas and amend the wrongs of history. His book *Nationalists and Nationals (1870-1940)* fills a need. For many years now I have felt the itch to chastise the impostures of a right wing which calls itself "national" and wishes to monopolize the brand name and vintage "France"—château-bottled, of course. It has also, somehow, appropriated the slogan "love of the fatherland" and put it to its own use. You proud backbones of uncompromising nationalism with your horizon-blue eyes and that indefinable something which makes it clear that for all eternity you were destined to wear decorations in your buttonhole! Your aura of preparedness, of high-minded disgust, would deceive anyone if contemporary history had not revealed that they served mostly as ingredients for a pretty gamy stew! I had seen enough miserable lackeys of the German occupation straighten up again in the Gaullist takeover of 1958, seen them drink and eat and sleep again, urinate red white and blue, and berate the Left in the name of national interests which they alone seemed to understand. I had thought this phenomenon went deeper than the cynicism of mediocre opportunists and obeyed some law of public life.

The Nationalist Right capitulated in 1871 (preferring Bismarck to the people of Paris, the safety of their incomes to patriotic adventure) and again in 1940 (blaming the Popular Front *). In 1914 it revealed itself as vindictive (103 Socialists had been elected to the Chamber of Deputies, an all-time record) and irrefutably illustrated Guillemin's thesis that for right-thinking members of the ruling classes strong-box and patriotism go hand in hand. If a few irresponsibles among the bourgeoisie—they do exist—risk contradicting this postulate and get caught up in a nationalism which loves France, living or dying, and is indifferent to the power of money, they will be denounced and if possible put to death. (After June 18 de Gaulle was tried as a traitor and condemned to the ritual twelve bullets. Easy to guess who felt betrayed.) Henri Guillemin writes at the end of his book: "1940 is inscribed in that series of major dates which over a century and a half have marked the history of France and each time indicated that profiteers have resumed their threatened power: 18 Brumaire 1799, 24 June 1848, 2 December 1851, 8 February 1871, 26 August 1914, 10 July 1940. Repeated victories of the propertied classes."

Nationalists and Nationals is made up of ten interconnected accounts all illustrating the same parody. So as not to exceed the limits of this journal, I'll choose one which sums them all up and tells of the vicissitudes of income tax. You will be amazed at the opportune occurrence of coups d'état, armed repressions, ministerial crises and even foreign wars each time the fiscal system which protects the privileges of the wealthy is threatened. Thus, in 1799 the Five Hundred † voted for the principle of progressive taxation. But under pressure from the group of bankers who fi-

---

* "Front Populaire" was a coalition of Leftist parties brought about in 1936 by Léon Blum, then head of the French Socialist Party.

† The "Five Hundred" was the name of the Political Assembly created by the Constitution in 1795. It was abolished during Napoleon's 18 Brumaire coup (November 9, 1799), when Napoleon returned to France from Egypt. With the help of the army and a few friends he overthrew the Directory and established the Consulate. This governed until the return of the Bourbons in 1814.

nanced the 18 Brumaire, Bonaparte revoked this measure. In 1848 Lamartine included income tax in the program of the Executive Commission. No further mention is made of it after the bloody days of June. Once the Commune had been suppressed, Adolphe Thiers could go straight to the heart of the matter when he exclaimed, on June 20, 1871: "No taxation! No inquisition! No violation of the secrecy of private property! Never!" Six years later, reassured by the victory of moral order, he can state: "Moral epidemics, like other epidemics, last only a certain time" and that "right to work, progressive income tax, are words now forgotten among us." Combes, Clemenceau, Caillaux, renewed the attack under the Third Republic only to be rapidly gotten rid of. In 1894 *Le Temps,* the paper which set the tone for correct morality, denounced income tax as "an attack on the honor, even the life, of citizens." At the same time Raymond Poincaré considered that this "incursion into private fortunes" envisaged by "the extreme Left" was infamous. France, "the real France," could breathe at last. ("Be quiet, Mr. Jaurès, France is speaking," *L'Echo de Paris* wrote on March 9, 1913.) And then in 1914, contrary to all predictions, the Left won the elections. On July 15, a financial law was voted instituting the accursed tax (three years were to go by before it was enacted). In 1920 this law inspired François-Marsal, banker, managing director of the "Parisian Union," president of the Syndicate of Commerce and Industry and minister of finance under Millerand, to say: "In the midst of war, while we struggled against the spirit of Germanic Kultur, we borrowed from the same Kultur that feature which is most odious to the spirit of France: fiscal inquisition." No less!

It is a pleasure to watch Guillemin strip the mask from this bourgeoisie which has no policy—not even in foreign affairs, where the safety of the country is at stake—save that of protecting its own class interests. He does it in his own impetuous, seething fashion. But he criticizes the failures and the retreats of the Left without sufficiently taking into consideration the economic conditions of the moment or the extent of social antagonism. Success is not possible everywhere all the time. His book throws light on the phenomenon of class war but misinterprets the balance of forces beyond which battle is in vain. Marx analyzes thus the events of

June 1848: "It was not the revolution that succumbed with these defeats. It was the traditional prerevolutionary appendages, the outcomes of social interrelations not yet sufficiently sharpened to become violent class oppositions: people, illusions, ideas, plans that the revolutionary party had not yet cast off and from which it could not be liberated by the February victory but only by a series of defeats." In the light of these words I feel more indulgent than Guillemin toward the early endeavors of the forces of the people. To each season its fruit. I sometimes feel that the author of *Nationalists and Nationals* wishes to pick them while they are still green. This historian who sets your teeth on edge at least gives you an appetite.

SATURDAY, APRIL 26

Moscow. Leonid Brezhnev grips my shoulders with both hands, we link arms as he leads me to his office and a chair. He sits down opposite me at a long table with Boris Ponomarev and the interpreter on his left. Charles Salzmann, who had come in after me, sits at my right, a little behind. (As he understands Russian, he will give me his account of the conversation later on, having missed neither inflection of voice nor choice of vocabulary.) An intercom near Brezhnev emits now and then a nasal and metallic voice, distorted by the instrument. He answers it good-naturedly till the third call, when he mutters in an aside, "I wonder what they'd do without me." Ponomarev smiles vaguely. Brezhnev then resumes a long softly spoken monologue. He talks passionately of peace, his love of peace, his desire for peace. "Twenty million dead, that's the price we paid for the last war. The dead are counted but not the unhappiness, the misery, the destroyed homes, the abandoned fields, the lost work, the misplaced energy. The time needed to rebuild a country, to make a man, is not counted. Those in the West who tell you that détente is only a diplomatic pretense, a tactical move, deceive you. We'll make war only if we are forced to." He stops and asks, "Do you believe me?" I feel his conviction and am moved by it. Could a long speech be enough to settle the affairs of the world? I hesitate before giving him the answer he expects. "Let me think it over. I would really like to believe you." He rises brusquely, comes toward me, opens his jacket, and with two fingers imitates the snipping of scissors, exclaiming, "You don't believe me, do you? It's exactly as though you had cut my suspenders." There is a pile of photographs on a little table near him. He picks one and hands it to me: himself as a young officer; then another, again of himself, risen in rank, company or perhaps regimental commander; then another, this time as a general. "I've seen war from too close up. One can only loathe it." Then his face lights up and he hands me a large photograph, a rather stiff studio portrait of himself in civilian clothes with a handsome felt hat pulled low over his forehead. "I wasn't bad looking when I was twenty, was I?" And looking at his companions, "They don't like my showing this one. But after all it is possible to live in civilian clothes!" He looks me straight in the eye. "You're a comrade in arms. I know what you did. I know your war record. Those who have lived through what we have must understand each other. Wherever you go, Leningrad, the Ukraine, Uzbekistan, ask questions, see the people at work. Our country is making an enormous effort to produce, to create riches, to ensure its well-being. We do not want to be forced to go on indefinitely producing more and more sophisticated, expensive weapons to protect our safety." Seated again between Ponomarev and the crackling intercom he goes on like that for nearly an hour, now and then asking me questions about France. "We here love your country. So much has come from there. But are your people interested in ideas, in events that occur outside?" Just as Suslov had done, he reels off statistics and figures glorifying the Russian people.

I have met two types of Russians, or more accurately of Soviet Russians. Those who are stiff and icy, knights of a system whose apparatus is the armor that keeps them upright even when lying down. The others, who are lively and spontaneous, going from tears to anger and from anger to laughter without transition, banging on the table or slapping their bellies, swayed by a vast range of intense feelings. Only in retrospect does one realize that all these variations have never departed from the rules of dialectic. Khrushchev belonged to the second category. In 1963 Gérard Jaquet was a member of a delegation of the French Working Class International visiting Moscow as guests of the Soviet Union. He remembers that after a long and copious lunch Khrushchev had given a detailed account of the difficulties he had had after his denunciation of Stalin's crimes. "In spite of all my efforts, a Stalinist current still persists in the Party even at the highest levels," he sighed. With a circular sweep of his arm he included all the Soviets present, among them ten or so members of the Politburo and the Central Committee, including Kosygin, Podgorny, Ponomarev, punctuating his gesture with the words, "Stalinists? You find them everywhere." Silent and embarrassed, the others took notes.

Some time later I described this scene to Carlos Rafael Rodríguez, who countered with the following tale: "During a similar reception after an enormous lunch, Khrushchev jumped into the swimming pool of the dacha, inviting us to follow him. One diplomat, who could not swim, had nonetheless jumped in, and feeling sick had to be helped out of the water. Others were paddling round, feeling foolish. I had followed the crowd though I dreaded being in the water right after eating. I reviewed all I had been through; I had survived dictatorship, revolution, arrest, torture and gunfire. A feeling of melancholy swept over me as I imagined my obituary: 'Drowned in a swimming pool.' Khrushchev roused me from my gloomy thoughts by shouting with a great gust of laughter: 'Look at them all! Scared stiff! Stalin trained them well.' "

Less eccentric, less provocative than his predecessor, Brezhnev is still of the same breed. He feels, and he expresses himself. But something tells me that this warmth, this ease of communication, is a subtle way of occupying the no-man's-land between himself and others; it serves as a strategically placed sentinel which allows him to stand well back and observe the world. Concentration and silence lie behind all the noise. I ask him, "Why these troops and arms massed on the soil of Europe? And those rockets pointing toward our cities? Our specialists have never before located so many nor such powerful ones. The state of NATO forces in that sector does not justify such excessive armament. This weakens your thesis." He avoids answering and launches into an attack against what he calls the German threat. When talking of the United States it is obvious that he misses Nixon. Brezhnev wants to know to whom he can talk.

He then changes the subject and with a sort of lyricism starts describing a future full of investments, equipment, exchange, scientific conquests, technical marvels, and buying power. Like all popes of transition Brezhnev wants to hang on, and he is hanging on; braced against time he endures. His power comes from instability and he wields it through equilibrium. But no reign can survive immobility. Motionless, the king falls. Brezhnev knows this, and by constant adjustments he must contain the liberal thrust coming from the frontiers of the empire and gradually gaining ground. He must dam the great longing to change centuries, to forget that it had all been said in 1917, to hasten the coming of other worlds, other fashions, perhaps even other concepts. He must repress the simple urge to live outside history, to dream on his own porch, to find his own answers, to shout each passing thought aloud, and even more, to escape from the vacant eye of that deity which thinks of everything. The spring that died in Prague puts forth dark blossoms under hidden suns. The earth protests: the laws of gravity do not apply to rising sap. In Moscow, in Budapest, in Warsaw, isolated man can now raise his voice above the towers of silence. That voice has become a tumult heard everywhere. Something tells me that Brezhnev is aware of all this. In spite of Solzhenitsyn, I am far from sure that the gulags are still a system within a system that lacks confidence in itself. Hence the need to maintain equilibrium. A German friend said to me recently that he was not unduly worried by the presence of massed Soviet troops near his country. "Brezhnev must keep his generals busy." The army keeps watch. It is worried by the convulsions that shake all the satellite countries, save Bulgaria; it is resentful of the decrease of Soviet influence in Africa and Asia; and ill at ease in the face of the stalemate with America. The army has made itself the conscience of the Party vis-à-vis the diversity of Euro-communism. After Thermidor * the captains start dreaming.

---

* "9 Thermidor" (July 27, 1794) was the day Robespierre was arrested. He was executed the following day.

But Brezhnev is there, his stature and his wisdom still act as a brake on the advance of history. Posterity, which usually despises men of transition, will grant a privileged place to this one. It is not given to everyone to terminate a revolution without compensating it with a war.

SUNDAY, APRIL 27

Mikhail Suslov has neither the rigidity nor the truculence of a member of the apparatus that he is rumored to have inspired. He resembles a pedagogue, attentive and thorough, giving himself time for thought between sentences, and then suddenly, peremptorily pounces on his adversary. I could easily imagine him teaching mathematics; he has that slightly untidy appearance which so often goes with teachers of exact sciences. Perhaps the word untidy comes to mind because of his thick gray hair, casually parted, an undisciplined lock falling over his forehead with a tuft standing upright atop his skull. This impression is strengthened by the ascetic face, the tall, slightly stooped body of a man of seventy-six, and the pale eyes in constant motion behind steel-rimmed glasses. There is nothing stiff about him, he rubs his beautiful arthritic hands together, blows his nose, shrugs his shoulders, consults his companions, loses his temper. He describes the successes of the regime without any criticism. Nevertheless, I venture one, "The economic crisis is beginning to affect you." He shakes his head and answers drily, "No." He compares Russia and France to the constant advantage of Russia. Systematically he enumerates: "Before the war you produced twice as much steel as we did. Now we produce four times more than you. We have enormous reserves of oil . . ." I interrupt him, "Do you think a Communist France would have more oil in her subsoil?" He looks at me in amazement, pauses for two seconds, and declares, "Well, yes," but this time with a half smile.

That was my impression of Mikhail Suslov. He has been a member of the Secretariat of the Communist Party of the Soviet

Union since 1947, a member of the Politburo since 1955; he is the
only enduring high-ranking participant in and witness of history
as it is lived and made in the most secret places of the Russian
empire. He is the guardian of theory, the prosecutor of deviation;
he has no number in the Soviet hierarchy but, in spite of his
inflexibility, or perhaps because of it, he is endowed with a certain
capacity for survival. He read practically everything that he said.
His text was written on large sheets of copybook paper. Sometimes he hesitated, crossed something out, and pointed out the
alteration to the interpreter. He talked slowly, as Communists do
the world over when speaking in public, the mission of each syllable to convince. As a matter of fact, no Communist official, from
the most modest secretary of the most modest cell to the secretary
general of the Party, can begin a discussion without reading a
carefully prepared text. The internal mechanisms of these documents reveal a well-rehearsed dialectic, and as I listen I wonder
from whom the speakers get them. They are undoubtedly able to
produce unaided motions, declarations, the drafts of communiqués—no political party pushes the schooling of its militants as far
as the Communist Party. But that is a long way from the
master hand which puts the subordinate clauses each in its right
place; and the identical use of semantics and rhetoric by cell sec-
retaries to the north and to the south cannot be entirely explained
by telepathy. I can see in my mind's eye some murky den where
documents are hatched. But what sort of den? We are dealing with
an international movement—communism—founded on a universal
theory—Marxism-Leninism—having as its point of departure the
revolution of 1917 which is recognized by its members as the
dawn of a new era. In imagination, can we climb the ladder of this
organization and, reaching the top rung, surprise the supreme
scribe in the exercise of his prerogative? It is wasted effort, for
Suslov himself—even Suslov—reads!

In two days of talks we were able to broach, and even on occasion investigate, a number of subjects. Enough to fill a long report.
But I will note only three observations. First: the Soviets' obstinate
denial of the existence of any sort of Third International, as this
dig of Suslov's illustrates: "French Communists who take no orders from outside . . ."; this just after he had stressed the an-

noyance his party had felt at the renewed activity of the Socialist International. It was ludicrous, but the insinuation made me understand Georges Marchais' words at our last meeting: "Unlike you, we do not have to take into consideration exterior factors which would affect our decisions." It was as though Suslov had wanted to put his seal on the French Communist Party's campaign of independence from the ussr and at the same time let it be known that this campaign was developing not in spite of Moscow but with its agreement.

My second observation is in the same vein as the first, since it was presented as the touchstone of peaceful coexistence. It concerned Portugal, which we discussed for over two hours, while the Middle East received only brief mention. Suslov passionately defended Cunhal and justified his attitude and his alliance with the Left: "I know him, he is not an adventurer." (*Adventurer, adventurism*, have a precise meaning in Communist terminology. "He is not an adventurer" has the value of a certificate of orthodoxy.) Taking over from Suslov, Ponomarev denounced the brutal, direct intervention of Frank Carlucci, the American ambassador in Lisbon; the pressure brought to bear on Soarès and his friends by high finance; and once again, the steps taken by the Socialist International. Exactly what had been said to me in my house one morning by the Russian ambassador in Paris, Tchervonenko: "The Central Committee of the Communist Party of the Soviet Union wishes you to know that our leaders will not tolerate any foreign interference in the affairs of Portugal," to which I had replied, "An amazing situation! A Russian ambassador in Paris, talking to the first secretary of the French Socialist Party about Portugal's right to decide her own fate!"

I make no secret of my friendly relations with Mario Soarès. Do the Soviet rulers wish to use me as a go-between to make him realize the risks he is running by his continued refusal to negotiate with Cunhal and Gonçalvez? The Americans have retired into their shell since Watergate and Nixon's resignation; their diplomacy and their army have been humiliated in Vietnam, in Cambodia, in South America, in the Near East; their strong man Kissinger is reduced to punching air. The moment seems propitious, as at no time since the Berlin crisis, for a limited and controllable trial of strength, which—should it succeed—would pave the way for a new balance of power in Europe. It is as though the Russians, attracted by the idea, were feeling out the West's capacity for retaliation. Who at Yalta could have dreamed of a Communist, or near-Communist regime in Lisbon, of the Azores seceding in reaction, and Portuguese partition pushing the dividing line between the two worlds several thousand miles westward? The high Soviet functionaries' extraordinary fixation on the narrow stage where the last act of the carnation revolution is being played out proves that such a dream can haunt the coolest heads.

This argument was in full swing when—third observation—Ponomarev interjected, "It is extremely important to help the new Portuguese government." This remark set our debate on a new, and to us unexpected, tack. For Ponomarev added, "We must not forget that the obstinate refusal of German Social Democrats to joint action with the Communist Party put Hitler in power." I countered, "While it was in the majority, Social Democrats had lacked foresight, even before they had—as a minority—practiced a policy of 'lesser evil.' As for example in 1932, when it allowed its votes to be counted with those of the traditional militarist Right in support of Hindenburg against Hitler. (Hindenburg was elected by 19 million votes against 13 million; Thälmann, the Communist candidate, obtained only 3 million.) It had not discerned the true nature of Hindenburg's interest, which a few months later made him hand over power to Hitler. History, even rewritten by ideology, cannot erase the overpowering responsibility of communism, shackled by Stalin's policy of 'class against class' which, without any shadow of doubt, allowed the emergence of the Nazi Party." Why, in a private meeting with very well-informed people, did Ponomarev see fit to bring up this old argument? Was it an expression of irritation at our refusal to bring pressure to bear on Soarès, as he wished? It was hard to imagine Ponomarev giving way to nerves. Especially as the Portuguese situation in no way resembled that of the Weimar Republic. The government in office in Lisbon was the result of an alliance between the Communists and the army, with the Socialists in opposition requesting a Common Program! I pointed this out. Nobody took me up on the point and the conversation resumed its course. But something told me that this incident was meant as a warning that we should not have too many illusions as to the fate Moscow would mete out to a union of the Left in France. The hour had not yet struck for a truce between the Second and Third International, between the two separated factions of the working-class movement, between communism and our socialism. I shared my doubts with Gaston Defferre, even though the hospitality extended us seemed to belie them. The attentions, the courtesy, the cordiality shown us were somewhere between the traditional relationship of members of the same party and the relationship between state and state. We interpreted this nuance as a gamble on our chances of success at the next elections. I drew the conclusion that our partners were torn between their wish for a genuine and lasting understanding with the future government of France and their fear of a new experiment capable of offering Europe the model of a Socialist state different from, even antagonistic to, the Soviet model—and were preparing for any eventuality.

MONDAY, APRIL 28

We had been talking since early morning. By the time the clock struck one, all of us round the conference table were beginning to stare into space or start up conversations with our neighbors. Quite obviously the Russians were as keen to move about as we were and to head for the dining room and a meal which would no doubt live up to Kremlin standards of hospitality. This moment was chosen by a Soviet delegate—economist and academician—to announce his talk. Suslov nodded in agreement and the speaker mouthed a greedy O in announcing the title: the "Grossplan." On every face, horror was followed by resignation. Food! Oh food! Then the toneless voice of Ponomarev filled the silence. "Relax, comrades, our comrade academician will not be long—surely less than three hours." The Grossplan was dispatched in less than ten minutes and we raised the siege.

Ponomarev once more. On leaving the Kremlin he accompanied me to my hotel; rush hour traffic held us up. He leaned toward me confidentially and murmured, "Comrade Suslov told you of our rapid progress in many fields. He forgot to mention one—as you can see, we now have traffic jams."

MONDAY, MAY 4

We dined with Fidel Castro on the evening of our arrival in Cuba. Our group consisted of seven delegates of the French Socialist Party, three of whom had brought their wives. One of the latter complained of travel fatigue and subsequent headache, and asked for aspirin. Fidel sent someone off to find the greatest possible variety of suitable remedies. While they were being rounded up the conversation turned to insomnia, which afflicted most of us—too much work, too many responsibilities, a tendency to anxiety. But I must introduce Carlos Rafael Rodríguez. He is one of the principal leaders of the regime, vice prime minister for economic affairs and a respected adviser of the Revolution. He had been a member of the government under Batista, whose twice-repeated dictatorship terrorized Cuba. However, he was there as representative of the Communist Party. The Cuban Communist Party had put into practice, long before its European comrades, the strategy of historical compromise and denounced Fidel Castro, that adventurer, who proposed to liberate the people by armed force. Castro did not forget, and once in power he arrested and condemned the secretary general of the Party, Anibal Escalante, before packing him off to the Soviet Union. Carlos Rafael Rodríguez, subtle, sparkling, cultured, was wise enough to espouse the course of history. He became Castroite without ceasing to be Communist, while waiting for Fidel to become a Communist without ceasing to be a Castroite. I have seen him in Paris several times since and hope to see him again, for there is much to be learned from this pleasant companion who, while he believes in what he does, is able to keep a sense of humor.

The medicines had still not arrived when the whole table heard Carlos Rafael's gentle voice murmuring: "Dear lady, I know an infallible way to ensure you sleep, and thus oblivion to all woes great and small. I use it myself every time I feel the need. I put a copy of *Granma* (the Cuban Communist Party newspaper) on my bedside table. I get into bed, I open the paper. Infallible! I read four lines and I'm fast asleep. I have to be shaken in the morning."

I was watching Fidel Castro and the other dignitaries present. No one seemed shocked at what would have been sacrilege anywhere else. Someone merely remarked, "Tell them you're joking, Carlos, or what will they think of our literature?" Everyone started laughing and the aspirin was forgotten.

Recently Carlos Rafael spent three days in Paris on his way to Moscow. He wanted to sound out the extent of the good intentions expressed by the French government toward Cuba. We met at the home of Edmonde and Gaston Defferre. Carlos was in excellent form; I have already mentioned that this sardonic character has a great gift for understated barbs and anecdotes. Nothing in common with what passes for wit in Paris nowadays—the cold ashes of Voltaire's, Rivarol's, Joubert's wit. I know whereof I speak. For ten years, ten too many, I moved on the fringes of that set known as "Le Tout Paris." It goes on tirelessly repeating the same things in the same tone of voice, never wearied by its own boredom, still convinced that it sways manners and behavior, whereas it does not even influence fashion. I used to be fascinated, I can't think why, by the very elements that today exasperate me: a society which drugs itself with a mixture of minor narcotics, thinking it satisfies its passions, whereas it has nothing but needs.

Economy of words is a quality I appreciate above all others. Carlos Rafael wastes no time. What a joy to follow the inference of sentences he has not uttered! And what a handsome Spanish face; just the sort of handsome Spaniard one can imagine stepping out of a portrait by El Greco (this is not an esthetic judgment; I prefer Velásquez). An elongated face destined to haunt heaven but loving its own body; a face old age will fill out, for if opposition doesn't kill you it fattens you!

Less than a week after my return from Russia I can write that I have heard no more penetrating remarks on Russia and the Russians than those of Carlos Rafael that evening. On the Communists also, and he is one. Some day I will explain why.

SATURDAY, MAY 10

The publicity brochure I am looking at vaunts the comforts provided, the unequaled "services rendered" when needed, by R. Funeral Parlors, and its branch offices. First, a special vehicle "having no sort of funereal appearance" manned by "two white-coated bearers" will fetch me from wherever death has found me to convey me to a trim villa (or thanateum), where—so I am informed—"the parlors are air-conditioned and of different sizes and decorations." Having chosen one for me, my family can also have the use of a reception room in the Louis XIII style favored by country inns. A hostess will be on hand to receive the guests, put their flowers in vases, and graciously offer them hot or cold drinks—the advertisement makes it quite clear that there is no extra charge. Visitors pausing here will find pleasant nooks to chat in and can nibble at the buffet or smoke expensive cigarettes. Color photos emphasize the care given to detail: a dainty lamp, a marble-mounted calendar, a chintz-covered hassock on top of the wall-to-wall carpeting. There seems to be only one anomalous element: the coffin. But clever interior decorators have found excellent solutions to this problem: velvet pedestals, Napoleonic columns, draw drapes. They have in fact integrated the object into the philosophy of the place: Death does not exist.

There is even better. Denise Fuchs, the friend who sent me this document, informs me that a thanateum in the south of France has reached a sort of perfection in the genre. Slightly raised on pillows, blush foundation on his cheeks, carmine on his lips, the hollows filled out with cotton wool and the puffiness ironed out, the departed receives his guests. On request, overhead cameras at desired angles film these last moments, and concealed bellows imitate the rise and fall of breath.

From my description the reader will have gathered that this ceremonial surprises me. Some will say that the cult of death also has its fashions, that there is no fundamental difference between the funeral pyres of Benares, our Catholic Requiem, and these boudoir obsequies imported from the United States; that the genteel refreshments can be compared to the trappings, complete with silver tears, of a first class funeral, and the twentieth century's cotton wool is a very modest element when compared to the bitumen of Egyptian mummies.

But this denial of death bothers me. I feel that a society which hides death from the eyes of the living, paints it over like a lie, removes it from daily awareness, is not magnifying life but corrupting it. Birth and death are the two wings of time. How can man's spiritual search come to fulfillment if he ignores these dimensions?

WEDNESDAY, MAY 14

Who is fooling whom? The government in Paris considers and declares that thanks to the merger that it has brought about between the American firm Honeywell-Bull and the French firm CII (Compagnie Internationale d'Informatique), France will at last "play a significant role in the world market," as they say in officialese, in this advanced industry. But the echo which comes back from New York through the mouth of Mr. Eldson Spencer, managing director of Honeywell, gives a different sound. "This merger is a very positive step forward for the computer section of Honeywell and represents a major return for the efforts made in Europe by our firm to put its activities on a more competitive footing in the field of data processing. This affiliation will give us access to important new markets, especially in France." And Mr. Spencer magnanimously concludes: "To achieve this we obtained significant help from the French government." "Affiliation"? "Significant help from the French government"? Mr. Spencer's words are in such brutal contradiction to those of Messrs. Chirac and d'Ornano that curiosity prompts one to ask: Who is fooling whom?

1. Let us compare the two parties. On the American side: Honeywell, a group specializing in automation and data processing with sales of two and a half billion dollars (say ten billion francs); the data processing subsidiary of this group (Honeywell Information Systems) with five-billion-francs sales and 40,000 employees; and finally Honeywell-Bull (Honeywell holds the controlling stock) which has sales of a little over two billion and 10,500 employees.

On the French side: CII (sales of 900 million and 9,000 employees), which has been limping along for some time and, as everyone knew, was looking for outside help. In 1972 it had signed an agreement with the West German firm of Siemens and in 1974 had formed a holding company called Unidata with Siemens and the Dutch firm, Philips. At this point, the principal shareholder, the French Compagnie Générale d'Electricité, had forced it to change tack and replace the European partners for the American one.

2. The French government, unable to remain indifferent to the fate of our data-processing industry, hesitated for a long time. The choice it has just made means that in the next four years the state will spend one billion two hundred million francs in subsidies, to which must be added tax rebates and guaranteed orders, in exchange for 17 percent of the shares of Machines Bull, which itself will own 53 percent of the shares of the company formed by the merger of Honeywell-Bull and CII. In other words, French public funds will control barely 9 percent of the enterprise (17 percent of 53 percent), the remainder being in the hands of private French and American interests.

3. Those who think it is important that French interests, whether public or private, should retain a majority of Honeywell-Bull shares (53 percent), will be alarmed at the nature of the ties uniting this firm with the Honeywell group—even if the nature of these ties were altered. For the computers made by Bull will be sold to Honeywell on the basis of a price fixed by Honeywell, whereas increases in capital could at any moment intensify Bull's dependence.

Nothing guarantees that research will be continued in France, that the range of products will be decided by France, or that the technology will coincide with national interests. Nothing allows us to assert that the power of decision will not leave France. Nothing forbids us to imagine that once French data-processing achievements have been digested by Honeywell, the directors of IBM—by far the largest firm in the world—will not then step in and take over the whole thing, by buying Honeywell, for instance.

The nationalization of Honeywell-Bull and CII by the Left would seem to be more in line with public interests.

4. Everything will be clear when it is shown that 50 percent of CII's sales in France came from government orders. So that when Mr. Eldson Spencer declares that American industry now has access to "important new markets, especially in France" he seems to be closer to the truth than Mr. d'Ornano.

The other day at Mourmelon Mr. Giscard d'Estaing gave a heartfelt speech on the subject of national independence. To quote Jacques Prévert, "Words, words!"

SUNDAY, MAY 25

As others had been before me, I was conscious that the major principles formulated by the Constituants in 1789, the year of the birth of political democracy in France, were showing signs of wear. I therefore proposed a charter of freedoms as one of the goals of my presidential campaign last year. I was guided by four principal aims. First of all, it was essential to restore to the people as a whole those gains which the bourgeoisie had appropriated by clever takeover. The new ruling class had come to power after years of effort at the precise moment when an industrial society in full expansion offered its masters an unlimited increase in profits. They had used the principle of economic liberalism as their favorite weapon against newly acquired freedoms. An apparent paradox which is only a question of vocabulary. All men who have a free spirit should proclaim aloud in front of the fortresses built at

the crossroads of production and exchange that "liberalism is the
real enemy." For public law, born of the Revolution, has only
served to translate the law of the jungle into the language of
capitalism.

Then came the need to update legislation on working conditions and adapt it to reality, to change the relations of production,
to prepare the way for control by the workers, to decentralize
decision-making. All things essentially bound up with the advent
of those two freedoms I am weak enough to consider fundamental: the right and the time to live.

Third aim. It was intolerable that our laws should remain two
generations behind our way of life. It is well known that Giscard
d'Estaing, who at the time had carefully avoided upsetting the
most conservative fraction of his electorate, had in this respect
annexed the program of the Left. A legitimate adoption that does
not annoy me; far from it. It stresses the validity of our projects:
All the better if legal age is now reached at 18, if birth control is
allowed and contraception encouraged; all the better if unhappily
married couples are freed from the degrading difficulties of
divorce.

Finally. Science and technology have put new means of interference in the private lives of citizens at the disposal of the State.
It is essential that these be inventoried and steps taken to guard
against them. This is the task of the study committee which under
Robert Badinter will start work this very week on the charter of
freedoms, that same charter I announced a year ago.

MONDAY, MAY 26

A newspaper bearing the fine name *República* was published in
Lisbon until a few days ago. It was a Socialist paper and for forty
years had stood up to the vicissitudes of dictatorship: censorship,
interdiction, and occasional imprisonment of the staff. In Portugal
liberty was spelled in four syllables. But *República* no longer exists.
The editor, Raul Rego, a regular guest of Salazar's jails, has

been confined to his own office and the printing presses taken over by a force of workers. Portuguese Socialists suspect that this commando was recruited by the Communist Party. The Armed Forces Movement dispensed justice like a one-eyed King Solomon by shutting down the paper. Farewell, freedom of the press! Unless everyone rallies to the rescue of democracy in peril. The Communist parties in Spain and Italy have already condemned this maneuver. The attitude of the French Communist Party is more confused. Freedom of expression is among the basic rights, and seen from this angle the *República* affair is very, very simple. Perhaps too simple. The question it poses can only be answered by yes or no.

TUESDAY, MAY 27

Inexhaustible subject! The inquiry into the bugging of the *Canard Enchaîné* * has come up again. The preamble to the Constitution of 1958—which in its entirety refers to the Declaration of the Rights of Man and of the Citizen—has not stopped the Fifth Republic from systematic censorship, from stifling radio and television, and from card-indexing citizens. The current minister of the interior goes on listening at keyholes and recommends the boycotting of those artists who, in the exercise of their freedom, used their talents to help the left-wing candidate during the presidential elections. Last week we saw the head of state put the crowning touch to a year's near-daily appearance on television with an insolent and childish festival of full-blown confessions. It was as though France had stopped living and was absorbed in self-adoration: seeing herself in the yellowed mirror-image of an old young man, quite evidently first cousin to Madame de Ségur's perfect little girls.

* The offices of the *Canard Enchaîné* were wire-tapped by two "painters" during a redecoration. The government, often lampooned, was thought to be responsible, but the "bugs" were discovered by the newspaper before they could be of any use.

WEDNESDAY, MAY 28

From Raymond Aron comes this blazing shaft: "The drama of Giscard d'Estaing is his not knowing that history is tragic."

MONDAY, JUNE 2

I am in Dublin heading a delegation of representatives of my district, the Nièvre. To an aged politician I express amazement that there should be in Ireland two apparently identical Conservative parties. He was silent, but as I insisted, finally volunteered, "What keeps them apart? The contempt they have for each other."

TUESDAY, JUNE 3

Shannon. Before I took off for Ireland I had been given notes for next Thursday's opening speech at the 1975 Suresnes Conference. I worked on it yesterday in Dublin and this evening in Shannon, after a day spent on the river of that name. I steered a little boat between the banks of a narrow backwater where wild irises and reeds grew. I saw a heron rise, three migrating Russian swans fly overhead, and numerous moorhens paddling around. A strong wind from the Atlantic whipped my face. An excellent preparation for the work awaiting me.

I remembered similar hours at Jarnac spent with my father when he went fishing on the Charente. His flat-bottomed boat was hidden in the rushes three hundred meters from the house and I had noticed that he was not much interested in fish. I asked him why and he answered that life was often like the river. At first sight nothing seemed to happen; the hours went by, then the days—sometimes longer, sometimes shorter—the seasons slid away . . . But if you looked more carefully, gradually your eyes saw more and more, till you realized that nothing changed, yet everything changed. How was it possible? The instrument capable of registering the constant and variable dimension of time was still to be found. I listened. My father seldom spoke. He cast an occasional word into the silence in much the same way as he cast his line into the river. It no longer quite concerned him. So I got used to filling my childhood with the skies of my birthplace, travelers' skies crossed by migrating birds; with flat fields swept by the swell of waving grass, and the smell of earth at the water's edge. I learned to recognize the call of wild duck seeking shelter and the cry of alarmed tomtits. My most marvelous memory is of an otter; reassured by our silence it cast a liquid look on us and turned away. Any vocation I might have had for fishing never overcame two obstacles. I loathed grubbing in the mud for the worms I needed to attract gudgeon, minnow or perch, and on the rare occasions when I overcame my disgust, I balked at putting them on the hook. But this did not stop me from continuing to haunt the river and the closed world of the marshes.

WEDNESDAY, JUNE 4

I have just finished the introduction to my speech. Christian Goux's suggestions guided my thinking. He was an engineer and seemed in no way destined to become one of the most acute and intuitive observers of monetary movements, nor yet one of Marx's most reliable interpreters.

Central idea: In the fight against the ruling classes by exploited people the world over, intellectuals, especially economic theoreticians who feel involved in the historic struggle, have a decisive role to play. They must simultaneously contribute to the collapse of the ideological bloc now in place, to the dismantling of its mechanisms, and, assisted by the ideas and experiences of the workers, pave the way for socialism.

Official strategy has endeavored to reduce these people to the role of prestigious scientists whose neutrality is guaranteed by the image of the sciences they study. Inviting their involvement may appear imprudent, save that some of the most brilliant have already given their answer. They know that economics is only a branch of the humanities, that is to say a discipline whose approach and methods are not bound by the precision of the exact sciences. Economics is fundamentally political, and the humanities differ from the exact sciences in that the necessary experiment which makes it possible to conclude that a proposed hypothesis is right or wrong does not exist. In spite of the perennial values which constitute the common good of humanity, the various social classes visualize and interpret past, present, and future in different ways. It is therefore desirable to resume and to elaborate—as Marx did over a hundred years ago—a critique of current political economy, that of the ruling classes. Numerous theoretical studies based on the actual economic and social state of affairs should be embarked upon to provide the tools with which a decadent order can be analyzed and challenged.

TUESDAY, JULY 8

Giscard d'Estaing likes to play at "doctor-so-much-the-better." But I refuse to play at "doctor-so-much-the worse." When I correct the figures and estimates of the president of the Republic on unemployment, budget, balance of payments, or rate of growth, I am very careful not to give in to the pleasure of contrariness. I do not ascribe his mistakes to secret or malevolent designs. I think he deceives us because he deceives himself. Not that he passes up the little nudge that enables all statistics to go from the negative to the positive. The French people do not seem to resent his numerous firecrackers that fizzle, nor the extraordinary elasticity of his monetary principles, whose chief characteristic seems to be the waving of a white flag at the slightest alarm. (We saw it with gold and fixed exchange rates.) So why shouldn't he promote to the status

ıw what used to be merely a convenience? Especially as it suits
/ nature; he loves predicting events but hates preparing for
em. We must accept that if it also suits his purpose it would be
asking too much to expect him to change his methods.

And yet I wish he would. I can understand that he should think
it important to allay anxiety by offering a picture of calm. But I do
not accept that a head of state should flatter a nation's hopes
without arousing its awareness. In small doses drugs anesthetize;
in large doses they kill. You don't medicate history with LSD. That
is what I wanted to make clear at this afternoon's press conference. Some journalists felt that my remarks were pessimistic. That
was not the impression I meant to give. France's game does not
depend on just one deal.

TUESDAY, JULY 15

If I had to describe Georges Marchais' * rhetoric, I would say that
it sounds like special pleading. The tightly knit speech gives the
impression that the orator is endeavoring to sway the attentive—
though perhaps reticent—assembly of his peers. Not that he runs
any immediate risk of disavowal. There is no instance of a report
accepted by the Politburo of the Communist Party being rejected
by the Central Committee. But as Marchais says, the Common
Program is a text without precedent. The Communists have been
working toward it for a long time; a first draft was drawn up by
Maurice Thorez in 1959. But they must now negotiate with a Socialist Party whose situation has changed considerably. Ahead of
them lie vast prospects with which they are rapidly coming to
grips. They are united and renewed. Far from being small change,
they are beginning to reestablish the internal equilibrium of the
Left and are aiming at becoming once again the first party in
France. The agreement submitted to the Central Committee bears
witness to this change in the balance of forces. Georges Marchais

* Georges Marchais has been secretary general of the French Communist Party
since December, 1972.

reveals that after tough and strained discussion, the Communist negotiators were obliged to give in on the automatic dissolution of the National Assembly in case it failed to respect the legislative contract; that they were forced to accept the insertion of the sentence, "If the country were to refuse to show its confidence in the parties of the majority, these would renounce power and resume the struggle in opposition," reminder of a principle to which they had only timidly adhered. They were also obliged to agree that the present state of security did not allow France to leave the Atlantic Alliance; they were forced to come round to the idea that a left-wing government would participate in the development of the European Economic Community, as well as in its institutions and joint policies. They were unable to obtain the interdiction of tactical atomic armament, or the destruction of existing French nuclear weapons. They had to consent to reducing from twenty-five to nine the number of industrial groups due for nationalization in the following five years—plus four cases of government majority shareholding. These were the main points.

It is therefore not surprising that Georges Marchais does his best to minimize in the minds of his audience the extent of the gap separating the Common Program from the Communist program. This explains the forcefulness with which he stresses the concessions made by the other side (necessary in any contract) and the wealth of unpleasant and sometimes abusive remarks he aims at the Socialist Party. Two quotations will serve: 1. "The Atlantic Alliance and the EEC are class alliances whose nature and function are to enslave our country to the imperialist system headed by the United States. It is for this fundamental reason the Socialist Party is so deeply attached to the Atlantic Alliance and the integration of the EEC countries of Western Europe." 2. "The permanent features of the Socialist Party are fear that the working classes and the masses will start to move and hesitate when faced by the struggle between class and capital . . ."

Excess of language is a well-known diversionary tactic. I will dwell on it only to note the comical cynicism of a strategy based entirely on an alliance with a partner judged incapable of being other than he is, that is to say, a hardened traitor. The cause defended by Georges Marchais before the Central Committee deserved better than this contradiction.

The three years that followed the signature of the Common Program were rich in conflicts from which the Left emerged united and loyal in spite of the dark predictions of the secretary general of the Communist Party. But it is true that this program is not Socialist and that it survived only because all points of ideological controversy had been removed. On our side, we made our partners admit that, systematically and exclusively, we must see everything from the point of view of joint government action—including the settling of our own differences. We accepted no compromise that infringed on our principles, the conduct of our congresses, the interests of the workers, of our international duties. In short, we have no intention of swapping our program for the Common Program; and we cherish as the apple of our eye the points of view that are inherent in our Party, its freedom of expression and action, and the expansion of its influence and organization.

Some of my readers will no doubt be shocked by these last remarks, typical of the Socialist Party, they will say. Let me reassure them: I have quoted them word for word from the resolution adopted by the Central Committee of the French Communist Party two days after drinking, in an atmosphere of euphoric sincerity, the champagne of friendship.

SATURDAY, AUGUST 30

Latche. Every day, or nearly every day, I visit my oak trees. This ritual amuses those around me, who laugh when I insist I can see them change. It's quite true though. I planted them in November. In spring the hungry deer attacked the fragile bark and mangled it. Helped by my friend the horticulturist I sealed the wounds with grafting wax and protected each tree with barbed wire. This summer a drought killed off the tender leaves—how heart-breaking to see the vigorous young branches suddenly wilt and turn brown. Now that rain has fallen—it always does after August 15— I'm watching for the appearance of new shoots to tell me that life has won out. Seasons are not propitious to men or to trees.

Last year in June, on a plot of land called Maroye, south of Latche, a tornado uprooted, or broke off half-way up, 80 fifty-year-old pine trees, each weighing about a ton. I acquired this plot in 1971 through an exchange with a neighbor; the peasants here call it an abandoned field, for there is only first-generation growth in this forest clearing. Previously corn and grapevines grew on this plot. The pine trees are less sturdy and the timber not as good as in the older plantations. Only after they have been felled a first time and been replaced by a new growth can one hope that the trees from abandoned fields will become as straight and as handsome as those of this area of Marensin where we are, which is generally considered to be the finest pine forest in the Landes.

Those who saw the tornado say that it came and went in twenty minutes. First the west turned black and then the whole sky. Twelve months earlier I had seen the same phenomenon. It was pitch dark at noon. Animals are forewarned of these things as also of earthquakes, and ours were all upset; the dogs yapped and ran round with raised hackles; the birds who live under our eaves (I have counted over twenty nests) circled round the beams fighting for a refuge. In the house, doors and windows were closed in a great hurry, and force was used against the recalcitrant ones to make sure they were firmly latched. A necessary precaution, for some of our neighbors who had lacked the time or the foresight to do the same saw their roof fly off. Even though they have occurred two years running these tornadoes are rare. How capricious they are! Whenever the fancy takes them they cut rectilinear swaths of forest. A laser could not do better. Across a front measuring precisely thirty meters nothing was left standing. The only survivors were the hollies, arbutus, thorn bushes, and woolly-leaved oaks which stay small as they are deprived of oxygen by the over-shadowing pine trees. It was the hardiness of these oaks which encouraged me to go through with a long-standing idea and plant enough of them to earn the title of forest. I am not there yet and I will have to live to a hundred or more to get the slightest shade from them.

There is no tree I love so much as the oak, except perhaps the willow, which never fails to evoke my personal landscape of France. Sufficient reason to dedicate to my oak trees this farewell to my holidays.

FRIDAY, SEPTEMBER 5

While preparing a lecture on "Socialism and Science" a few years ago, I read a short book entitled *What Is Labour?* written by Harold Wilson. At the end of July, 1974, a lunch at Chequers—residence of British prime ministers—had brought together the leaders of the Socialist International. On this occasion I asked our host, Harold Wilson, "Tell me, what is labor?" and quoted a passage from it on the role of computers in the society of tomorrow which had particularly interested me. A very slight doubt seemed to cross his mind, and then he said in a matter-of-fact tone, "I don't know the work in question. Please tell me the name of the author."

SATURDAY, SEPTEMBER 6

Still at Chequers. I was going round the Council Room sometimes used by the Cabinet, contemplating the full-length portraits of Nelson, Pitt, Wellington, and others painted by British masters, hanging on the walls, when I heard Wilson say: "If the presence of these paintings upsets you, I can have them removed." I thought he was joking and told him so. "Do you know that to avoid a diplomatic incident we once exiled these portraits to various London museums?" Wilson answered. And he told me that Georges Pompidou had considered that French sensibility was offended—nay! the French flag insulted—by his being forced to sit beneath the gaze of France's conquerors. Edward Heath, then prime minister, bowing to the presidential request, had had these seeds of discord replaced by still lifes. Some time later, after

Heath's defeat, the Labour Government rehung the portraits of Nelson and his illustrious contemporaries back where I had seen them.

MONDAY, SEPTEMBER 15

Two years ago—it seems a century—Salvador Allende was murdered in Santiago de Chile. His enemies, who were the enemies of the people, had not been niggardly: To kill this man, army planes had dive-bombed and tanks had fired at close range on the lovely baroque façade of La Moneda palace. Machine guns had finished the job. "Surrounded by smoke and flames, Salvador Allende waited for them in his office, with no other company than his noble heart," Pablo Neruda wrote on the final page of his memoirs. "His body was secretly buried in an obscure spot," the poet adds. That obscure spot haunts my dreams.

As for Pablo, he died twelve days later on September 23, 1973, of cancer—and that other disease that is killing Chile. The army harassed his last days and kept a close guard on the small cortege of friends who followed him to his grave, with express orders to shed no tears. With advance payments of royalties on his *Canto General* he had been able to buy a house in 1939. ("I needed a place to work in. I discovered a stone house overlooking the ocean in a place unknown to all called the Isla Negra.") This house was pillaged, the furniture smashed, the books burned, the manuscripts defiled and torn. "The yellow leaves about to fall and the grapes which will live on in the sacred wine will stand out from all that I have written in these pages," Neruda wrote in the introduction.

A short while before, I had seen Neruda in Paris where he was the Chilean ambassador. He was lying, rather than sitting, on a deep divan; his voice, always low, was already beginning to break as he said to me: "You haven't read *A Hundred Years of Solitude*? It's the most beautiful novel to come out of Latin America in the last twenty-five years." So I read *A Hundred Years of Solitude*, and since then Macondo has haunted me. That village of clay and water, born with the Buendías family and fallen into decay with them: From the first Aureliano who fought thirty-two civil wars and lost them all, to the last Aureliano, who forgot his dead and their sorrows, and locked himself up in his room. He boarded up the doors and the windows so as to be disturbed by no temptations of the outside world—including the temptation to live. The author, Gabriel García Márquez, tells of one of his characters, Alvaro, who left Macondo with no hope of returning but who sent postcards to his friends remaining in the village from every station where the train stopped, and says that this for him "was like tearing the long poem of transience to bits before throwing it away." The long poem of transience! Has mankind any other history?

For the second anniversary of Chile's entrance into solitude, neither French television nor French radio sent postcards to the dead; to those who had been tortured. Silence. Silence also for Neruda and the forest of signs and words he planted round the earth. ("How beautiful is the language we have inherited from those grim-eyed conquistadors. They took away gold, but left us gold, they took away everything and left us everything . . . they left us words.") Silence for Allende and that simple action which consists in never giving up what one holds in trust from the people. Silence for the living who fight on.

Though the floodtide of interest in Portugal is receding for the audio-visual media, I was nevertheless asked this week for several short interviews on the situation in Lisbon, which I refused to grant. But nobody has questioned anybody on the subject of the Pinochet regime: "Tell us, Mr. Poniatowski, what is your opinion about the respect for freedom in Chile?" "Mr. Chirac, can you explain why the economic crisis in Chile is worse since the Right came to power than it was with the Left?" Some people have specialized in pointing out the shortcomings of Soviet Russia with regard to the freedom of movement of men and ideas. A very honorable pastime. And journalists are being kept busy these days, what with the thwarted love of a young French girl who wants to marry Spassky, the Soviet chess champion, and the writer Amalrik who has just been released from a concentration camp but is still being persecuted in Moscow. But which of these journalists has worried about the free movement of men and ideas in countries such as Spain, Brazil, Iran or Chile? (Not to mention the United States, if one is black or a half-breed and claims to have a brain to think with?) I know their answer: It's not front-page news, and it does not interest the French public. Chile! Chile again! But last July all three television stations and all four radio stations reminded their audiences throughout the day that seven years earlier Russian tanks had entered Prague and put an end to spring. What strange geography!

MONDAY, OCTOBER 13

What does Giscard want? To conserve. Having made this assertion I must amend and complete it by making two remarks. First, the Giscard of whom I speak is the politician, so his actions allow me to pass judgment on him. Far be it from me to interpret the deep personal sentiments of the private Giscard whom I do not know, though certain character traits lead me to believe that he is open and approachable. And then, Giscard is too intelligent and too subtle to want to conserve in the way that X or Y does. I mention no names. People of the Right contemplate suicide when they are told that they are of the Right. Let us have no mass suicides!

But Giscard has understood that to conserve the essential it is often necessary to change the inessential. Why did he find it nec-essary to saddle himself with legislation on abortion and divorce which cannot be enforced and is daily flouted, and moreover makes the Establishment and the ruling classes objects of hatred to thousands of Frenchmen who would remain perfectly indif-ferent to the nationalization of the chemicals industry? By adapting legislation to current morals in those areas that his elec-tors—and others—find to their advantage, he has gained a reputa-tion as a man of progress, which has relieved him of the necessity of doing any more. And if he has offended a minority of die-hards, they have not been so deeply wounded in their faith as they would have been by taxation on large fortunes or by a property tax.

In short, Giscard is there to conserve. If this were not so, he would not be there. His campaign slogan for the elections was "Change within continuity"—an amusing association of words which proclaims that change must bow to continuity. In truth, politics has its own laws which are more logical than might appear at first sight. Before finding out what Giscard wants, let us enumerate what he used to want: electoral reform, regional reform, a federated Europe—all things now forbidden him. What in fact does Giscard want? What Chirac wants! This is the real change: Rome is no longer in Rome, but at Matignon.

The France that Giscard wants does not interest me. I do not want the France that he is making.

WEDNESDAY, OCTOBER 15

It is not the accuracy of its pictures that I hold against pornography; it is the falsity of its myths. The fable that happiness can come from well-studied postures or picturesque situations distresses me. Alissa in Gide's *La Porte Etroite* taking her hand out of Jérôme's because they are warm after climbing to the top of a hill, tells me far more about love than explicit miming of other so-called pornographic films. If physical love, the games and lusts of the body, brought happiness—I mean that state which leads the human species to believe it has come upon one of the secrets of life, which thereby gains its justification—we would not have had to wait for "Emmanuelle" to discover it. This polished, oiled, deodorized sexual machinery which porno films put together in ingenious combinations like pieces of a Tinkertoy—always the same and limited in number in spite of attempts at imagination in the scenario and the goodwill of the actors—can produce only so many, or so few, permutations. Unlike computers—when they work—these films do not integrate all the data fed into them by the questioner. An answer is always lacking. To think that "the amorous octopus made up of arms and legs" which Cocteau celebrates will have revealed its secrets because its various possible combinations have merely been inventoried is a vulgar mistake.

However, let us not exaggerate the evils of pornography as a social phenomenon. After all, it is no more than the product of a mercantile society whose only morality is to serve its own interests in all things. Porno pays. Long live porno! But its limits are in sight. I am more alarmed by the drugs in "More" or the violence in "A Clockwork Orange." Degradation and death wait at the end of the "always further" myth. We need not take at face value the arguments deduced by cinema professionals from the success of porno films: "The fact that audiences can and do give free rein to their pleasure proves that such films fulfil a need." Is this argument sufficient to let things go on as they are? No, a thousand times no! *O* raped, lacerated, a ring placed in her sex, being painstakingly trained under the eyes of record crowds, makes one think all too easily that in the garden of tortures, the only flower is blood.

But how can censorship be applied to pornographic films? To give up automatic subsidy of film makers strikes me as dangerous; it is insufficient to put a surtax on films forbidden to minors; and impossible to forbid distribution. I would prefer to limit showings to special channels and allow them only at certain times. Programs could be controlled so that in medium-sized towns the movie theaters would offer the inhabitants a wide range of films.

THURSDAY, OCTOBER 16

The Communists are now our allies—more than ever before in history—since this alliance is based on a program agreed on in 1972 for a period of five years, one that is a program of government.

anti-Socialist offensive launched by the Communist Party
time last year, and kept up with its usual perseverance, an
sive intended to "improve the quality of the alliance" as it
es with a curious brand of humor, worries us to the point that
e commission led by Lionel Jospin wonders whether it is not a
move intended to postpone the coming to power of the Left. It is
as though the Communists could not bear the idea of victory
unless they themselves were the principal actors. But let us not
commit the sin of hastiness. A definite answer to this question
will become essential once we are closer to the goal.

The new element—no doubt unexpected, except by us, which
upset everybody's calculations, except ours—was the rise of the
Socialist Party. The Right had gotten into the habit of thinking,
with a mixture of fear and satisfaction, that France had become
bogged down in the same situation as Italy (a strong Communist
Party and a weak Socialist Party), so that our progress was met
with incredulity.

The Communist Party was scandalized that the alliance should
fail to behave with the docility expected of it. When we had three
million electors we were liked; when we had five million we were
tolerated; above that number we became a cause for alarm. We
like being liked, but now that there are more than six million of us
we can feel resigned to not being liked quite so much. We know
our weak points. Being the first party in France is not measured
merely in terms of votes. We fall short in many other fields and
we would be foolish to feel over-confident. When I think of our
finances, our organization, the level of training of many of our
members, I realize that we are open to criticism. All these matters
will keep us busy for years to come.

There is one point, however, on which we are sensitive. We
certainly take the tricks of vocabulary—which oppose our "re-
formism" to "revolution"—for what they are worth. It is a favorite
theme with the Communist Party and on occasion with a minority
in our own party, which goes even further, distressed at the idea
of not being in the very forefront of action, in the vanguard of the
first commando. But let us first of all agree on our definitions: If
the word "revolution" is used with the first meaning that comes to
mind, that is to say a brutal, total, sudden breakaway from the

previous order of things, after a test of strength in which the adversaries have staked their last chance of survival—the situation in which Lenin found himself in 1917—then this is not the type of action we have chosen. But I do not know any party of the Left in France which acts differently—with the exception of a few groups which at this time have no influence on events, either owing to their extremely limited numbers, to their remoteness from, not to say unawareness of, the masses, and even on occasion to their infiltration by the police.

The Communist Party's tactics are not founded on some possible miraculous Great Day, any more than ours are. It progresses from compromise to compromise, as when it agreed to be included in the parliamentary system; when it established regular, open, relations with the officials of the regime: prime minister, ministers, prefects (the refusal to go to the Elysée Palace was merely going along with the circumstances of the movement, since Georges Marchais agreed ultimately to go there in August 1974); or when it accepts the risks of universal suffrage. Its program of "advanced democracy," first presented by Waldeck-Rochet and then by Georges Marchais, recommends structural reforms which would lead one to believe that capitalist society would eventually be liquidated, step by step. But the steps in question are not linked to any precise timetable, whereas the Common Program proposes a five-year plan. I should add that it is grotesque to suggest that fifteen nationalizations represent class collaboration, while sixteen make a revolution. An accurate evaluation of the forces confronting each other, and the nature of the conflict, leads the Communist Party to temporize with the existing society until it is strong enough to change it, while its public pronouncements accuse the Socialists of betraying a theoretical plan whose details are only parsimoniously revealed, though one can surmise that it looks like the twin of the Soviet system.

These contradictions do not alarm me. Socialists are not Communists; they are Socialists. As soon as the Communist Party has accepted these two complementary propositions, a united Left will emerge from the desert where a regrettable mechanical breakdown has stranded it.

MONDAY, NOVEMBER 3

At Château-Chinon I endeavor to preserve any traces of the past
which seem worth it. Truth to say, they are rare in this country
over which the kings of France and the dukes of Burgundy battled. After the death of Charles the Bold the war came to an end in
a field three leagues east of the town. Driven this way and that by
the fortunes of war, victors and vanquished left only ashes behind
them. Château-Chinon went up in flames six or seven times; nothing is left of the castle and not much of the old city. Nevertheless,
the houses built of hard gray stone which hug the side of a steep
hill, the narrow streets that still follow the medieval plan, the
arches, the fountains—which have taken on the color of the earth
and of the autumn sky that you find only in these Celtic lands—all
need to be protected. In the old days the roofs were thatched, but
the long rye straw has become a costly luxury now that combine
harvesters break it to bits. The flat roof-tiles which followed
thatching became less used during the last century and are now
found only near the Morvan. The eye immediately notes that slate
has taken over. It is a question of attunement to the setting, of
harmony with the texture of the surroundings. As mayor of the
town I have decreed that all roofs shall be covered in slate, genuine Anjou slate. As you can well imagine, there was much opposition. Asbestos shingles or some sort of roofing material
imitating tiles would have been acceptable. People balked at the
cost of real slate. In spite of their doubts, my Municipal Council
stuck to its guns. And soon, even the most hardened objectors
realized that it was to their advantage to use the long-wearing
slate and began to love this beautiful material which gave them
brilliant, long-lasting roofs.

It was a very different matter with my feudal lords; I mean the
administration, the banks, the Public Works Department. The
Electricité de France used the forbidden shingles; the Crédit Agricole covered its roof with mud-colored tiles; the Public Works
Department was less daring and asked for a waiver. I had the

Crédit Agricole tiles removed, and though I put up with the Electricité de France shingles for the moment, I refused to grant the Public Works Department a waiver. In retaliation has come the threat to divert promised funds elsewhere. The project for a Finance building is likely to remain blocked since the semiprefabricated structure chosen by Paris calls for an aluminum roof; the same applies to the hospital extension. And I am barely on speaking terms with the national education authorities, who have put a miserable sort of fence around the high school. My obstinate "Have some respect for the harmony of my little town" is countered by a stubborn "We haven't got enough money to pay for your fancy ideas." So that is where I stand in this most recent war of mine.

At Nevers, my neighbors have been blessed with a quite unmentionable Post Office building right in the middle of a charming baroque district. The recently erected Treasury Department building will have a choice place in the catalog of the Universal Museum of Monstrosities. And let us say nothing about that enormous lump of lard that some misbegotten pork-butcher of a sculptor dumped on the banks of the Loire as a tribute to Sport and Culture. Thus it is that bit by bit, France—unloved by her own central government—has become a shantytown. We will soon have forgotten what stone and glass and concrete can express in the hands of a talented nation.

MONDAY, NOVEMBER 10

Régis Debray could not have found a better title for his novel than *The Undesirable*. It was among the first books selected as candidates for the Goncourt prize; it disappeared in the second round and was thus out of the running for the final choice that will be made on November 17. I have read three of the seven books that remained as final contenders for the prize. Two of them are not worth much; Emile Ajar's *La Vie devant soi* is the only one that has the style and tone of a good vintage. On the basis of comparison with the other books alone, nothing justified the rejection of *The Undesirable*. It is true that Régis Debray had committed the unforgivable sin, as far as Paris circles are concerned, of acquiring his fame by means other than writing. Many people fail to appreciate that real life made a character of him long before he ever thought of inventing one. It is as though he must be made to understand that he has gone far enough for the moment and that he still has a lot more to prove before being recognized as belonging to the literary establishment. He is a graduate of the Ecole Normale Supérieure and has earned a degree in philosophy, but these accomplishments, which usually bring laurel wreaths in their wake, seem, in his case, rather to annoy people. What was this professor doing in Bolivia, anyway? To a certain extent I share this complaint. *The Undesirable* and its author are so similar that we are forced either to accept them both or to reject them both. This is not my only criticism. As I read on, I had a feeling that the author had bridled that inspiration more than was necessary, that he had held in check that tendency to follow fancy where it takes him which suits him so well and manages to surface here and there throughout the book in spite of his precautions. I believe I now know why. Our mutual friend Françoise Castro informs me that the manuscript submitted to the publisher was in fact three times longer than the book which finally appeared. Pared down to the bare bones of the story, it has lost much of its impetus.

But what subjects for debate he proposes, what questions he asks, and what a writer he is when he confronts himself squarely! To quote Debray, I like to listen to "that imperious little night music . . . which always turns our ear inward . . . the cello underlying the brasses, muted at first, then at last dominating them all." Unlike him, I do not think that this is a defect—which might be labeled "Western individualism." After all, that music is his; he has made it his very own. All the better for him, all the better for us. It is a tenacious passion, and therefore a habit—dear Régis, there are no good habits—which makes him deplore the fact that three thousand years of history weigh on a society which he sadly considers to be insufficiently "undivided." As for me, I do not miss "the days of landmarks and set courses." I would tend rather to dread their return. Dear friend, be sure that on this dark night where no lodestar points the way, in this unfortunate century lacking a compass and cardinal points, no man can sift out ideal from idolatry, nor myth from mystification, unless he lays bare the diamond point—I mean that incorruptible particle of the spirit called conscience. As for Franck, the undesirable, a hail of bullets pierces his body and he slides into the "undividedness" of death. The book closes on a last image: Franck sees the dawn of a new world and feels "a great joy bear him aloft." I am certain that he was smiling, too, at the strangeness of life. Nothing is lost in advance. He who finds his own unity is very close to attaining the unity of the world. I recommend *The Undesirable*.

Régis Debray offers us a wealth of tenderness and charm, though some indefinable modesty or refusal to reveal himself holds him back from the freedom of being and writing all that he owes us. As this song of love bears witness: "Franck foresaw his future and was resigned to it. He knew that between their two memories a river would always flow to separate them, an Amazon of silence and inadequate words; that even if he loved her a whole year through, Celia would never become for him that faceless and incomparably comforting warmth with which one has slept three hundred nights: his woman, his wife. He knew that the endless weaving of love, all that meticulous braiding with which a man surrounds a woman day by day, would capture nothing but water."

TUESDAY, NOVEMBER 11

"Zionism is a form of racism and of discrimination," in other words, "Zionism equals racism." This is the new dogma that 72 countries against 35, with 32 abstentions, promulgated last night at the United Nations General Assembly. Robert Badinter just phoned me to ask for my signature on a protest. I would give it to him twice if I could. I already knew that fanaticism was one of the attributes of stupidity. This morning I feel like writing that it is stupidity itself. To be convinced of this I do not need to have seen the faces or heard the words of these pronouncers of anathema. The fabric of man's history is woven of his immemorial hatred of his own species.

Let us be sparing of lapidary words, and retain only one: contempt. And for the edification of all, let us scan the ridiculous list of "fors," "againsts," and "abstentions." On one side Amin Dada and Franco, on the other Duvalier of Haiti and some Tonton Macoutes. In the middle, Pinochet.

Yesterday I wrote about Frank the undesirable. Association of words, association of ideas. Frank, Anne Frank, that wonderful and heartbreaking undesirable, flower of life, poor corpse. It is of you that I am thinking as I write the word "forgive."

MONDAY, DECEMBER 1

I first met Mikis Theodorakis at the Continental, a big hotel in Paris where he was holding a press conference. He had arrived from Athens, having just been liberated after three years' internment and house arrest. Papadopoulos had decided to let him go free so as to sidetrack the ministers of the Council of Europe meeting in Strasbourg to determine whether it was time to make public the report of the Commission on the Rights of Man concerning the practice of torture by the regime of the Greek colonels. No one will have forgotten the rescue mission organized by Jean-Jacques Servan-Schreiber which resulted in Mikis' arrival in France. The day before, I had myself been approached to undertake this mission. But I was at Château-Chinon and there had been delay in contacting me so that I had not been able to charter a plane at such short notice. On my return to Paris I was informed that this mission had been successfully accomplished by the editor of L'Express.

As I entered the room where Theodorakis was speaking, I was

immediately struck by his stature and by the ardor with which he spoke. He was like some beautiful athlete who has exceeded his strength and gives himself time to breathe while getting set on his starting block for a new race. Untidy curly hair surrounded a face that was at once drawn and puffy with fatigue. With rapid passionate words, he talked about Greece: about the brutal stupidity of the dictators, and the struggles of the resistants. The flow of words, the timbre of his voice, emanated from a sense of rhythm which revealed a familiar music.

The second time I saw him he was playing the piano in a flat in the Saint-Augustin quarter. There were too many guests for the very small room. Shoving and standing on tiptoe, people peered between heads and shoulders to get a glimpse of Mikis. He was bent over the instrument, his fingers running over the keyboard as though writing a poem. He played with long silences and that obstinate concentration which is a form of absence, an inner journey, though at the same time a shortcut for crossing the border which joins one to the rest of the world, when one knows the way. Now and then he accompanied himself in a half-muted voice. The emotion which gripped us all transformed this small crowd into a single body, animated by the soul of the instant. We were the sun and the river and the lonely valley; and we were the steps of the upper town, edged with flowers and blood. We were the devastated gardens and the burning forests. O Greece, O freedom, twofold and unique homeland! We were exile and hope, vine and sea, the traveler not to be turned away from the path that leads homeward. In my mind's eye, I could see great migratory birds tracing their course above the curve of the earth, the vast sweep of their wings erasing our geography. I could see them alighting beside that marsh or on the branch of that tree which thousands of reincarnations had foreordained as their refuge. I cannot guarantee that Mikis' technique was perfect, but he was the medium who transmitted his own creation. The dulled or broken echo he awoke in us bore the music he was playing as far, if not farther, than the art of the best interpreters could have done.

I was again aware of this at our third meeting: a concert given in the hall of the "Mutualité." Maria Farandouri and Pedros Pandis had sung "the sorrows and longings of the Greek people" to music by Ritsos, Christodoulou, Seferis, and Mikis himself. Maria, hieratic in her Oriental gown, disdaining all theatrical effects, stood with her arms at her sides, motionless save for her right hand beating time, her generous contralto dominating the orchestra. For me Maria incarnates Greece. This is how I see Hera, strong and vigilant. I do not know any other artist who for me illustrates so well the word sublime. Pedros, just as motionless, with eyes and fists tightly closed, opened the doors of that kingdom to which dreams and regrets go. I could hear him calling to all the living witnesses of so much bloodshed, so many unheard cries. Would the walls fall if his cry were repeated seven times?

Facing his companions, Mikis embraced the music with open arms. It was as though he were harvesting a field of sound. With the tips of his fingers he drew to himself each note of the bouzoukis and the guitars, and knotted them in sheaves which the next phrase unknotted. His great height bent and straightened as though he wished to defeat in single combat "that angel, horned as old Moses, who, knowing he did not know his face" still intended to break him. Suffering and laughter, attack and defense, flitted across his face. He seemed totally engrossed in this brotherly close combat when he turned suddenly toward us and started to sing. I have already said that he doesn't have much of a voice, but this is of no importance. He makes this music his, he re-creates, invents it once more; through it he transforms stone and metal till they fuse and become words. The crowd was on its feet.

I have met Mikis frequently since and presume to call myself his friend. Each time he comes back from Greece, either on a concert tour or for personal reasons, he lets me know. He is still waiting for me to visit him in his home in Corinth. I promised to go there this summer—someday I will. I was invited to rehearsals of Neruda's Canto General and thus was present at the birth of a masterpiece: the meeting point of two major inspirations which came together at the exact place where the history of our time is being written. Where Mikis is concerned I will not talk of artistic commitment to a cause. Political involvement is the source of his music—not the opposite. The whole of his creative output is battle and the means of doing battle. The dictatorship knew what it was about when, five weeks after the coup d'état, it promulgated the following decree: "We have decided, and we decree, applicable to the whole country: that it is expressly forbidden to reproduce or to play the music or the songs of the composer Mikis Theodorakis . . . citizens violating this order will immediately be brought before the military tribunal." On November 9, 1967, the court of Thessalonica condemned Konstantinos Daoutis, a shopkeeper, to four year' imprisonment for having sold a record by this forbidden author.

It is essential to read in *Culture and Political Dimensions* the analysis that Theodorakis makes of his poem "The Song of the Dead Brother." He writes: "Song is the substance of the people in its march forward and in its historical continuity. . . . It sums up the quintessence of the national and popular character caught up in the flow of troubles and centuries." The poem should be heard:

> O tender mother, you had two sons, two trees, two rivers
> Two strong Venetians, two sprigs of mint, two great joys,
> One joined the party of the East, one of the West
> And you, alone in the middle, you speak and you question the sun.

Mikis Theodorakis belonged to the Greek Communist Party when it split in two, and Mikis went off on his own in search of "a Left freed from the shackles of bureaucratic dogmatism, intimately in tune with the requirements, problems, and idiosyncrasies of the Greek progressive movement." I see him such as he is, advancing with giant footsteps. His task is far from finished. "The taste of freedom is bitter," he told the French journalists who greeted him at Le Bourget one spring evening in 1970. Bitter and necessary, dear Mikis, bitter and delicious.

MONDAY, DECEMBER 8

The scene is now ritually set. As soon as I arrive on the rotunda at Roissy a small group of journalists rushes forward; I am blinded by flashbulbs, questions get muddled. I emerge from a crowd of passengers who are either irritated or amused by the scuffle. Claude Estier leads us to a less crowded part of the airport and there begs my visitors please not to speak all at once. At last a question gets through to me. "What do you think of America?"

How to answer, must I answer? The cameras are upon me, great eyes whose retinas feed the collective memory of my contemporaries. Until recently I had a tendency to pronounce every word recorded by these machines as though it were a final truth. It took me some time to rid myself of this failing, not entirely lacking in merit. But whatever humility daily use may have taught me, I do not have sufficient courage to declare, just like that, in forty seconds, what I think of America. It had already started in New York. Suitcase in hand, I was halfway into the revolving door of the hotel when a reporter from the *Herald Tribune* shouted at me, "Sir, quickly, quickly! What do you think of America?" And now once again, Claude Estier, of *L'Unité*, has been after me for the last week, "Write us an article on what you think of America." Well, I don't feel like it.

When traveling I jot down on bits of paper, which I frequently lose, the impact that a word or an image has made on me. Later, if the opportunity presents itself, I use these scribblings when the components of a subject or a portrait have taken shape in that submerged region where the spirit orders its material. I have not yet told of my trip to Cuba last year, of Fidel Castro, my companion for a week. Some day, should I feel the need, I will write of Brandt dreaming aloud in the train to Stuttgart. But anecdotes tend to bore me when they are divorced from history.

I know more about countries and people in a flash than years will ever teach me. Nonetheless, I am wary of intuition, the wisdom of globe-trotters: True knowledge is sedentary. But I survive as best I can, snatching from the constant agitation of my life its earth and its water, that is to say, silence.

I have been to the United States five times. I had not been back for seven years. I stayed there for six days. I talked for an hour and a half with Henry Kissinger; I lunched, dined, breakfasted, with fifteen to twenty congressmen, those of whom it is said that

they matter; I spoke before journalists of the National Press Club
and diplomats and businessmen of the Council of Foreign Relations, those testing grounds of politics. I liked this country where
everyone goes out of his way to meet those who are passing
through and throws the doors wide open. I liked this boundless
country. While in Washington I took advantage of a moment of
respite to drive up the valley of the Potomac. A few miles beyond
the suburbs I was already in the South of *Gone With the Wind.*
Under a sky as pure as on the day of creation, the splendor of an
Indian summer lent the woods, the rivers, the fields, the colors of
a fire. I must add that my head was filled with the short stories of
Ambrose Bierce, on the War of Secession, read the previous night
on the plane, collected under the title *Sudden Death,* and including
that masterpiece "An Occurrence at Owl Creek Bridge," that En-
rico used as the subject of a wonderful short film. Once again I
was overwhelmed by that feeling I had felt so strongly on my first
visit in 1946: America is still to be conquered.

Propeller planes were then still in use, so I crossed the Colorado
desert in a DC-3. The flight lasted for hours. (What! is America
this empty land, this abandoned satellite?) In Palm Springs, where
the gentry of Los Angeles spends its weekends, if you leave the
lawn where tea is served, your host will warn you, "Look out for
the snakes, they're deadly." In Las Vegas, you must be careful, in
the center of town, not to leave the sidewalk. Automobiles on the
one hand, scorpions on the other: Stick to the straight and narrow!
North of Seattle and on into Canada, a wide mountain range
awaits its explorers. I know neither Texas nor Louisiana. The
plane carrying Marie-Hélène Lefaucheux got lost in the marshes
where alligators slumber. No, I'm not describing Borneo or Man
in the Ivory Coast. It is the United States I am talking of: the
country of Cape Kennedy and Westinghouse. But all travelers see
America with the eyes of Christopher Columbus. It is a voyage of
discovery. Mine was space.

On my last evening we viewed New York from the sixty-fifth
floor of Rockefeller Center. If the term pure poetry has any meaning, it is to be found there. The geometry of this city has the scope
and rhythm of a poem. Beneath us the entrails of the earth were
revealed between the walls of sunken towns. The play of light and

shadow erased even the idea that man might exist. I was amazed that morning to see a flight of mallards take off at the mouth of the East River. They had flown straight through a cloud of starlings, just at the point where the fresh river water meets the salt water of the sea.

I relished the idea that the flow of the seasons still continued to rule the order of things.

WEDNESDAY, DECEMBER 17

Describing America (I gave in at last) by talking of wild ducks banking at 80 miles an hour over the prow of Manhattan may seem frivolous. I hope to be forgiven if, however, I insist. Deciphering fate in the flight of birds is not new, and I read in those birds more signs than the mere passing of time. America is on the brink of something impossible to imagine. Too many blows received have made her huddle in her corner like a groggy boxer. The questions of yesterday seem to have faded in the daze of a terrible uppercut: no more angry blacks, no class war, the Mafia now a tourist agency, the universities cozily at home again—I mean back in the nursery. But wait till she rises to her feet once more and heads for the center of the ring. Heaven help the cardboard decor and the knickknacks in the hall. My friends know that I would like to write the chemical history of societies. In the entrails of America the pockets of mine gas are waiting to explode.

This makes the actual political maneuverings seem all the more futile. The one thought of Gerald Ford, the most powerful man in the world, is not space, nor détente, nor monetary stability, but beating Ronald Reagan for the Republican nomination at next year's convention. While Schlesinger, in disgrace, ponders the forward leaps of Russian strategy and Kissinger weaves his cloth on the surrealist loom of the new prewar period, the president criss-crosses the United States, shakes hands with Nebraska station masters, strokes the napes of the neck of little girls from Wyoming, and throws footballs at the boys from Missouri, seeking and counting the votes of the king-maker committees. A poll having revealed that Reagan was in the lead, Ford trembling for Ford is ubiquitously in all the places where history is not made. Apart from this, the race for the White House is off to a slow start. In the Republican ranks, Ford's only serious rival is that Reagan whose name has just appeared for the third time in the last twenty lines, with no desire on my part to write it once again. The ex-governor of California, who got his reputation thanks to the qualities he revealed in the exercise of his profession as a television master of ceremonies, has seduced the old machine that once produced Lincoln, thanks to the fact that he is even farther Right than the others—which is not all that easy. In the final analysis, the Goldwater precedent taught nobody anything.

Everyone seems to agree that if the Democrats could get together on a suitable candidate, they would win. But the total failure of McGovern against Nixon eliminates him; McCarthy, raised to a pinnacle by the youth of 1965, sank at the same time that that youth grew old—so fast! ; Muskie's image has grown dim; Connally has changed parties; Sargent Shriver has not managed to put across the point that he really is the husband of John Kennedy's sister. Jackson, who has the best organization, has installed his men in the key posts of the party in state after state, but has upset the liberal contingent by his hawkish foreign policy. Ted Kennedy would be chosen if he accepted, but he refuses. Wallace, wiser now, remains marginal, and nothing is known about the others.

That the party of Roosevelt, Truman, and Kennedy, which has a majority in Congress and holds thirty-six governorships (also an elective office) out of fifty, having been given a boost by the senility that has attacked its traditional adversary, should—less than a year after the ousting from office of the Republican president— be incapable of wielding a power no one questions, makes it necessary to inquire into the fossilization of institutions. That a country as rich in the fields of art, science, technology, and industry should reveal itself so lacking in responsible politicians capable of governing, that is to say of deciding everything for

everyone, this discredit of the *res publica* in a regime which claims
to be the direct expression of the will of the people, indicates that
the system has reached its extreme limits. Because it has become
divorced from the values which heretofore inspired it and has not
invented any others, it now obeys only a reflex of self-defense and
is rapidly closing in on itself. It is from this angle that Kissinger's
actions must be observed and judged. An unplanned policy can
take as its point of reference only "Realpolitik," whose very nature it is to copy what has been done before. After the rupture
brought about by the French Revolution, Metternich clung for
thirty years in the same way to the Europe of pre-1789. Perhaps
such men take pride in forcing history to march backward. Henry
Kissinger's face bore a half-smile as I suggested this comparison.
He pointed out to me on the wall of his office a painting repre-
senting the globe—or perhaps not the globe, but just a circle, any
circle, or perhaps simply a blob made up of ten thousand other
blobs, themselves marks, signs, points, craters, or nothing more
than the exploded outlines characteristic of abstract painting.
"That's my table of organization," he said to me.

THURSDAY, DECEMBER 18

Surrounded by a cloud of photographers, Henry Kissinger greeted
me at the State Department with these words: "I'm pleased to see
you again." It is without false pride that I confess that through a
lapse of memory I still cannot explain, the idea of any connection
between the all-powerful secretary of state of the American empire and the modest Harvard professor I had received in my home
some years previously on the recommendation of the president of
Columbia University had never struck me. Kissinger, who was
then working on his book, *American Foreign Policy*, was touring
Europe to meet the political leaders whose opinions mattered to
him. He arrived at my house late in the afternoon and spoke more
than he listened, which in this case I greatly appreciated. Long

enough, at any rate, for another place to be set for dinner. That evening, that conversation, that impromptu meal, all came back to mind as I listened to the words of welcome of the secretary of state. Kissinger pretended not to have noticed my slight hesitation, took me by the arm, and led me to his office, a spacious rectangular room, light and comfortable. There we sat down according to the set pattern, he in an armchair, Robert Pontillon in another, myself opposite in one corner of a sofa, the other being occupied by Jacques Kosciusko-Morizet, French ambassador to Washington. Having nothing to say that had to be kept secret, I did not resent the tenacious presence of the ambassador, who adopted to the end of the interview the embarrassed reserve one would expect of a stowaway. But I heard later that Kissinger had resented his presence. "I was not able to talk as freely as I would have liked," he confided to the person who later repeated it to me.

Our host started off by talking of the situation in Italy, which seemed to cause him more concern than the state of affairs in France, unless this was a roundabout way of warning me of the consequences of allowing Communists to participate in an Atlantic Alliance government, while seeming not to interfere—at least in my presence—in French internal affairs. He spoke favorably of Berlinguer, praising his subtlety and charm; talked about Eurocommunism, which he saw as a tactical move in a worldwide strategy; of Christian Democracy, which he described somewhat mockingly, though he admired its dexterity in making people forget its many failures and muddles by playing on their fear of greater calamities when the worst was already at hand. He said ironically, "The Italian Communist Party allows its country to remain in the Alliance. That is very good of it. They may like it; I don't. The Atlantic Alliance was constituted to contain Communist expansion. We don't need a Trojan horse." I replied, "The United States has the right to choose its allies, but having made its choice, it should not feel aggrieved if those countries of Europe that prefer their freedom of decision to your protection, seek the safeguarding of their security elsewhere." To which he replied, "That is quite true, but I'll get over it. My sleep wasn't disturbed one single night by the thought that France had left NATO. And I would sleep just as well if you left the Alliance. Of course, I'd much rather that you didn't." He had drawn his sword. I merely answered, "I cannot see the United States giving up its worldwide presence quite yet, nor returning to isolationism. Unless, of course, it aimed at becoming another Switzerland." Kissinger unbent, smiled, and lifted a hand in a weary gesture. "Ah, Switzerland, Switzerland," he murmured. "I dream of a Swiss canton, it's so well organized." I looked at him and reflected that in spite of his intentional changes of humor and tone, my host had only one way of being himself. His capacity for astonishing ended there. He is always described as being in a hurry, agitated, forever on the point of rushing off to the other end of the world for a fifteen-minute conversation. I think rather that he lives up to this image of himself as a means of gaining time. Nothing is less double-faced than his diplomacy. He either charms or attacks. Of course, it is easier for the princes of this world to scorn false pretenses. And those who automatically expect trickery have lost from the outset. Mere ability is not sufficient to explain great destinies. The last yards are run alone; one can only judge a man when he has run his race. Those who use up all their energy on a career have nothing left for history. I do not envy the lot of such of our contemporaries whose long uselessness has in the end made them indispensable.

Kissinger is of a different stamp. He knows he skirts disgrace, he lets it be understood, and as his power diminishes he does not conceal his bitterness. I realized this from remarks such as these: "America is going through a fit of virtue. Whoever is in power here is automatically presumed guilty. There is not a single senator who wouldn't like to sink his teeth into the secretary of state." Or: "I'm off to China this week. Maybe I'll settle there. There is no extradition agreement between China and my country." But he deals with the problems of the world as though he had all eternity ahead of him.

The conversation came back to the Atlantic Alliance. I asked him, "Why does the United States practically always give its support to dictatorships rather than to democracies? It is making the country lose its old reputation which used to be so great that in French provincial families Jefferson, Franklin, and Lincoln were revered to the same extent as the sages of antiquity. At least that was so in my family and I expect it was the same throughout the Western world. We admired and loved this type of man who lived a simple life, respected others, and fought for freedom. This image was even brighter when your army came in beside ours in the First World War. In our eyes, you were the army of Right. Without wishing to appear naïve, it seems to me that this was worth more than the precarious advantages of war in Vietnam or the colonels in Athens." The word "dictatorship" made Kissinger flinch. I had a feeling I had offended him. "No, no. We hate dictatorships. In contrast to your history, ours has not known any. But communism is also a dictatorship, and the worst: one can never escape from it. Build democracies that know how to stop its advance and we will help you." I protested: "We are the only judges of our choice. But if you think that you are protecting your interests by playing on the threat of a coup d'état each time the established order is threatened—in other words, if you make the Atlantic Alliance and democracy incompatible, it is the Atlantic Alliance that will perish." I did not wish to hurt his feelings but neither could I conceal my thoughts. However, he regained his composure and said, "The Germans, the English, the Dutch, to mention only them, do not define the problem in those terms. And yet they are our faithful allies. Whatever form it may take, we respect the orientation of their internal politics. Their common denominator is to have no indulgence for communism. We ask nothing else of our friends." I felt like saying, "Have you never had any doubts? The West will not be able to resist the power of attraction of the system against which it fights, until it breaks away from the system which inspires it." What good would it have done? I could not expect him to condemn a society when his function was to be its prime defender. As though he had followed my train of thought, Kissinger changed course and remarked, "You may say it is none of my business—just put it down to curiosity on my part—but tell me why you plan so many nationalizations in your Common Program. I do not want you to think that they alarm me because they involve the expropriation of private interests. I am quite indifferent to that aspect. The United States, the major capitalist country in the world, has far stricter antitrust laws than you have. You are quite right in wishing to impose your views on those who control the banks, industry, and commerce. They will always try to govern in your place. I am aware of it here every day. But allow me to give you this advice: Nationalization is not the best solution. First of all you overload the State machinery, which needs to be adaptable and able to act quickly. The Italian Communist Giorgio Amendola recently confided to one of our senators that the first task of a government of "historical compromise" would be to get rid of at least one third of the present public enterprises, which paralyze the economy of his country. But that is not the most important factor. Private enterprise has lost its prestige, what I might call its moral weight, or better still its mythological power inherited from the great adventure of the nineteenth century. Money for money's sake will never awaken man's feeling of the sacred. It is permissible for the State to bargain with capitalists, to corner them, to dominate them. If a conflict does break out, public opinion sides with the State, not with General Motors. Whereas by nationalization you confer power on thousands, hundreds of thousands of officials purported to represent the national collectivity, just as you do. The power you give them is a portion of yours, is of the same nature as yours. You are handing over to them your own mythology. When they fight you, they will fight you on your own ground. In the name of what can you then persuade the people to decide in your favor?"

I appreciated the value of his arguments, but the discussion he had started involved too many ideas for us to pursue it then. Our meeting was coming to an end, so I merely remarked that he was mistaken, that our mythology was not based on the State (of which he spoke as Suslov speaks of the Party), that the State was nowhere the mouthpiece of the nation, but of the ruling classes— whether they were Communist bureaucrats or capitalists and their agents, the managers. I said that the mastery of the major means of production and credit represented, in the West, the *sine qua non* for a change of society. However, we were not confusing ends and means, and nationalization represented for us only a necessary passage toward another revolution, a revolution at once great and humble, which would make it possible for each individual to become, first of all, himself, and then to make his own decisions. We parted with mutual promises to resume this conversation some day.

Some day, perhaps.

1976

SUNDAY, JANUARY 4

I do not expect the three television channels to broadcast only what pleases me. There is little chance of that. But the year-end broadcasts force me to return to this irritating (irritating and wearisome) subject of audio-visual information. I hesitate to broach it once again, especially as I do not like repeating myself, and even more, I dread hurting the feelings ⸴ ᴄhose journalists who do not deserve being accused of platitude, conformity, and boot-licking. In truth, nothing is more difficult than the profession of journalist where a monopoly exists. Party newspapers are aimed at a public which freely chooses them. By definition a monopoly imposes its point of view. This is the case—quite legal and above-board—of French radio and television; it is also the case beginning to prevail in the provincial written press. And, even if they compete commercially, the magnates of the mass-distribution illustrated weeklies all belong to the same milieu, all represent the same interests, and when necessary show a united front. I have yet to forget that press magnate—a provincial one—who took the liberty of banging on the table (quite literally: we were lunching together) to persuade me, when I was secretary of state for information, to grant him more than his normal allocation of paper. (During the post-war paper shortage one of the functions of the ministry of information was to allot the stocks available, and the fate of a newspaper published under the German occupation could depend on my signature.) I do not know who had given these lordlings the habit of applying undue pressure for more paper, nor the freedom to pursue this practice with impunity. But on the other hand, I do know what it cost me, for many years moreover, to be hard of hearing.

By comparing then and now I can evaluate fairly well the obstacles that today's journalists encounter. Caught between a State monopoly of television and radio on the one hand, and the control exercised by money on the written press, their freedom resembles those icebreakers which can advance only by pushing their way through mountains of ice. Capitalist takeover is increasing in this field as in others, and—with a few rare but noteworthy exceptions, including for example the daily *Le Monde,* or the weekly *Le Canard Enchaîné,* and *Le Nouvel Observateur*—written and spoken news is subjected to repeated censorship, made possible by the fact that a journalist who is rejected from the closed circle of monopolies is, in fact, excluded from the profession. Competition, which is the mainspring of freedom in liberal theory, exists only within a closed world dominated by a single power. The freedom of expression vaunted by the masters of the information media serves no other purpose than to provide them with a façade. It is therefore extremely important that a democracy worthy of the name should establish a stringent set of rules; these are essential when the State has been mandated by the nation to manage, in the name of all, an instrument as powerful and as sensitive as radio and television.

Proposed rules of this sort are outlined in the Common Program, but the president of the Republic prefers to have recourse to a jesuitical dialectic of orders and incantations. God will recognize his own. The managing directors of the four groups which took over the Office de Radio-Télévision Française (ORTF), the government-owned radio-television network, were nominated with sovereign authority by Giscard d'Estaing, acting in this case not so much as head of state, but as leader of the majority party placing sentinels on the watchtowers of the fortress called power.

What freedom of judgment do they have? I can already hear them yelling like scalded cats, protesting that it is an insult to set the problem in those terms. But I need only listen and watch to be quite sure that where the theory is bad the practice cannot be good.

No person in charge of radio or television is free until he dare grant the opposition the right to answer for itself under conditions comparable to those enjoyed by the leader of the majority. And what has become of the great public debates?

TUESDAY, FEBRUARY 3

I have just reached the six hundred twenty-fifth and last page of *Montaillou*, and can't tear myself away from this book which has so occupied my mind for the last weeks. I linger over the photographs of Montaillou in 1975 which the author, Emmanuel Le Roy Ladurie, had the good idea of reproducing at the beginning of the book. At the top, on the left, can be seen the ruins of the castle silhouetted against the mountains which rise above it. In the middle, though slightly lower than the old village, lies the huddle of houses which constitute the present-day hamlet; farther down, the village church which has replaced the old one where Pierre Clergue officiated around the year 1300. He was priest, confessor, and tithe-collector, lecherous, wily and loud-mouthed. He was nicknamed "the little bishop of Aillou County" because of the importance of the role he played there. He was the real lord of the village, along with his brother Bernard, the *bayle*, a sort of judge and police commissioner combined. The one held his authority from the counts of Foix, the other from the Church—rather, the Inquisition. I already very much wanted to visit Montségur. Well then! I shall go by way of the Plateau de Sabarthès, where, near the source of the Hers, the village of Montaillou with its fifty hearths climb up a rocky escarpment surrounded by pastures and forests. I discovered in the telephone directory that there is still a Clergue to perpetuate the name.

For a whole month, with Ladurie, I shared the daily lives of the
two hundred and fifty inhabitants of the medieval village, peasants and shepherds, not forgetting the chatelaine, Béatrice de
Planissoles, mother of four daughters, whose only true loves were
always ecclesiastics. With the exception of the children below
twelve or thirteen years of age, they were all to be arrested on
August 15, 1308, and taken to the "wall," that is to say the prisons
of Narbonne, Carcassonne, and Pamiers, to answer charges of
heresy. Twenty-eight of them were to be subjected to a thorough
interrogation, which was recorded in detail in a "Register of Inquisition," kept admirably up to date by the bishop of Pamiers,
Jacques Fournier. He was elected pope under the name of Bene-
dict XII and was so proud of this "Register" that he brought it to
Avignon with him in his baggage. Thus it was that minutes and
parchments eventually found their way to the Vatican Library.

I had always felt curious about this man who succeeded John
XXII. It was he who started building the famous Palace of the
Popes in Avignon, and distinguished himself by his canonical in-
transigeance. I knew that he came from the county of Foix, but I
did not know of the passionate zeal he showed in the service of
God, not only by imposing an agricultural tithe on the production
of cheese, turnips, and rutabagas which were previously ex-
empted, but also by scouring the souls of his flock contaminated
by the Albigensian "deviation." Fournier is a model inquisitor. He
uses physical torture as little as possible but tracks down error in
the mind. He does not seek punishment so much as confession.
He questions, but he also listens. He allows the accused neither
rest nor dark corner; neither solitude nor forgetfulness. Each suspect must reveal the smallest detail of his life: family relations,
love affairs, seasonal movement of flocks, conversations. All are
grist for his mill. "I was enjoying the sun at the back of the house,
and Guillaume Andorran was four or five paces away from me,
reading a book," Raymond Vayssière states. "I was standing in the
square of Montaillou with my little girl in my arms, when my
uncle Bernard Tavernier, from Prades, came along and asked me if
I had seen his brother . . ." Guillemette Clergue testifies. And
Raymond de l'Aire reports, "About twenty years ago I'd bought
some grass or hay, still standing in a field somewhere near Juniac

belonging to Pierre Rauzi of Caussou. We had agreed to meet on a
certain day in that field to cut it. And when we met there—he'd
come from Caussou and I'd come from Tignac—Pierre Rauzi
started sharpening his scythe to cut the grass in the field. And
while sharpening his scythe he said to me, 'Do you believe that
God and the Blessed Virgin Mary really do exist?' "

A fundamental question. At Montaillou they practiced a little
magic (the nail parings of the head of the family were kept after
his death so as to bring good luck); and a bit of animism (the
quarters of the moon and the flight of magpies were interpreted as
auguries); they were fatalists too ("When something good or
something bad happens to someone, it was bound to happen, it
couldn't have been any different," says old Raymond Franca to
the terrible Fournier); they are deeply conscious of the sacredness
of certain things: "The soul's salvation is the great concern" says
Ladurie. But one can't talk of salvation without talking about the
absolution of sins. And bitter competition arose with regard to
this vital point. "The priests cannot absolve a man of his sins;
only the Goodmen can," Bernard Gombert, Albigensian, assures
his cousin Bernadette Amiel. And the *Parfait* Guillaume Authié
teaches that "his own power of absolution is equal to that possessed by the apostles Peter and Paul." The best path to salvation
is the subject of heated arguments. The shepherd Pierre Maury
never stops discussing it with his friend, the Goodman Bélibaste.
The village gossips sitting together on their flat roofs interlard
their chatter with metaphysical considerations while their daughters remove the lice from their heads. It is at this point that Jean
Fournier's keen ear becomes all the more attentive. Nothing escapes the bishop, who compares testimonies, and from interrogation to interrogation, closes the gap between two facts differently
reported. Across the years he has left an account of this village for
his twentieth-century readers. Emmanuel Le Roy Ladurie has
made it live for us thanks to extensive research and an extraordinary imagination, which never goes beyond the bounds of scientific investigation yet manages to reconstitute the daily gestures of
prayer, hygiene, courtesy, or sexuality. The two collaborators of
the bishop of Pamiers, Guillaume Barthe the notary and Jean
Strabaud the scrivener, took down everything. The "Register"

grew daily till it became a textbook on ecology, archaeology, eth-
nography, sociology, theology, and semantics all rolled into one.
Jean Fournier's zeal knew no limits: "He took fifteen days to convince Baruch the Jew, summoned before his tribunal, of the mys-
tery of the Trinity; eight days to make him accept the double
nature of Christ; and as for the coming on earth of the Messiah, it
took three weeks of commentary administered to Baruch, who
could have done with less," Le Roy Ladurie notes in his introduction.

It is only his zeal for the greater glory of God which makes this
patient prelate mete out burnings at the stake, confiscation of
goods, prison for life (or death), the wearing of a yellow cross, or a
pilgrimage of penitence. And as we get deeper into this book, it is
not so much the portrait of his victims, as his own, which emerges
from these dialogues. As we read on and his personality is revealed—awe-inspiring and transparent in its single-mindedness—
this senior official of truth, as I must call him, seems ever more to
be a modern figure. We could change the title of the book: *Montaillou* or *Stalin at Pamiers*. But why bring Stalin into it? In 1308 it
was a different Church. The historian who has just finished this
masterpiece seems to be telling us that the worst tyranny is that of
the spirit. After reading it one cannot fail to be convinced that the
beast will lie in wait for its prey until the end of time.

WEDNESDAY, MARCH 31

As a footnote to the mainstream of history, the death of Field
Marshal Montgomery reminds me of a strange journey. It was
during the war, at the beginning of January 1944. I wanted to get
back to France after a three-week-long mission I had just completed in Algiers for the Resistance, to which I belonged. I had to
trust to luck, for even then, General de Gaulle made quite sure
that nothing escaped him and did not easily release any of the
people in authority inside France who came within his reach—
unless they swore allegiance to him, something that was not at all

to my taste. It is well-known that these clashes continued. So, as things stood, if I wanted to leave Algiers I was on my own. Having realized this, I wasted no time mulling over the irony of fate. I did not know the town, nor anyone in it, and what with the wartime atmosphere I had the feeling I had gotten lost in some dead-end of the world. To get to London from there was a challenge. But Josephine Baker, who welcomed all wandering "little Frenchmen" in a palace in the Medina, commissioned a young Afat girl who was stationed at the airport to let her know of any plane stopping over. Great idea! I waited only four days, when one morning the Afat girl appeared all out of breath, to inform us that an English general, whom she did not identify, was willing to take me aboard. Two other Frenchmen had preceded me: Camille Paris, Claudel's son-in-law and a career diplomat, and Major Pierre de Chevigné, with whom I was to sit on a government of the Fourth Republic, five years later. What an odd crew! Four or five British officers and one German soldier still in uniform rounded out the little group that Montgomery, returning from El-Alamein, was ferrying through space like an amiable host. Supreme courtesy: Nobody asked me either for identity papers or travel orders. A useful courtesy—for I had none.

The flight was uneventful save for a storm which shook the sky above the Irish Sea. Tea was served to us twice. The coast of England was in sight when Montgomery told me what was on his mind: As he did not know who I was, he apologized for not being able to drop me off in London, where the security services had no sense of humor, and proposed letting me off the plane in Glasgow. Which he did. Alone at the end of the runway from which my companions were taking off, I stood waving at them for a long time as a mark of friendship. Thirty years later, I would like to do so all over again.

SUNDAY, APRIL 11

I learn from an article dated 1849 that in London, when an omnibus stopped and the coachman left to relieve himself, an employee was ordered onto his seat to crack his whip and make the horses believe that their master was still there. In contemporary France, this stratagem is not restricted to horses.

MONDAY, APRIL 12

The declarations of the Right set out to prove that the Socialist Party's program betrays the ideas of Jaurès and Blum, who have suddenly become worthy of this bare-faced praise. What this belated eulogy is meant to suggest is only too evident. For my readers' benefit I was curious enough to have a look at the records of parliamentary debates and press archives of the first half of the century. It would take a whole volume to reprint the abuse, both verbal and written, that was heaped upon our models. The bourgeoisie waited till they were dead before honoring these men it now holds up to us as examples. On occasion, in fact, it was in a considerable hurry for them to reach that point! Antipatriot, antimilitarist, enemy agent—these accusations are part of the inexhaustible common fund of calumnies employed by Jaurès' enemies. One day in June 1912 he opposed the Moroccan policy of the Caillaux government, only to be told by the minister of foreign affairs, "With you, Monsieur Jaurès, it is always France who is in the wrong." A familiar tune which has come down to us and is trotted out against us when needed. Méline and Déroulède * both sang it a few years earlier, each in his own way: Méline accused Jaurès of "inciting soldiers to rebel against their leaders," and Déroulède proclaimed that he considered him to be "the most odious corruptor of public conscience ever to have played the enemy's game." Traitor. The word had not yet been uttered, but it is easy to guess that it was on the tip of the "nationalists' " tongue, and that only a more daring polemicist was needed to cross the vocabulary bar.

*Jules Méline (1838–1925) was head of the French government from 1896 to 1898. Paul Déroulède (1846–1914) was a writer and president of The Patriots' League.

The conservative and liberal (!) press embroidered endlessly on this theme. *Le Temps* deplored that "In every instance, Jaurès is the advocate of foreigners and against the national interest"; *La Croix* published his portrait next to that of William II, under the title "Two friends"; *L'Echo de Paris* reproached him for having "lost the habit of being French," of having "allowed himself to be given a foreign mentality," of even having "taken on a German appearance: a heavy squat figure, a tangled red beard, a professor's features, and a dogmatic and pedantic style . . ."; Maurice de Waleffe, writing in *Paris-Midi,* thinks "he has vowed to himself to give Paris to the Prussians," while *La Liberté,* which had called him Herr Jaurès, lays it on even thicker: "This civilian title will not do, we should say Major General Jaurès. He has well deserved a high rank in the German army, for no German has served it better in the last ten years." Maurras, who could not allow himself to be outdone, asserted on July 18, 1914, in *L'Action Française* that "A serious investigation, set up by a national authority, could not fail to reveal, throughout the entirety of his articles and speeches, the taint of German gold" and added that "it would be well to keep an eye on this traitor." The word had been uttered. Thirteen days later Jaurès was assassinated.

Let us transpose the situation, and for the Germans of 1914 substitute the Russians of 1976 as the focus of the phobias of the rightists. Then we can understand the precise import of Michel Poniatowski's warning when he announced two days before the second round of presidential elections, that if I were elected, Soviet tanks would take up their quarters on the Place de la Concorde the following Tuesday (admire his precision). Or again when he compared Georges Marchais, who was deported to a labor camp in Germany in World War II, to Jacques Doriot, who was an officer in the Nazi army. The accusation of crimes against the homeland, referred to by the Right—which calls itself national but preferred Bismarck to Gambetta, and Vichy to the people of France—would be laughable if I had not found among the documents I examined these words of Juarès's dated July 4, 1914: "In your newspapers, in your articles, among those who support your party—mark my words well—you have constantly called for our murder."

I will take my comparison no further. But let the politicians in power who prophesy "national disaster" and "collectivist penal servitude," should the Left win the election, spare a moment to think about it: Inevitably, somewhere, whether they like it or not, there exists a citizen, at least one, sufficiently sincere or sufficiently mad to take what they say seriously.

WEDNESDAY, APRIL 14

Roland Agret is a young man sentenced to fifteen years at hard labor for murder. He is seeking his own death in an attempt to obtain legal recognition of his innocence. In his favor and alas too late, there is the testimony offered by a witness, a self-confessed gangster, which would clear Roland Agret of the accusations which led to his sentence. His wife, Yolande, is ending this evening the eighth day of a hunger strike. Here and there a few people protest, a few are alarmed; a defense committee has been formed. On Saturday, after a demonstration that brought five hundred people together in the Place Vendôme, Claude Mauriac and Father Cardonnel led a delegation to the Ministry of Justice. But the minister of justice did not bother to receive them. And Roland Agret will have to wait. So now we can only hope that the inquiry launched by the Central Office of the Judiciary Police will succeed and its conclusions be submitted to the appeals commission.

Order is order and the machine goes round and round at its own speed. Should the majesty of justice be perturbed for so little? I mean, for the life of an individual whose only argument is to risk that life? I am not unaware that all this is very difficult. The innocent and the guilty look alike. As much alike as brothers; yes, exactly like brothers, except that the innocent one is not sufficiently gifted to explain that he is not guilty.

At this time of collective catastrophes, when the screams of the tortured in Santiago have ceased to echo through the walls, when in Cambodia death is meted out on an assembly-line scale, some people will be surprised that anyone can still waste time on one lost child.

Two days before a certain Friday which may remind them of something, I will answer that for nearly two thousand years in the world in which we live, a civilization, our civilization, has been asking that question.

SUNDAY, APRIL 25

It is useless to search for excuses—there are none. Neither in the dramas of the past, coups d'état, oppression, repression, nor in those of the present. No, there is no excuse for the government, for the system, for the methods of the Khmer Rouge in Cambodia. I understand and I accept some of the arguments put forward to excuse them. First of all, that the news available to us in Europe contains a considerable proportion of false information, of faked photographs—in other words, of provocation. Second, that one cannot wipe out history with a flick of the wrist, especially lived history, when written and endured in blood. The greatest crimes are always founded on greed or on desire for power.

But when stupidity enters in, the machinery becomes implacable. If the American government instigated the palace revolution which eliminated Norodom Sihanouk, considered too neutral, in order to impose Lon Nol, with the intention of protecting the flank of the Vietnam War and reinforcing their containment of the Communist world, it shows the extent of their contempt, which has nothing lofty about it, for small nations, the pawns on the chess-board of imperialism—and also their ignorance of the values and incentives of our time. As a result, they have lost two wars at one stroke. "It wasn't worth it, it really wasn't worth it," the words used to be sung to an operetta tune. Nowadays the accompaniment is tears.

I repeat it now for the third time: The American crime does not excuse the crime in answer to it. It is possible to expatiate endlessly on revolutions, clean slates, starting over from zero. But nothing and no one can break the chain of generations or the interaction of ideas, even if they are antagonistic. A social class conquers only where it has already infiltrated. When the bourgeoisie, which had furnished barbers to the kings, took over the task of overseeing the kingdom's finances, it was not long before it started dreaming of better things and rose from advising to governing.

My mother was in the habit of saying that all wars are wars of religion. She had not read Marx and was perhaps mistaken. But had she been familiar with the Marxist-Leninist adventure, I expect she would have found even more reasons for clinging to her convictions.

The duty of educating, of forming people's minds to cope with the choices and duties involved in the break-up of any society, is one thing. That hideous machinery set up nearly everywhere to crush consciences at the cost—where necessary—of breaking bodies, is quite another. To confuse the two is to run the risk of doing considerable damage with unforeseeable consequences. Yet this is the point which has been reached at Phnom Penh.

WEDNESDAY, MAY 5

I have just finished the draft of a letter I have been itching to write in answer to the tirade delivered against the Common Program by Jacques Ferry, vice president of the Confederation of French Employers. After a few more corrections I shall send it off to Le Monde, which is expecting it.

> It is with interest that I read your comments inspired by my declarations of April 26 before the Senior Officials' Association for Social and Economic Progress. With interest but also with surprise. I had expected from someone in a position of authority, who is also a well-informed observer of economic matters, a more accurate appraisal of the reality of French capitalism and a more precise knowledge of the Socialist project, which is the project of my Party.
>
> Having no doubt as to your competence and appreciating your

culture, I can only assume that being the mouthpiece of employers must be an uncomfortable task. However, I do not disdain any opinion and endeavor to learn as much as possible from all disagreements. As the essential part of your criticism bears on nationalization, in which you see the first step to collectivism—the theme chosen as a slogan by our political adversaries, but which deserves to be taken more seriously—the burden of my answer will bear on nationalization.

You know the Socialist theory on this subject. It was formulated at the beginning of the industrial era by a few great minds who demonstrated that private ownership of the means of production and exchange had allowed the bourgeoisie to set up the present structures of exploitation of man by man which originated and justified the class struggle in the modern world. They demonstrated that capitalism, by following its own logic, necessarily vitiated the laws of supply and demand and reduced free competition to the point of extinction, thus denying the principles upon which it based its own system. The evolution of industrial society has confirmed the accuracy of this analysis: Capitalism lives only by devouring itself. True enough, it started off by devouring others, but watch it now, turning to eat itself. Let us add up the bankruptcies, judicial liquidations, takeovers, and mergers. Let us observe the decline and then the disappearance of industrial and commercial concerns on a local, regional, and even national level, all taken over for the greater profit of multinational capitalism. Let us put on record the position of dependence into which banking capitalism puts industrial capitalism, and grant me that though the proletariat and the salaried classes have been, and still are, the first victims of the system, it is now the turn of the entrepreneurs to suffer the effects of its implacable laws.

I would like to remind you of a few facts.

The only monopolies you recognize in France are those in the public sector. If that is true, I would like to know how to define the position of the firm of Dassault in the field of military aeronautics; of Péchiney in that of aluminum and copper processing; of Saint-Gobain-Pont-à-Mousson, through its subsidiaries, in the fields of thermal insulation and cast iron; or the Compagnie Générale d'Electricité or the Thomson group in the field of electrical equipment and television components. You cannot be unaware that this group has acquired a technological monopoly in various fields and is now the only supplier of heavy medical equipment and military electronic equipment to public entities; nor that Péchiney, which is the biggest client of Electricité de France, will soon be its chief supplier. Contrary to what you say, when we describe these private groups as monopolies, we are not indulging in verbiage or pandering to fashion; we are describing the status of these groups such as it really is, and such as they wish it to be.

To follow your argument: You consider that the law of the marketplace would be better safeguarded by reducing the role of public enterprise and increasing that of private enterprise. In my opinion you are falling into a threefold error.

The first is that public enterprise does not necessarily equal monopoly. For example, in our country the energy-producing concerns are in competition with each other, as are the national banks and transportation companies. (A government of the Left will have to intensify this competition as much as possible.) The concentration of large capitalist firms over the last years has been much more rapid than that of public concerns. Thus, the nationalized banks exercise far less control over the French economy than do the private banks such as the Bank of Suez and Paribas, whose industrial shareholdings increase daily in an ever wider range of sectors. I do not have to tell you that Paribas' interests weigh heavily on the scales at Hachette, Babcock, or Thomson, for example. Nor that the Bank of Suez controls La Hénin or La Lyonnaise des Eaux. This immobilization of capital is neither economically useful nor politically acceptable, as it strengthens the hold of a small group of men on the vital centers of the economy.

On the other hand, you know that public enterprises play a vital role in our social development and that they are making considerable progress in productivity.

The second mistake is ignoring the very favorable financial record compared to that of private firms to which you understandably attach considerable importance. The recent past has shown us, on a European scale, that some of the most outstanding successes have come from nationalized industries. I will only mention Italsider in Italy, Dutch State Mines in the Low Countries, and at home, Renault, Electricité de France, and the national railways (SNCF).

And finally, the third error. Today there is no real competition between the private groups which constitute the pole of the economy, channeling in the direction of their own particular interests investments, production, commerce and even our consumption on the one hand, and the bulk of French concerns which must submit to the decisions of these groups, on the other. Competition is distorted by prices, but also by technology, commercial networks, and after-sales service. It follows from the process which I have just described that a small number of private enterprises now control an entire sector. Let me say that a "law of the marketplace" that for many years tolerated scandalous agreements—now officially recognized—between the oil companies; or that allowed certain automobile manufacturers to raise their prices at a time of decreased demand and diminished purchasing power, is a very strange law indeed. One might also find it surprising that in a regime which supposedly encourages a "free market" it is always the provincial branches of the big contractors who divide important State contracts among themselves to the detriment of local firms, without ever rousing any hue and cry.

To sum up my argument and make it clear: Contrary to what you say, it is incorrect to maintain that capitalism and free enterprise are identical. Do you really believe that anyone wishing to set himself up on his own account as a manufacturer, tradesman, artisan, or farmer can count on genuine freedom of enterprise, in view of the financing necessary, the cost of credit, and the various difficulties which impede the initiative of anyone wishing to enter into competition with the established powers? Do you really believe that a small and dynamic firm could grow and survive without eventually becoming dependent on private industrial or banking groups? The barriers to expansion put up by large-scale private interests are insurmountable nowadays. In the last ten years we have not seen a single firm break into the aluminum, chemical, or telephone markets.

But, over and above these considerations, I would like to correct the way in which you present the industrial future which the Socialists propose for France. I must remind you that we do not consider profit itself as evil. Far from it. It is the proof that wealth is being produced, which is the basic condition for general progress. We consider that the real problem is its distribution, and with it, the distribution of power. Neither profit nor power must be reserved for a small number to the detriment of all. As things stand, the growth of certain enterprises has led to such an accumulation of capital, and therefore to the possession of such powerful means of pressure on economy and politics, that it has become necessary to formulate as rapidly as possible the criteria which will enable the nation to exercise the right of State appropriation, or the assumption or control of, and participation in, private enterprise which the Constitution allows. This applies to enterprises producing goods on which the entire national economy depends; to those whose principal income derives from government contracts; to those which have virtually reached the status of monopoly in important sectors. It applies also to key sectors likely to fall under foreign control. These were the criteria applied in 1972 when the Common Program of the Left was evolved, and led to the decision to nationalize nine industrial enterprises, along with credit and insurance, and to make the State the majority shareholder in certain other companies.

Do you also include among the trifling items our desire to give the country all the trump cards necessary for its own independence? Isn't the choice between public and private sector often outweighed by the dilemma of nationalization versus internationalization? Since the endorsement of the Common Program of the Left, less than five years ago, two of the industrial enterprises I mentioned have been absorbed by foreign groups: In the field of data processing, Honeywell—after digesting Bull—has secured technological control of CII; and in the pharmaceutical industry, the German firm of Hoechst has taken over Roussel-Uclaf. A third firm, Rhône-Poulenc, is at the mercy of any foreign company that wants it. In the same category, though in different fields, the fate of nuclear energy is a source of concern, as are aeronautical construction and the food industry. Further enumeration would only add weight to my fundamental argument.

Finally, I must confess that I do not understand your remark on the incompatibility of the public and the private sector, or on the impossibility of their coexistence. I think, rather, that there is no free enterprise or economic independence possible without a strong public sector. Moreover, in the process of industrial expansion which the Left intends to promote, it is essential that the respective roles of the public and the private sector be clearly defined and known by all. Thus, once credit has been nationalized, it is essential that the private sector retain a significant number of shares in industry, which merchant banks currently render unproductive. For us, nationalization is a tool, and it has no meaning if not taken in conjunction with a definite and coherent industrial policy. It must also serve to create and promote pilot enterprises in such fields as machine tools or the agro-alimentary industry, which will then attract private competitive firms in their wake.

So that there may be no misunderstanding, I wish to state that it seems essential that five rules of management be respected by all State enterprises: 1) avoidance of excessive growth, which inevitably leads to unwieldiness and inefficiency; 2) refusal to isolate French enterprises from international competition; 3) better control of and genuine sanctions for management; 4) a guarantee that their own funds will be able to grow in a regular and healthy fashion; 5) democratic planning as the framework within which the industrial apparatus is made to serve the national interest. Bureaucracy is not inevitable in the public sector, nor is high-quality management the prerogative or the lot of the private sector. Recent examples have shown that bad capitalist management has led to massive dismissal of workers, and that unjustified grants of public money have served to camouflage the mistakes made by management. Can you not feel how aloof senior personnel remain from a capitalist system that can grant them neither genuine promotion nor responsibility? Their awareness of their situation should give you pause.

I hope that these statements, in keeping with those I have made over the last years, as also with the spirit and letter of the Socialist program and the Common Program, will enable you to judge our intentions more accurately in the future. You have had the courtesy to consider that our intentions were good, for which I thank you.

But you have also spoken of the relationship between hell and good intentions. Am I to understand you to mean that General de Gaulle, to whom we owe the majority of French nationalizations, has cast our country into Gehenna? That would be the subject of yet another discussion.

I think it would be better to admit that, faced with a worldwide crisis of capitalism, there is no other solution for our country than the establishment of a new system, which to my mind can only be Socialism. In this letter I have not raised the subject of democracy in industry, nor the Socialist project for self-management, nor the social demands to which we attach so much importance. I have kept to the actual subject of your criticism. I am sure I will have further occasion to talk of it. And though I harbor no illusions of having convinced you, I ask only one thing of you—which I ask of all Frenchmen—that is, to know and to judge our proposals for what they really are.

SUNDAY, MAY 9

In 1790, Lucile Duplessis lived at 22, Rue de Condé. Camille Desmoulins was an habitué of the Café Procope, 13, Rue de l'An-
cienne Comédie. When they were married, they went to live at 2,
Place de l'Odéon. Since my arrival in Paris in 1934, I have always
lived in their neighborhood. In *Le Monde* the other day, Georges
Michel evoked these two gentle ghosts, and his article brought
back to memory the familiar itinerary (I used to go that way to the
Sorbonne and the Law School), which led me several times a week
under the windows of the curved building opposite the theater.
On March 31, 1794, from the third floor of that building, Lucile
saw Camille, who had been arrested, taken off to the Conciergerie
and his death. I never failed to greet the grief-stricken young
woman with a little friendly thought as I passed by. Incriminated
in the plot of the "Indulgents," Camille Desmoulins, who had
preached mercy during the worst of the Terror, was condemned
out of hand, the Tribunal not even deigning to hear his defense.
The execution followed immediately upon the verdict.

One evening at Saint-Privat when we were talking of friendship, Claude Manceron spoke endlessly on the subject of this
scene and of the love which bound Lucile and Camille. I asked,
"Why Lucile?" She had written to Robespierre to protest, to beg.
In reply she had been arrested, sentenced, and executed in her
turn—exactly eight days after Camille. Yes, why Lucile? Claude
had then told us their story: The Collège de Clermont in the heart
of the Latin Quarter, the friendship between two schoolboys,
Camille Desmoulins and Maximilien de Robespierre; their days at
law school together, their first revolutionary struggles, how they
had always agreed until the end, nearly the end. How Robespierre
had twice saved Camille from the scaffold. He told us of Camille
and Lucile's wedding, celebrated in a side chapel of the church of
Saint-Sulpice; the witnesses were named Pétion, Brissot, Danton,
and naturally, Robespierre. I phoned Manceron to confirm the
accuracy of my memory and he added the name of Louis-Sébas-

tien Mercier, who wrote *Tableau de Paris* and a science-fiction novel which came out in 1772 under the title *The Year 2440* with the subtitle *Dream, if Ever There Was One.* We too have dreamed.

On December 29, 1790, after the religious ceremony, the friends, who had lunched together at Lucile's home, lingered round the table, talking of everything and nothing, and chiefly of the world they would build. Happy to be alive and to love each other, the friends parted company late in the night. Lucile was nineteen years old.

Their lives ended sooner than was right. Brissot was beheaded on October 31, 1793. Pétion killed himself in Guyenne and his body was devoured by wolves on June 20, 1794. Danton's head was exhibited to the people on April 5, 1794. And Camille, and Lucile . . . and Robespierre. Louis-Sébastien Mercier was the only one to survive the tempest.

MONDAY, MAY 10

On my first trip to the Ivory Coast shortly before entering the Ministry of France Overseas, I was not able to meet Félix Houphouët-Boigny. This young doctor, who was his country's deputy in the French National Assembly, had made himself hated by the white settlers for having organized a trade union of black planters. He was president of the Democratic African Assembly, whose members had established connections with the Communist group. The government in Paris had decided to eliminate him by any means and he had been forced to flee so as to escape the repression practiced on the spot by a strong-arm governor. He was reported to be hiding in his native village of Yamoussoukro, or on the move along the Gold Cost (present Ghana) border. Back in France, I learned that the political climate had further deteriorated thanks to the administration's delay in starting coffee trading. At Dimbokro, an important commercial center, the military had opened fire, leaving thirteen dead and sixty wounded. The government was pressing its demand that Houphouët's parliamentary immunity be waived, a demand which had been renewed in 1949 by the attorney general in Dakar. At the beginning of 1950 the National Assembly had set up a commission of inquiry. The prisons of Abidjan and Grand-Bassam were packed with African militants; others had been sent to La Santé prison in Paris. Arrests and sentences proliferated. In his deposition, the strong-arm governor was to mention the figure of 1834 people sentenced for the whole of the Ivory Coast by April 1950. One deputy requested the death penalty for Houphouët.

I am not bringing up these facts for the pleasure of reviving ancient history. I left the government in June 1951 because nearly all the white members of Black Africa's parliament—the majority of them active members of the Rassemblement du Peuple Français, General de Gaulle's party—had demanded it of the president of the French Republic. In their eyes I had handed over that same Africa to "international communism in the person of Houphouët-Boigny."

All's well that ends well. So I hope I will be forgiven if, last week, while listening to Giscard d'Estaing's speech of welcome to the president of the Ivory Coast—that same Houphouët-Boigny—I could not help smiling, when, after congratulating himself on the friendship between our peoples, he uttered the sentence which no doubt struck only me as comic: "What a lesson for ideologists of every complexion."

TUESDAY, MAY 11

"Astonish me," Diaghilev used to say to Cocteau. Monsieur Poniatowski is always astonishing us; but he differs from the poet in that nobody asks him to. Immediately after the local elections he scandalized serious observers by discovering equal gains for the Socialist Party and the Party of Independents, his own party. The actual figures: a gain of 204 seats for the former and a loss of 34 seats for the latter. This morning I heard him commenting on the legislative election in Tours: "A retreat for the Left" he affirmed. In actual fact, the figures coming out of the machinery of his own ministry and announced officially show that the Left has gained two percentage points, while the Center, a flabby version of the Right, has collapsed. It is a strange morality which leads the minister of the interior of the French Republic to adopt as his intellectual master that nineteenth-century murderer, Pranzini, who from the scaffold sought to warn his likes by crying out, "Never confess!" After all, a setback is not a crime.

MONDAY, MAY 24

On Saturday we dined on a slice of ham and some cottage cheese at the inn of Anzy-le-Duc, in Brionnais, where Paul Duraffour, its mayor and deputy, received us with all honors—including one of the most beautiful Romanesque steeples in a part of the world where there are a number of them. There were twelve of us round the table, the conversation was slow-paced and peaceful, and the moment held that mysterious something that takes one outside time. The smell of the oilcloth on the table, the sound of a clock striking, the post office calendar on the wall, all brought back my childhood; this and the intense silence when words are no longer spoken but thoughts continue in the depths of the mind, had kept us there till a late hour. It was past midnight when we set out to find our cars parked some distance from the village. We walked along the wall of the Duraffours' park, heads lifted, enveloped in the milky night, when a nightingale began to sing. How trite! a nightingale singing on a night in May. And why not moonlight and mist in the valley, you will say? The moon was high and from the mist blanketing the valleys there emerged islands of groves and the little hills of the high plateau which is nudged gently downward toward Charolles by the thrust of the Lyonnais range.

I am a child of my province and intend to remain that way. It shows in my writing as an accent might show in a person's speech. To give an example, I am proud to be able to call trees and stones and birds by their name. I would consider myself learned enough if I could identify all creatures and all things. Alas! I must confess that I am like an infant learning to talk. But I seek to learn more and when I no longer feel this need, I shall know the end is at hand. It will not be necessary to tell me. Isn't death the ultimate confusion?

As a matter of fact, I was not sure. That bird singing in the sky, caroling its escape from earth in the freedom of space, could be a garden warbler or a song thrush, those tender messengers of the rites of spring. It was years since I could remember hearing a nightingale sing. It is generally believed that nightingales sing only at night. This is not true. My ear is still enchanted by the dazzling trills poured forth during the heat of the day in the Saintonge of my childhood. Had nightingales disappeared with the hedges, victim of the regrouping of plots of farmland? Or had they fled the chemistry of fertilizers that seep down and spread their pollution to the water table? This plenitude welling up from the poignancy of a perfect sky, this tragic sense of happiness, is unmistakable. Standing there in the middle of the path, we listened to the nightingale of Anzy-le-Duc. Proud, ecstatic, pure. Not one of us moved, not one of us spoke. When it fell silent we remained there a long while contemplating a night as bright as in August—the exploded sphere of the original world. Then we went back to Cluny.

The following day, Whitsunday, fulfilled the promise of the splendid night before. If you ask me what I did, I'll have to confess that I did not go dine with the 41 out of 42 voters of the commune of Pech in the Ariège who had cast their ballots for me, following the example of Valéry Giscard d'Estaing extending his thanks from the glorious heights of his present position to his loyal constituents of the commune of Arhansus, in the Basque country (59 votes out of 61). No, the details of my day lack spice. I spent it as I have spent Whitsunday for the last thirty years: Cluny, Milly, Saint-Point, Pierreclos, Solutré, Cluny—home port and ports of call unchanged. Family and friends get together, the same ones year after year save for those whom death has winnowed out. From one year's end to the next, we may not write or phone each other, or cross the boundaries which separate one part of the same town from another. But at the appointed time the flock comes together again for these two days—and these two days only. We simply walk into each other's houses without ringing or knocking; no need for complicated polite formulas to enter the circle: "Hello, how are you?"

WEDNESDAY, JUNE 16

I do not approve of Pierre Boutang, because of what he is and because of what he professes, and there is no doubt that his election to the post of senior lecturer in philosophy at the Sorbonne alarms me. Will I sign the petition drawn up by those researchers and professors who violently object to this choice? No. For Pierre Boutang practices his profession, and from this point of view—which is the only one that concerns me here—he does it well. I will not use against him his opinions, his fanaticism, or his inquisitorial zeal, which have often led him to make outrageous statements. It is not in the name of his principles that I accept him, but in the name of mine. If I used his teachings as an excuse for dismissing him from the University it would only prove—heaven forbid—that I had become his disciple. My freedom has meaning only if I accept the freedom of others. I have been told that the name of Jean Cassou, whom I know slightly and respect greatly, figures among the signers of the petition. His writings still delight me and I frequently quote to myself, for the pleasure it gives me, lines from the posy of poems of Hugo von Hofmannsthal which he translated so perfectly:

> With a cup at his lips
> He walked with a firm stride . . .

Jean Cassou, his body drenched with blood, barely escaped death during the last days of the German occupation in Toulouse. He has the right to speak and to sign. Cassou against Boutang; any day. Long live Cassou! But my dear Cassou, is not our adversaries' freedom also our freedom?

SUNDAY, JULY 4

Having learned that I must go to Hyères, Dorothy Léger wrote asking me to stop at Vigneaux. I had not been back to that house since February 1973. Saint-John Perse was then eighty-six years old, still straight-backed and clear-minded. As a form of discipline he used to make himself clear the land of his property which sloped steeply down to the sea at the tip of the peninsula of Giens, opposite the Ile du Levant. Four or five times a day he went up and down the steps which led to the sea. (How many are there? Seventy, eighty?) He told me that the work and fatigue that resulted made him one with the elements, like wood eroded by salt. Only a certain fixity in his gaze called to mind how old he was and revealed the irreducible gap between himself and the forward movement of things. He had always been passionately interested in politics and reminisced about the days when he directed the foreign affairs of France at the side of Aristide Briand and Philippe Berthelot. Then he questioned me at length about current events. As usual, I found it difficult to bring him back to the subjects that mattered to me. I wanted to hear him talking of birds and ships on the high seas. This conversation, which came to an end only at his death, had started a few years before in my Paris home after I had received a note from him saying quite simply: "May I see you?" Do I dare speak of friendship? Each landmark of my life was thereafter greeted by signs: short letters in his beautiful handwriting, telegrams, dedications—until that telegram on September 22, 1975: "Deeply regret to inform you of death of Alexis . . ." signed Dorothy.

Dorothy Léger opened the door. There was nothing I could say. She led me through the rooms that Saint-John Perse had loved, surrounded by his books and objects. The old house was shedding the heat of the day and the evening filled it with the scents of Provence. I was unable to stay to dinner but promised my hostess to meet her again soon in Aix, where an exhibition on the theme "Birds and the Work of Saint-John Perse" was to be inaugurated on June 19. A popular fête at Mialet, that beautiful solemn village of the Musée du Désert in the Gard, would give me the opportunity. But getting from Mialet to Aix across the Camargue and the Crau on the first Sunday in summer was a difficult undertaking.

It was well after 8:30 p.m. when I arrived in front of the town hall where Dorothy, my friend Félix Ciccolini, the senator and mayor, and Pierre Guerre, the director of the Saint-John Perse Foundation, were waiting for me. Blessed delay! For now our little group had no further pressing duties and could enjoy to their fullest those precious hours when everything contributes to the plenitude of the moment. Within the town hall the exhibition was housed in the main rooms of the Foundation, which follow those of the Méjanes Library. It was divided into two parts: One on the first floor, where there had been brought together several dozen beautifully chosen objects—drawings, pictures, itineraries, sculptures—all having to do with familiar or fabulous birds; those "dreams of creation," to be found where space and man come together. Here also were the poet's notes and manuscripts dealing with birds and his ornithological research. The other section was reached through the paved courtyard. It was centered on *Birds,* the book which Georges Braque and Saint-John Perse composed together. Two documents throw light on the meaning of this encounter. One, a letter from Janine·Crémieux: "Yesterday I went to Georges Braque's . . . I read him a passage from "Noon, its fierce animals, its famines": 'The bird gliding in its vaster space sees man freed from his shadow on the confines of its territory.' He asked me for a copy, he was so overcome by the identity between these lines and certain of his own birds." The other document is a quotation from a poem by Alexis Léger: "A white seagull unfurled against the sky like a woman's hand against the flame of a lamp, lifts up in the daylight the rose translucence of a pure white host . . ."

Poetry is rigor, the rest is verbiage. Saint-John Perse's manuscripts are proof of this; though infinitely crossed out and corrected they never looked muddled. His handwriting, like Chinese calligraphy, expresses art for art's sake. This alone arouses the desire to reach ever further toward an exact understanding of words and the things they represent. These two messages, for

instance. To a friend he writes: "My ignorance of all nautical practice makes me stumble over the 22 points of the compass, having
expected 24." And another: "Have a good journey, Hoppenot, and
bring me back the name of that European bird which for two days
followed my little sailboat along the coast of England (rat-gray in
color, the legs of a nightjar, and the size of a seagull)." We can
understand more easily why Braque's (and Alexis') birds "can no
more escape earth's fatality than a rocky particle in Cézanne's
geology."

TUESDAY, SEPTEMBER 14

God, giant, lighthouse, Mao's departure for the unknown shore
has been greeted with a fine assortment of superlatives. Beyond a
brief formal communiqué, I have chosen to remain silent, refusing
to add my voice to the concert. I am in no hurry to talk about
Mao; the marks he has left on history are too deep to disappear
before many years have passed. As to adding to the confusion and
nonsense fed to public opinion, no, a thousand times no. Mao co-
opted! And by whom! The farce has gone on long enough. I see
him again in his winter-wasted garden, and hear him say to me,
"It is the good season." He contemplated the earth beneath a pale
sky like a peasant who knows that spring will be born of long
obscure work. Mao's personality flatters the West, which finds in
him food for its need for hero-worship. But this particular hero
does not belong to the West.

WEDNESDAY, SEPTEMBER 15

I was dining with friends on the day we learned that Russian
tanks had entered Czechoslovakia. The ambassador of an Eastern

European country was among the guests. As the focal point of the agitation caused by this news, he remained silent for a long while before answering the questions fired at him: "Forget Prague. Think only about Yugoslavia." This advice comes back to me at a time when alarming communiqués concerning Marshal Tito's health are being broadcast over the radio. It is not that I think Russia has aggressive intentions. In spite of the expansionist complex inherent in every empire, forced to go ever farther if it wishes to keep what it has, I sincerely believe in the Soviet desire for peace. This country, which suffered more than any other from the Second World War and which badly needs to assimilate all it has acquired through the sacrifices of its people, will not alter its strategy just for the charm of Belgrade and a sizable stretch of Mediterranean coast. History obeys the laws of physics. After Yalta, Czechoslovakia was joined to the Eastern bloc, and could not leave it without upsetting the balance of power. Lyndon Johnson was well aware of this when he did not postpone his weekend by one single hour for Dubček. But as far as the two great powers are concerned, Yugoslavia does not belong to either side, and there is no room for a vacuum in Europe.

On the banks of the Danube, a stone's throw from that very spot where Tito watches what soon will cease to be recede from sight, one can still visit the watchtowers where, in the last century, the sentinels of both worlds continually kept watch on each other.

MONDAY, SEPTEMBER 20

The upheaval has already taken place in the two Scandinavian neighbors of Sweden. In Norway, the referendum which revealed the country's hostility to joining the Common Market ousted the Socio-Democrats, who had been in favor of joining, from power in 1973. They were out of power less than a year. At the next elections, they again obtained a majority and returned in force to the direction of public affairs. It was also in 1973 that Denmark

succumbed to a Poujadist type of movement and the Social Democrat Party was beaten. However, eighteen months later the parties of the right-wing coalition collapsed—having demonstrated
their inability to come to an agreement on a responsible political
program—and the Socialists, headed by Anker Jörgensen, returned to government. I believe that the same phenomena are at
the origin of the setback suffered by Olaf Palme and the Swedish
Social-Democrats. The three bourgeois allies just barely won (50.7
percent of the votes) and had not previously agreed on a program
of action. So it is inevitable that they should now pull in different
directions. The clearest example of their failure to agree is provided by their quarrel over nuclear power plants. The party of the
Center, the principal party on the victors' side with 24.1 percent of
the votes (whereas the Social-Democrats, by themselves, obtained
42.9 percent), assured the success of the coalition—even though it
had lost ground itself—thanks to its fierce denouncement of an
atomic energy program. But on this point it was in total opposition to the Conservative Party.

By writing this I do not pretend to diminish the worldwide
shock caused by the end of an exemplary experience, temporary
though it may be. I note that the "Swedish model" remained
true to itself to the very last. In how many countries could the
transition from one economic system to another be accomplished without giving rise to extreme tension? Neither Communist regimes, as we know them today, nor capitalist power, in
spite of its virtuous petitions of the principle, are willing to va-
cate their position merely as a result of a majority vote against
them. Everyone knows that, if necessary, they would set off the
mechanisms of repression or sedition. I am impressed that in
Sweden, on the contrary, Social-Democrats attempted to convince voters simply by the use of reason, and that having failed
to do so, withdrew without a word. I must confess that I prefer
this example to the outrageous propositions that proliferate
nearly everywhere. This is indeed what our revolutionary experts hold against the Social-Democrats. Never wearying of de-
manding of others the aptitudes they lack, these experts go on
repeating that class struggle is an art of war, that any victory
implies the categorical elimination of the adversary. In other

words, that Socialists who remain oblivious to these supposedly self-evident truths are potential traitors.

I do not accept this argument, even though the crimes of Santiago de Chile give it the added weight of all the blood that has been shed. Should Allende, or should he not have abandoned the legality to which he adhered and which expressed his political philosophy, for the sole reason that this legality had been conceived by and for the ruling class that was waging a merciless war against him? This is a difficult question that history has not yet answered. As for me, I am far from convinced that socialism would have gained anything by denying its own essence and setting up a dictatorship which had no hope of escaping from the terrible and monotonous logic of all dictatorships, rather than perpetuating the tangible message of the Chilean president in the collective memory of the people of Latin America.

Regardless of what the truth may be, it is interesting to compare these two countries. Nothing illustrates better the relativity of the conditions of the struggle—which depend on the moment, the geographical situation, and the state of development of human societies—than this lack of dramatic coloration to highlight the Swedish event. Does this stem from the nature of its citizens? Or from the nature of socialism practiced in Stockholm? Personally, I see its main cause in the conviction shared by everyone—save a few minority conservatives—that the progressivist transformations brought about by the tenacity of the Social-Democrats are, without any doubt, irreversible. Who would dare touch the contractual policy, the various guarantees of security, and even the redistribution of incomes which has no equal anywhere else, including the Soviet Union? The parties of the Right and of the Center will discover that if they shake the edifice they run the risk of bringing it down upon their own heads. Would anyone dare force Sweden back into the cycle of social conflicts from which it had liberated itself by 1931, with the exception of the wildcat strikes in 1970, little sparks presaging the breakdown of the system?

I have on occasion expressed my criticisms to Olof Palme on two points. The first, to voice my surprise that the Social-Democrats did not carry out the social appropriation of the major means of production, thereby depriving the private monopolies and cartels of the power to sabotage his Socialist project. The other, to deplore the immutability of men and functions at all levels within a society which has a natural tendency to close in upon itself as a result of having been governed by the same party for a very long time. Surely the a b c of Social-Democrats is to obtain mastery of the economic poles and to organize the separation of power and counter-power. Olof Palme answered that they were progressing along this road, that direct responsibility of the workers was being extended, and that his party was putting younger men in key positions and modernizing its methods. I have seen Swedish Socialists at work on the spot and I have faith in their rectitude and determination. It is a paradox that the government which succeeded better than any other in controlling the crisis of the industrial world by maintaining employment without causing prices to skyrocket should be made to withdraw by the will of its own people. What remedy is there against the wear and tear of time? There is none save in oneself.

MONDAY, OCTOBER 11

A meeting at my home last week, riots in Hebron in the country of Judea, and the past comes back to my eyes in such crude, bright colors that they devour the precise shadings of the years which have gone by in the meantime. The present merges into all that preceded it and thereby loses its immediacy.

The meeting was with Kamal Joumblatt who had arrived in France a few days previously to plead the cause of the Lebanese Left. After dinner, with our coffee cups in front of us, we talked for more than an hour. Or rather, my visitor answered my short questions with a long monologue. He sat as he usually sits, his eyes half closed, his forehead held high under a rebellious shock of hair. He is sparing of gestures and his voice is soft as he carefully chooses his words out of respect for the language. His

French is elegant and precise though rather old-fashioned and interspersed with Anglicisms as soon as he uses technical phrases. Kamal Joumblatt belongs to the community of the Druses, a small irreducible people attached to its hills, faithful to its history, to its faith, and to its religious sect, which is an offshoot of the Ismailian branch (followers of the Aga Khan), which itself is derived from the Shiite schism which continues to divide Islam. (The Shiites refuse to recognize the legitimacy of Abou-Bakr, successor of Mohammed, and swear allegiance to Ali, the son-in-law of the prophet, who, according to them, had received the divine investiture; they thus oppose the law of obedience to a hereditary and infallible chieftain, to the tradition of general consent, and to its interpretation by the Imams.) Kamal Joumblatt did not speak of this, he had been sent as the representative of Lebanon, doggedly defending its territorial and political freedom. But the descriptions he gave me of the camps, the clans, and the spheres of influence, the explanations he provided for the deep-rooted reasons behind the civil war and the Syrian intervention, were so evidently the logical consequence of a thousand years of struggle and bloodshed that I had the feeling I was listening to the narrator in an antique tragedy, who, standing at the front of the stage, relates for the benefit of an ephemeral audience the timeless web of history woven by the passions of men. I will spare my readers the incredible, admirable, terrible diversity which made of this small area of the globe the meeting-place of all races and all religions, which were then to branch out, to divide, to disagree, as invasion, persecution, and tyranny succeeded each other. But the weight of spiritual exigencies was even heavier, as though the flames of all these certainties burned so intensely that they melted the stones, and harder than stone, the last reaches of reason. We went from Christian phalanxes (Joumblatt added, "Fascists") to crusades. Behind today's rival groups the past still looms: Islam and its antagonistic prophets; the Oriental Christian churches divided into Maronites, Greek Orthodox, Chaldean, Syriac, Latin, Jacobite, Armenian Catholic, Armenian Orthodox, Greek Catholic, and yet others. No choice was gratuitous and death was the price of them all—no doubt the necessary condition enabling each sect's beliefs to survive through time. The heresy of Nestorius, Patriarch of

Constantinople, who taught in the fifth century that the two na-
tures of Christ, human and divine, did not coexist, but that God
lived in the man Jesus as in a temple; and that of Dioscorus,
Patriarch of Alexandria, who affirmed that the human nature of
Jesus was lost in His divinity like wax in a brazier, still inspire
thousands of believers, Nestorians and Jacobites. At one point in
the conversation, Kamal Joumblatt remarked, "It is not possible to
understand Lebanon if one is ignorant of the quarrel between
the Monophysites and the Monotheists." For in fact, this debate
gave rise in the fourteenth century to the Maronite community
which, as is well known, exercises a predominant influence on the
Christian peoples engaged in the present conflict. And finally, the
judgment that Joumblatt the Druse passed on Assad, the president
of Syria, who is an Alawi, brought to mind the inescapable presence of the centuries.

I was arranging the notes I had taken during this interview
when news of the sacking of the synagogue at Hebron reached
me. This synagogue was recently built on the initiative of the
Israeli extremists of "the Coalition of the Faithful" near the cave
of Machpelah, which Abraham bought for the sum of 400 shekels
of silver as a burial place for himself and his wife Sarah, as the
Bible records in the Book of Genesis. Abraham and Sarah were
buried there and after them Isaac, Jacob, Leah, Rebecca, Joseph,
and Jawllya, patriarchs and matriarchs shared by Israel and the
Arab people. Immediately above the cave rises a mosque which in
the thirteenth century took the place of a church built by the
Crusaders, which in its turn had taken the place of a sanctuary
built by Herod. On the third of March, to protest what they took
to be a provocation, thousands of Moslems invaded the synagogue and tore up the scrolls of the Torah. A few days later, a
unit of the Israeli army, surrounded by a crowd of the faithful,
bore the sacred parchments to the old Jewish cemetery of Hebron
to bury them according to custom.

Anger confronting anger. From a distance of several thousand
years, two people, two religions, pore over the books of the law.
That ". . . field of Ephron, which was in Machpelah, which was
before Mamre, the field and the cave which was therein, and all
the trees that were in the field, that were in all the borders round

about . . ." (Genesis XXIII), to whose history do they belong? Shimon Peres, a responsible minister, wisely decided, after consulting with both sides, that the Jews would pray in the chambers where the tombs of Abraham, Jacob, and Leah are found, and the Moslems in the chambers with the tombs of Isaac, Rebecca, Joseph, and Jawllya. This did not prevent a heated debate in the Knesset—nor Arab and Jewish opinion from becoming inflamed, nor yet the exegetes from giving contradictory interpretations of the texts. It is rumored that this has shaken the Rabin government, or that Rabin is using the episode to embarrass his rival, Peres. What is the nature of this concatenation of events which goes from the purchase of a field two thousand five hundred years before Jesus Christ to the confrontations of today? Earlier I wrote of the stubborn presence of the centuries. Only the unwise hope to escape it.

MONDAY, OCTOBER 25

Valéry Giscard d'Estaing would do well to meditate on this *mot* of Talleyrand's at the time of Louis-Philippe. Someone in his entourage asked him "How do you think this government will end?" "Accidentally," he replied.

TUESDAY, OCTOBER 26

The Médan lectures were coming to an end. In beautiful, concise words Jean-Claude Cassaing had presented Zola to an audience of several hundred faithful admirers. I had myself spoken of the man and the creative writer whom time is restoring to his rightful place, not that far from Balzac and way ahead of Barrès—except for his style. We were chatting on the steps in front of the house while the shadows took possession of the valley and the setting sun lit up the greenery on the terrace.

Someone came up to me and said, "I am Dreyfus' daughter." I did not conceal my surprise. Jeanne Dreyfus was slim and erect, with short white hair. She went on, "I wonder why they did not kill my father." I answered, "No doubt they thought they had won. All these upright people who put reasons of state before everything else dislike actual physical killing when it is not absolutely necessary." The year before I had flown over Devil's Island. She had never been there. "When we were children our mother did not talk to us of those things," she said. Then asked me, "What is it like today?" As the plane flew low I had seen corrugated tin roofs. Was it there that Captain Dreyfus had lived? Zola, Dreyfus. If the twentieth century began historically at the end of the 1914 war, it was born twenty years earlier in those torments of the spirit which precede crimes of bloodshed.

THURSDAY, OCTOBER 28

Tel-Aviv. Golda is expecting us at the headquarters of the Labor Party. She came out of the hospital yesterday and gloomy faces greeted any inquiries as to her health. I found her unchanged. "What do you expect?" Jacques Attali murmured. "She's as old as Judea, and look how alike they are." Arafat's speech at the United Nations and the ovation he had received there filled her with bitterness. "While he was speaking I was visiting a kibbutz where his men had assassinated eleven members of the same family," she said to us. Her voice broke. "We have lived a life of hope and prayer, of work and suffering, and now everything is decided by money and oil . . . If you have billions you can buy anything, not only factories and universities and banks, but anti-Semitism too," she said to us. She glanced at those around her. "I can allow myself to be frank because I am an old lady." And the tirade went on. "As I was born in Kiev, King Khalid thinks I am a Communist. Whatever you do, you can't change it—a Jew will always be held responsible for his birth."

FRIDAY, OCTOBER 29

Jerusalem. Our delegation of the Socialist Party lunched with Itzhak Rabin, prime minister of Israel. I noted this remark of his: "We have achieved impossible things. We have not succeeded quite so well with the possible ones." And this from the president of the Knesset: "We will not sacrifice our national reality to fulfil an international duty." Had Israel's policy changed since my last visit to that country more than four years before? Very little, if one can rely on what its leaders say. The arguments put forward by Rabin and his ministers to justify their refusal to recognize the Palestinian Liberation Organization, and to accept the creation of a genuinely Palestinian state, a buffer state between Israel and Jordan, were identical in every respect to those I had heard from the lips of Golda Meir. As I said goodbye to her, she answered me, not entirely in jest and looking at her companions, "Hurry up and come back before they have let everything go." But our criticisms were received with more attention than previously, and no doubts were cast on the friendship which inspired them. I gained the same impression from the press. For two whole hours, day before yesterday evening, I answered the never-ending questions of journalists—one must understand that these questions mean life or death for those who formulate them—on Israel's right to exist, on the fate of occupied territories, on Resolution Number 242 of the UN on French intentions and, more urgently, on the threat contained in the arrival in Lebanon of a new army of thirty thousand Arabs.

I did not conceal my thoughts, especially on the controversial subject of the Palestinian situation. The courteous reactions of my questioners convinced me that something is stirring in Israeli opinion. Not that I deduce from this attitude that they have come round to our point of view. But a process of maturation has begun which it might well be imprudent to hasten. On Thursday I went to Masada, that awe-inspiring rock which stands like a sentinel above the Dead Sea. In the year 76 B.C., on this narrow plateau rising straight up into the sky, when they understood that the Romans had won, the last Zealot defenders chose to die by their own hand—there were eight hundred of them, men, women and children. Unity of time for this people who have learned to die in order to endure.

MONDAY, NOVEMBER 1

Milan Huebl is a Czechoslovak historian sentenced in 1972 to six and a half years' imprisonment for subversion by Gustav Husak's judges. He had communicated to the Italian Communist Party documents on the situation in his own country and the actions of his own party. At the time I had protested against this sentence which added a supplementary note to political persecution, as ten years previously Milan Huebl had made himself conspicuous by the passion he had shown in obtaining from Antonin Novotny, then in power, the rehabilitation of one of his friends, the victim— before and after so many others—of arbitrary despotism. The name of his friend: Gustav Husak. This had not earned me exclusively friendly sentiments in Prague.

I am not seeking now to renew a fellow-feeling which would cause me more embarrassment than pleasure. But I see no reason for concealing the fact that I thought I had discerned the desire for a certain détente in the recent actions of the regime. What I hear of the treatment inflicted on Milan Huebl forces me to recognize my error. The prisoner is not only the object of ceaseless bullying (the prison authorities confiscate nearly all of the six hundred crowns he earns per month reweaving the straw seats of chairs, on the pretext that he must pay back the costs of his trial), but he is also being attacked through his family. His son Dusan, aged twenty-one, is an ordinary laborer who has passed the entrance examination to a technical college several times, but continues to be refused admission. Magda, his daughter, aged seventeen, has been forbidden to continue her high school studies for the last three years. Milan Huebl has just begun a hunger strike. There is little likelihood that he will ever see these lines. But I am writing them for a purpose. Madame Hueblova asked me this summer to participate in a commission of inquiry into the trial of 1972. She will find my answer here. It is yes.

I do not intend to confuse the issue by bringing up without transition the Lesage de la Haye affair. The secretary of state for universities is requesting the dismissal of this assistant professor at the University of Paris-VII. In addition to an old, though serious, prison sentence—he served his term, thus to a large extent paying for his offense—he has recently incurred a minor sentence for participating in the illegal occupation of a diplomatic building by a dissenting group. The administration, which had previously put up no opposition to the hiring of Lesage, has suddenly taken-fright, and put the matter before the courts and the Council of State and driven the unfortunate recidivist from its ranks. I repeat that no connection must be sought between the case of the political prisoner Milan Huebl and that of the undesirable French professor. Nor yet do I compare our democracy, however lame it may be, with the oppressive methods of the Czechoslovak system. But really! Is our civilization so lacking in self-confidence that it cannot allow itself to forgive or forget? This common-law malefactor who can extract from his misfortune enough strength to live and to teach others how to live inspires my respect. Far more than I feel, at any rate, for those who knife him in the back. I don't like manhunts.

TUESDAY, NOVEMBER 2

> Dear Otelo, I deeply regret not having been able to meet you for reasons which I deplore. Nonetheless, I wish to send you my most heartfelt greetings and tell you that I hope to see you again soon— free. I came to Lisbon to meet my Socialist friends gathered together for a congress, and you know that I am bound to them by brotherly ties. I said to them, as I say to you, that there is no socialism without freedom and I am sure that this is their belief. With kindest regards, dear Otelo . . . etc.

Before leaving Lisbon I entrusted this letter to Otelo de Carvalho's lawyer, as he himself is under house arrest, and sent a copy to Mario Soarès.

WEDNESDAY, NOVEMBER 3

Harry's Bar, the famous bistro in the rue Daunou, voted for Gerald Ford. Since 1924 the straw vote of its American customers had never once turned out to be wrong—so we are told. "France Inter" radio used this test as a point of reference. Listening to the commentaries it was easy to guess who our national radio favored. However, as the hours went by, the tone changed, as did the vocabulary. Jimmy Carter, who was nothing but a peanut vendor last night, has climbed several rungs on the social ladder and is now a groundnut planter. There is no doubt about it: If he keeps on at this rate, he will soon be president.

THURSDAY, NOVEMBER 4

Catherine G., Jacques Monod's niece, sends me these words of his as he sinks into a coma: "I am trying to understand."

SUNDAY, NOVEMBER 7

In December of last year I set down in these pages some impressions I had brought back from the trip I had just made to the United States. I noted the opinions I had gathered in Washington and in New York on the chances of the various candidates in the presidential election. They came from sources considered to be reliable: the secretary of state, influential senators, the pundits of the Council on Foreign Affairs, the leading journalists of the *Washington Post*, *The New York Times*, and *Newsweek*, presidents and professors of universities, diplomats, and the directors of two opinion polls. Fourteen personalities involved in the race were pointed out to me as covering the entire field of possibilities. So I listed them: Reagan, Connally, McCarthy, Humphrey, Jackson, Kennedy, Shriver, Udall, Church, Wallace, Muskie. I had also listed any potential dark horses, Brown for the Democrats, and Richardson for the Republicans. Really, nobody had been forgotten. Yes, one. Jimmy Carter. Not once was his name mentioned.

I will not blame my informants. They reasoned the way important people reason. But neither computers nor electoral machinery have managed to imprison dreams. And the American people were dreaming. What about? Something other than the important people. Quite simply: something different.

TUESDAY, NOVEMBER 23

André Malraux belonged to our neighborhood, to the landscape
of our life. It is as though a light in the house opposite had gone
out, leaving a few more shadows to darken the space and the time
ahead of us. It is hard to realize today the enormous impact made
by *Man's Fate* in the years before the last war. My generation
followed just after his, so it is thanks to him that as adolescents
we came into contact with the world that much earlier. I have
written elsewhere how I detached myself from him, when, at the
age of forty, I began to wonder what it was that had made us
succumb so hopelessly to his spell. One is not fair when disap-
pointed, and I was to remain so for a long time. When the charm
no longer operated all I could see were the mechanisms and the
fancy rhetorical tricks of his literary eloquence. Even *Man's Fate*,
even *Man's Hope* lost their appeal, not to mention *Museum Without
Walls*, which never had any for me. I would not write anything on
Malraux, who goes to his grave superbly escorted by the trumpets
of funeral orations, if the Malraux of the last works, who lived
and dreamed and philosophized, had not aroused echoes of long
ago in my mind. How many times I stopped at certain passages of
Lazarus to hear myself read them aloud! Lazarus resuscitated
leaves death behind him—before returning there. His path goes in
the opposite direction from that of other men, all other men, who
move forward from birth. Weighed down by the terrible burden
of a beyond he cannot remember, he endeavors to reveal a secret
of which he knows nothing. Shorn of all splendor, he speaks in a
voice burned by the fire of black suns. Alone and naked, groping
around his bed seeking once more the humble security of things,
his spirit voyages forth, pursuing strange dreams. Malraux-
Lazarus move me. I do not agree with Hervé Bazin that he is, with
Proust, the greatest novelist of the century. Between the two a
long list of names belies this judgment. Nor do I think that he will
be judged by posterity on his writing. Twenty years ago I spent a
few days with him. The man I knew then struck me as being a

medium: it was in talking, not in writing, that he really conveyed his message. Then he transmitted that dazzling light which dead stars are said to give, still brightening our darkness.

SATURDAY, DECEMBER 4

The partial elections having forced me to cram into the last week of November all the work I had not been able to do for a fortnight, I was unable to find time to see Moshe Dayan when he came to Paris to present his book, *The Story of My Life.* I regret not having seen that exceptional character. At the beginning of October we had lunched together in Tel-Aviv as guests of Shimon Peres, the minister of defense, and had planned to meet again. During the course of the meal Peres had expressed the wish that I waive the precautions of usage and language and give my real opinion on Israel's policy. He pressed me "not to leave Israel without having asked the questions which you put to yourself." I took advantage of this invitation to deplore the hostility shown by its leaders to the creation of a Palestinian state in Transjordan, while they assert they would accept, even encourage, the integration of this territory into the State of Jordan—on certain conditions, naturally. I added, "Hussein will not live forever and I cannot see what you gain by increasing the power of a neighbor who could within a short time become far more embarrassing than now." More in a spirit of fun than because he was at a loss for an answer, Peres said lightly to Moshe, "You first!" It will be a long time before I forget Dayan's answer: "No, you begin. You tell him what the government will do and then I'll tell him what the government ought to do."

MONDAY, DECEMBER 6

A long conversation before dinner (they dine late in Madrid) with Willy Brandt and Günther Grass, an unexpected member of the

Social-Democrat Party delegation. I had met Günther Grass three years previously at the publishing house of Le Seuil when the French version of *From the Diary of a Snail* came out (the translator, Jean Amsler, is an old friend of mine). He told us about his next book, *The Flounder*, from the name of the fish, both real and mythical, which symbolizes plenty in popular German tradition. *The Flounder* will describe the people of Germany by talking about their food. In it we will rediscover America at the time when beans, potatoes, cucumbers, tomatoes, corn, and eggplant started appearing in European households. Carried away by enthusiasm for his subject, Günther Grass exclaimed: "Why! the potato had far more influence on the history of Germany than the Seven Years' War ever had!"

THURSDAY, DECEMBER 30

At Latche, where I am spending the last days of the year, I always watch the news on television. So yesterday I witnessed the surprising spectacle of the minister of the interior, surrounded by the head of the Judiciary Police and the chief of the Criminal Brigade, giving a press conference on the state of the de Broglie* affair. If I understood Monsieur Poniatowski rightly, thanks to an accelerated investigation, as round and smooth as a billiard ball and a model of its kind, conducted by various branches of the police: "All those who have participated in the crime from near or far are under lock and key by now." The killer is known, as well as his associates, the go-between, and the people behind the crime. However, as the minister, wreathed in smiles, spoke on—very sparing of regrets at the murder of a man whom one might have taken to be his friend—I began to feel more and more uncomfort-

*Jean de Broglie, Deputy of the National Assembly for a Normandy *département*, was murdered December 24, 1976. An extreme Right terrorist organization claimed responsibility. De Broglie's alleged shady dealings have been rumored, but nothing has yet been proven. The investigation has been going on since 1976.

able. For propriety's sake and also on a point of principle. Propriety? This scenario, just after a session of the Council of Ministers during which they had congratulated each other on the fact that criminality had been reduced to its lowest level in fifteen years, the day after the president of the Republic had visited a Paris police station, was too pat not to look like a rather vulgar propaganda operation. Principle? I considered that it was not the function of the minister responsible for the police to decide that these people are guilty. And I remembered yet another occasion when two dignitaries of the regime had shown an indecent haste in their attempt to use the murder of a child for their own (political) advantage.

So you will understand how much I approved of the note put out by the Ministry of Justice and published in this morning's papers, expressing grave concern at the failure to observe the most elementary rules of the Rights of Man, of which Monsieur Poniatowski had been guilty—even though I feel no surprise at not seeing the signature of the minister of justice at the bottom of this protest. Monsieur Olivier Guichard is extremely talented at concealing his considerable height in the thickets of anonymity.

Though Jean de Broglie and I sat together in the Palais Bourbon through four legislatures, I never approached him and knew him only from having heard him speak on occasion from the roster of the Assembly. Nothing attracted me to this prolix and sententious orator, leader—he was secretary general of the Party of the Independents—of one of the two large parties of the majority, and member of several governments which I had never ceased to fight. But to tell you the truth, I am moved by his death. I do not know what will be discovered about him, or against him, tomorrow, since the fashion of the moment decrees that though the murderer may hope for attenuating circumstances, the victim may not. But the friends who kept quiet or turned away, the prime minister who had himself represented at the funeral by a symbolic Prefect, those three ministers—elected in Normandy!—who gave the weather as an excuse (cold feet perhaps) . . .

To die as a news item! I can think of no failure more bitter for someone who dreamed that his life would be noteworthy. An unfulfilled life and a botched death. That bloodstained, pathetic body, sprawled on the sidewalk one December morning, which one could push aside with a tip of a shoe—the bullet which pierced it destroyed more than an aorta. The title of a book by Jouhandeau comes to my mind: *Guilt Rather Than Scandal.*

1977

MONDAY, JANUARY 10

Since the Common Program of the Left was signed, several important documents have recapitulated, developed, or elucidated the proposals it embodies for national education, especially those concerning private education. On this subject the Federation of National Education and the Communist Party have published documents which reveal the same concern in approximately the same terms. As the Common Program affirms, they both wish to unite "all the sectors of primary education and an important part of permanent education in a single secular public service under the direction of the Ministry of National Education" and to nationalize "as a general rule . . . all private establishments, whether secular and run for profit or religious, that receive public funds." It must be noted that these documents did not reawaken old arguments or rekindle the war over education. Why is it then that the draft of an educational project submitted by Louis Mexandeau to the steering committee of the Socialist Party should meet a different fate—and it alone of all the others? It is not necessary to look far for the reason. All means are fair in fighting the Socialist Party. To confirm this one need look no further than the source of the attack: that Union of the Associations of Parents of Private School

Pupils (UNAPEL)—that trouble-maker we find confronting us on the eve of every general election. Behind this business there is an obvious desire to harm the Socialists, but I shall not use this argument to avoid the real issue. The coexistence of two educational structures, one public, one private, poses a problem which is not of recent date and which cannot be solved by resorting to clever tricks of language or by erasing history. Plain speaking will be my way of respecting both the gravity of the interests at stake, the ideas and preferences of those who oppose us, and the convictions which are ours.

Even when it has shown itself tolerant in actual practice where departmental and communal schools were concerned, the Left as a whole has never accepted any other rule than this: "Public funds for public schools; private funds for private schools." By contrast, the parties of the Right, which have been nearly continuously in power, have always attempted to increase the amount of public subsidies destined for private education. Thanks to the Debré law in 1959, they even managed to make the State bear the burden of certain expenses incurred by establishments which were not subject to its authority. This confusion of roles and types has led the organizations which favor public education to proclaim their desire to reestablish the previous state of affairs and to inform those in favor of private schools that they would be mistaken in believing that they could first take advantage of those benefits conceded by the Right and at a later date persuade the Left to perpetuate them. The Socialist Party shares this view.

But a step forward has been taken. The nationalization of education requested long ago by the militant lay associations was not included as one of my possible options in my presidential campaign of 1965 and did not become part of the Socialist program until 1972. There is no doubt that the offensives of private education compelled the Left to harden its attitude. But let no one attribute to bitterness what is in reality an invincible attachment to public education and its basic function. In any case, this evolution took place several years before the Mexandeau report, which does not propose any innovations as far as the basic principles that I have just outlined are concerned.

Let us get to the heart of the matter. Two points of view are in opposition. Both are based on traditions, convictions, and loyalties whose roots go deeply into the soul and body of the French nation. No one is ignorant of this. But let us not confuse the issue. We object strongly to any form of indoctrination, any idea of official schools, but we believe that a plurality of ideas, of beliefs, of cultures, and of races, that the right to be different, can and should be exercised within a system of public education. We feel apprehensive at the ratification of an educational dualism, the permanent institution of two parallel and competitive systems financed by the State. One—private, with a Right-wing orientation imposed upon it by the conservative notables who are gradually taking the place of ecclesiastics at the head of private schools. The other—public, all too easily and imprudently accused of belonging to the Left. The present climate is unhealthy. Those private schools that have a limited contract with the State in fact escape all control. Contracts of association between private schools and the State would permit many methods other than those that are the usual practice (witness the experiment carried out in the town of Laval), and would conceal many abuses. Employers are increasingly taking over technical training. In other words, the system is totally illogical and change has become necessary. Jean Poncet (president of the Federation of Private Education, affiliated with the CFDT—Confédération Française Démocratique du Travail), wrote in *Le Monde*: "The SGEC (Secrétariat Général de l'Enseignement Catholique) has never asked itself whether educational freedom necessarily depended upon the existence of two parallel structures." Well, we Socialists do ask this question—and answer it! And the answer can be found in the Common Program.

What does the Common Program say? I quoted two key sentences from it above. I will add that where private establishments receiving public funds are concerned, it uses the formula "as a general rule," and as far as private establishments not receiving public funds are concerned, it contemplates investigating their situation "with an eye to their eventual integration." What is the meaning of these details or nuances, which are not there just as a precaution? They mean that the endorsers of the historic agreement of 1972 never intended to impose integration, or decide on a monopoly, or order nationalization, without discussions, negotia tions, and periods of transition, without taking into consideration the multiple realities of France.

The other evening I was the guest of the "Club de la Presse" of Europe One radio station. As the subject came up again, I said that though it was easy to nationalize products (computers, bombers) or institutions (credit, education), it was neither possible nor conceivable to nationalize opinion. I will say no more.

TUESDAY, JANUARY 25

Mexico. Night was falling on the terrace of the Hotel Camino Real, whose architecture recalls the massive slopes of Aztec architecture. I talked for a long time with Andrés, the young university student who had taken us round the city since that morning. "Four million Mexicans are American citizens," he said to us. "Many of them occupy important positions. Two of them are state governors. Jimmy Carter was elected by the racial minorities, and, without flattering ourselves, we can claim to have been a determining factor in his election. Carter has promised to submit amendments to Congress which would grant American citizenship to our emigrants who had entered the country legally and make it easier for illegal immigrants, known as 'wetbacks,' to obtain work permits. It is not possible to know how many there are—certainly several million. They cross the border for short periods and then go back home. People in Europe think that the United States has seen the end of the incessant population movements which have marked her history, that the country has settled down. Or else that they pay attention only to the problems of blacks. They are wrong. People still enter and leave from many points, but mainly across our border in hundreds of places. In a century or two—that is to say in no time seen from Sirius—Mexicans will have penetrated all the arteries of the American body. It is not a question of a premeditated plan; it is a natural and constant flow. Humanity is shot through with currents, like the bottom of the ocean. Look at the endless border which stretches for

miles and miles from Tijuana to Matamoros. It doesn't just separate the United States from Mexico. Separate is the wrong word,
for as I have just said, it is more like a sieve than a barrier. It
marks the meeting place of the mobile geography of two worlds.
For truly it is there that East and West meet and confront each
other. Do not dismiss that as a paradox. We are Orientals. The
Indians came from the north, the shortest route from east to west,
and they are going north again. It is a wonderful about-face.
While the United States was endeavoring to establish its power by
war, war in Vietnam, war in Cambodia, and its soldiers were
dying far away from home, we were tilling their soil; while it was
extending its influence to the far corners of the earth—South
America, Thailand, Japan—we were building its towns. While it
was sailing the tropical seas to control all the straits of the globe,
we kept its factories going. In other words, the East is besieging
the citadel of the West, and the West pretends not to notice.

"Do not think I am a visionary or an angry nationalist. I value
our neighbors and wish them no harm. I am like someone observing the migration of birds. You don't take sides for curlews against
golden plovers. And as I can't penetrate the deeper meaning of
things, I try to decipher the signs. After all, the earth is round."

This afternoon we visited the Third World Institute, where we
were warmly greeted by its founder, Luis Echeverría. This man,
who forcefully governed his country during a six-year presidency—which came to an end two months ago—is putting the
same energy into his new task. It is easy to see that he is impatient
for Fate to smile on him again. He had hoped to succeed Kurt
Waldheim as secretary general of the United Nations. The great
powers barred the way to this exceptional candidate, who owed
allegiance to no one and had done nothing to reassure them. The
Americans had taken alarm at his enthusiasm for the Third
World, and Mexican business interests, closely tied to Washington, had reeled under the avalanche of legislation which he had
forced through (four hundred laws passed one after the other). In
Mexico, the law provides that the president cannot be elected to a
second term. Six years—how paltry! In that brief period, Luis Echeverría doubled the number of miles of roads, built thirty airports
and thousands of schools; drafted an educational reform thanks to

which the length of obligatory school attendance rose from six
years to nine; initiated fiscal reforms; decided on a mass increase
of wages in the lowest brackets; prepared the political reform
which his successor, López Portillo, confirmed last September 14.
But this effort to expand public facilities and bring about social
reforms has been costly. The foreign debt has reached twenty
billion dollars and there is a three-billion budget deficit. This autumn inflation exceeded 7 percent a month. The parity of 12.5
pesos to the dollar, which had been maintained with increasing
difficulty for twenty-two years, crashed, and the devaluation of
last August 30 brought it down to 22 pesos. Even though the end
of the "reign" of Luis Echeverría was marred by the economic
crisis, even though López Portillo could not continue investing
(the new president is a classical economist by doctrine, by temperament, and by necessity), the changeover has been effected
without strain and Echeverría and his team participate in the
López Portillo cabinet. However, public opinion is alarmed at the
return in force of the Americans, who do not lend their dollars
without usury. The intellectuals are already denouncing the infiltration of foreign capital, desired and encouraged by the bourgeoisie and the financiers. We know that Mexico must live
through this as one lives through an illness in anticipation of the
compensations of good health. I could discern in López Portillo's
entourage certain signs of irritation against what is called "collaboration" by some. Two or three ministers are obviously tempted
to branch out and join the informal groups which, either inside or
outside the official party, are endeavoring to prepare the ground
for a new political system.

Mexico's originality goes so far as to have a governing party
called the Institutional Revolutionary Party (PRI). Revolution and
established order backing each other up, guaranteeing each other.
Someone had to think of it! But the PRI has suffered from the
wear and tear which come from practically undisputed power for
nearly fifty years. Since 1929 it has not only controlled the presidency, the government, the legislative assemblies, and the civil
service, but it also guides the trade-union movement from a distance and its members are obliged to have their PRI card. To allow
the "nonregistered" parties to express themselves, Echeverría has

tried to introduce the beginnings of proportional representation. He feels strongly about this, having lived through a cruel experience: In 1968, as minister of the interior, he was not able to avoid bloodshed in breaking up a student riot. But tension has not been reduced by a rather half-hearted attempt at proportional representation. It is a difficult country to govern with its twenty races, a hundred languages, and the weight of thousands of years of history which are still present. It gives an impression of irresistible power, drawn from telluric forces which nearly touch the sun, for the earth is so old and so eroded that its own substance is all that it has left for nourishment. I liked this diverse people, strong in its self-pride, with eyes that in painting and sculpture reshape, with unequaled audacity, forms that have always existed.

WEDNESDAY, JANUARY 26

Mexico. Informed of our impending visit by Régis Debray, who had been able to make his journey coincide with ours, Gabriel García Márquez was waiting for us at the Mexico City airport. I have already related this anecdote. Pablo Neruda asked me: "Do you know *One Hundred Years of Solitude*? If not, read it right away. It is the most beautiful novel that Latin America has produced since the last war." I read it the next day, and later I met García Márquez in Paris. The man bears a strong resemblance to his work: thick-set and solid, laughter and silence. I do not use the word just for effect. Under the wealth of imagery and the prodigious joy in words, stretches a desert of silence such as tropical forests can create.

We breakfasted together on the following days. (Beatrice and Isabel Allende, the daughters of the assassinated Chilean president, had joined us. One lives in Mexico, the other in Cuba.) We talked chiefly of García Márquez's latest book, *The Autumn of the Patriarch*, just published in France. We discussed form—Régis feared that no translation could do justice to the rhythm and the sonority of this oratorio composed, written, to be read aloud in its original language—and also its theme, or rather, themes, which revolve around a character who is typically South American, though universal: the dictator. A mythical, thick-headed general who plays, enjoys, lives, and finally croaks, thanks only to that ultimate rapture: power. Power over people, power over things; convinced that he exists because others reflect his image in the mirror of his unhappiness.

We all agreed that though the dictators of today have taken over from the models of the preceding period those traits that are common to all dictatorships—order, uniforms, blood—they have nonetheless changed their political nature as economic structures have been transformed. The days of consuls are over. They were as cruel as was necessary, the adventurers of their own adventure. They sprang from the people whom they defended against the assemblies which called themselves democratic but were in fact the collective throne of the ruling classes. But today's dictator is no more than just another lackey in the pay of the masters of money. He appears at just the right moment, when patrician democracy is no longer able to protect its own privileges. At this point in the conversation I pointed out that our definition was inadequate, as it did not include that other type of modern dictator which the cult of personality has propelled, and still propels, to the top of the Marxist-Leninist pyramid. We agreed that the subject would repay investigation, but that in any case, the differences did not conceal the resemblances.

THURSDAY, JANUARY 27

Costa Rica. I have managed to combine three invitations to Latin America in one journey. One from Luis Echeverría, at the time head of state of Mexico, which for lack of time I had postponed from month to month. The other two, extended in December in Geneva during the Socialist International Congress, by Carlos Andrés Pérez, president of Venezuela, and by Daniel Oduber, president of Costa Rica. Preparing for the municipal elections and the tasks that the daily life of the Socialist Party impose upon me had made it impossible to leave France for more than a week. It was therefore necessary for me and the small and friendly delegation accompanying me—Gaston Defferre, Lionel Jospin, Antoine Blanca and Antoine Andrieux—to give up, not without regret, virtually everything that did not actually concern the object of our visit, that is to say politics. But in Mexico and Costa Rica, that same politics looked after us well, to the point of causing all fatigue to disappear. I had been warned about variations of both altitude and latitude one on top of the other. I neither noticed them nor suffered from them. On occasion and in certain places, I have been bored (though I am not naturally given to boredom and it takes a lot to make me succumb), but this time the hours seemed short. Here in Costa Rica, my day that is just coming to an end reinforces this impression.

Daniel Oduber lives in his own home. In Costa Rica there is no official residence for the head of state. This evening he entertained us in a restaurant, the sort of restaurant you come upon all over France, with tables of polished wood placed end to end, red cloths and rolled napkins, flounced curtains at the windows and little brass lamps. There were ten of us at table: Oduber, several of his ministers, Pedro Cardenal, the guerrilla priest famous throughout South America for always being in the thick of the battle, and the members of my delegation. All the revolutionaries of the neighboring countries eventually seek refuge in Costa Rica to give themselves a breather and wait for luck to change. There must be between six and seven thousand of them at this moment. The democratic heads of state of Latin America who have never had occasion to live their years of exile there are rare. Andrés Pérez, whom we were to see the next day in Caracas, spent nearly ten years in Costa Rica. In this part of the world where the fires of earth are as intense as the passions of the men they mold, Costa Rica appears as a haven of peace—a sort of Latin Switzerland. Not a coup d'état since democracy came in, except Teodoro Picado's abortive attempt in 1948. Institutions that jealously guard their integrity see to it that there is no leeway for intrigue or ambition. Elective terms of office last only four years. Reelection is forbidden by law—for life. One can imagine the consumption of presidents, of ministers, of governors and deputies (the single chamber has 57 members) which this small republic of two million souls allows itself. Logical to the end, Costa Rica has declared peace on the world and does not have an army.

FRIDAY, JANUARY 28

Caracas. From one hotel to another. We were sitting in deck chairs enjoying the cool of the evening by the pools of the Tamanaco Hotel where we are staying. It is an enormous block of concrete anchored like a watchtower on the slope of a hill which overlooks three valleys through which the town flows like a river—sometimes overflowing, sometimes receding, with wharves and lagoons and islands. Enrique Tejeira París, a senator and international secretary of Democratic Action, the ruling party in Venezuela, who had been ambassador in America during the Kennedy and Johnson administrations, told us that in 1963, at a reception given by Curtis LeMay, commander-in-chief of the American Air Force, he had heard the commanding officer of the American Air Force in Panama, just back from a study tour of Latin America, perorate in these terms: "The Venezuelan army has the best officers and the best military tradition; then comes Argentina's which is methodical and well organized." "What about Chile?" somebody asked. He laughed aloud and replied, "Don't talk to me about Chile. I questioned the generals there about the possibility of Salvador Allende—a Communist, or very nearly—being elected to the presidency of the Republic and presumed that in that case the army would settle the matter as you would expect. And do you know what they answered me? 'We are a constitutional army.' I said to them 'You're quite mad!' and dropped them like a brick." Tejeira expressed his approval of Kennedy who, having been informed of the incident, ordered within a week that the swashbuckler be removed from office. He added that shortly after, in Paris, he had received from the president, via his collaborator Ralph Dungan, a copy of *Seven Days in May* which tells of an imaginary coup d'état.

It bore the dedication: "This sort of thing can always happen anywhere."

The conversation veered to the actions of the CIA in South America; to American instructors sent to train the cadres of local armies, and to ambassadors whose diplomatic immunity protected a compact network of police and spies. Tejeira felt that Watergate, the coming to office of Carter, and the wave of moralism which had taken hold of public opinion had made the political climate much healthier, and that there was a genuine desire for change in the United States. But he very much doubted that good intentions, even if they became common currency in the White House, would be able to change the habits of the senior officials of the administration who were the real rulers of the country. "I do not believe that the teams which are just below the best-intentioned government heads will let themselves be eliminated. I can remember the ambassador who pointed out a little Bolivian colonel named Barrientos, lost among a group of officers, and said in a low voice, 'That one will soon be master in his country.' Eight days later, Barrientos' coup d'état succeeded. In Latin America dozens of would-be dictators like him are available, and in Washington there are plenty of specialists to pick them out several lengths ahead of history."

TUESDAY, FEBRUARY 1

Two days in Greece, six days in Latin America: these journeys to and fro do not allow time for the pleasures of travel. However, I will not complain. Everything I saw and heard, the subtle understanding between my traveling companions, the warmth of the welcome we received everywhere, and—more than anything else perhaps—the ease I feel in my relationship with myself when time and my life go smoothly, all gave me, in the exact measure in which I needed it, a feeling of continuity.

In Corinth, or more precisely, fifteen kilometers to the west, lies the village of Vrachati, on the northern seacoast of the Pelopon-

nesus. Here Theodorakis has built his house. (The first time he
slept there, after long, impatient, fond expectation, the police
came to fetch him and did not bring him back again for two whole
years.) I arrived there at night, with Mikis driving along one of the
most beautiful roads in the world. During the entire journey I
repeated to myself the names I spied on the signposts. Their sonority had irrevocably shaped the memory of my language—
Athens, Eleusis, Megara, Thebes, Corinth, Mycenae, Argos, Epi-
daurus, Delphi—the whole universe unfurled within the narrow
limits of one small stretch of earth. Mikis too was softly reciting
the familiar syllables, marveling that they had preserved the mys-
tery and charm of a poem read for the first time.

My bedroom, pine and sandstone, decorated with luxuriant en-
gravings by a Peruvian painter and sober portraits of Goethe and
Johann Strauss, gave onto a garden. I went out to walk in it for a
while. On the other side of the fence a cold wind whipped the sea.
At regular intervals the sound of the waves drowned the melody
that Mikis was trying out on the piano before going to bed.

The next day was a rush. Politics in Greece is fully as hectic as
in France. At Vrachati I met Papandreou, Protopapas, Mavros,
Florakis, Illiou, Dracopoulos—eminent men of contemporary
Greece fighting against dictatorship, and leaders of the six parties
in opposition. Around the table we lunched, dined, and talked. I
knew of the controversies, often fierce, which separated them, I
knew the freedom with which they spoke and their taste for blunt
talk. But—five of them had shared exile, prison, and torture—they
all had love for their country in common and freedom in their
very blood. Though they had signed an electoral pact at the time
of the municipal elections (thanks to which they had won several
towns, including Athens) they nonetheless remained divided on
certain capital points. Divisions which, I felt, were caused more by
their difficulty in surmounting their own history than by the realities of the present, though these must not be underestimated:
whether to join the Common Market; what tactics to use with the
prime minister, described by some as the unconscious forager of
the military Right, while others see in him a lesser evil and even
the guarantee of a progressive return to democracy. The stature of
Constantin Caramanlis, though diminished, is still considerable.

Everything goes through him. Should I meet him? Without exception, my visitors advised me to see him—including Florakis, secretary general of the Orthodox Communists, whose weakness is not
servility. I took their advice. Karamanlis received me in the vast
office reserved for the head of state, which occupies a corner of
the Parliament building. After he had recalled a few memories
of his eight-year exile in France, the conversation I had with him
bore entirely on the subject, the only subject, that occupies the
mind of every single Greek to the point of obsession: the latent
conflict with Turkey, whether over Cyprus, rights in the Aegean
Sea (and first of all its sub-soil), or the minorities in Thrace. I find
indiscretion repugnant; but I do not believe that I am wrong in
thinking that the prime minister did not voice his concern only for
my ear when he said that one could not exclude the possibility of
war. Everyone spoke to me of Turkey, in the same key and with
the same determination. On this point at least, national unity does
exist. The exasperation of the Greeks can be felt. The politicians
certainly remain cool-headed, and one must admit that given the
present state of public opinion, Karamanlis shows more courage
by putting a brake on impetuosity than he would by encouraging
it. This prudence can also be discerned in the arguments of the
principal leaders of the Left. But who can be master of a situation
where a word or a gesture could lead to an explosion?

The general irritation is focused on the Americans, with or
without nuances. Nearly everywhere (except in the spheres of influence of the CIA, which is extremely active) they are accused of
having preferred Turkish alliance to Greek friendship, either because the former was considered to be more useful to the Western
bloc, or because they feared that Ankara would turn to the Soviet
Union. They are accused of the blackest Machiavellianism, for
example in the Cyprus affair. One of the most trustworthy leaders
of the moment alleged in my hearing that the State Department
had organized the whole operation so as simultaneously to get rid
of Makarios, guilty of neutralism (it was only by chance that he
escaped death), and the colonels, who had become impossible.
This offered the double advantage of restoring democracy in
Greece—which would please the Greeks—while serving the interests of the Turks. As usual, these suggestions credit the powerful

with more imagination and ability than they really have. The mechanisms of the world are governed by simpler forces, that is to say disorder and chance. But when a stubborn idea, even though mistaken, seizes the minds of millions of men, then it is not very far from the truth.

FRIDAY, APRIL 1

These so-called Easter holidays allowed me a short visit to Latche which came to an end this evening. I am so much in need of peace that I have not moved out of my glade. My neighbors came to me. We talked about the weather. In my present mood, anyone trying to steer me round to the subject of the election of the Parliament of Europe by universal suffrage, or the Twenty-Second Congress of the Communist Party, would be wasting his time. I put politics aside when I change my clothes. If I let my mind wander according to the whims of the little world that surrounds me, I will see more clearly what I should do, what I want to do, once I am back in Paris. An exceptionally mild spell is slowly bringing winter, which lasted a good month longer than usual, out of its torpor. I was here briefly in March and the quality of the silence then gave an intimation that spring would be late. I am very rarely mistaken about such things. There is a sort of inner roar in the surge of life. Last week the thermometer rose to twenty degrees Celsius in the afternoon but fell below zero around dawn, with the result that, except for a few primroses and the clumps of daffodils under the magnolia trees, my visit to the flowers was disappointing. In the orchard it is even worse. Only the apple trees have any hope of bearing fruit—which the blackbirds and bullfinches will no doubt get before I do. Perfidious latitude! It is safer to plant in Lorraine or on the northern plain. The seasons there are less treacherous. But where would I find my breath come so easily? Nowhere better than on the coast of Gascony does the expression "the heart of the air" convey so exactly a physical reality. Here sea and space meet. Three thousand miles of water separate us from America—two

million acres of pine forest protect us from the cities. And at night
our glade touches the sky!

SATURDAY, APRIL 16

This business of trees—I mean the national holiday ordered by
Valéry Giscard d'Estaing—typifies his way of doing things better
than any other illustration. The idea of inviting the people of
France to plant a tree is a good one. His merit is in no way diminished by the fact that he is neither the first nor the only person to
have suggested it, nor yet (as some malicious commentators have
implied) that a certain electoral urgency seems to have prompted
these ecological reflexes. After all, not many presidents of our five
Republics have taken an interest in the matter. But planting trees
in April! Here the good idea becomes distressing. The fruit will
get no further than the blossoms' promise if one tampers with the
seasons. And why the hurry? As far as I know, voting doesn't start
before next year. It is a pity that Saint Catherine has lost her voice
since Domrémy.* Had she whispered in the ear of the head of
state that it is not as easy to play about with trees as it is with
statistics, she would have advised him better than his experts.
Nobody will be surprised if nature takes her revenge. To my certain knowledge she never undertakes anything without
forethought.

SUNDAY, APRIL 17

I love forests. The journeys of my life lead me from the forests of
the Landes to those of the Morvan. Whenever a trip makes it
possible, I never fail to go by way of Tronçais, by Bellème, or by la

*Domrémy is the birthplace of Joan of Arc, in Lorraine.

Margeride. According to my mood I prefer Rambouillet . . . or another forest, all the others. Chantilly or Fontainebleau, the Sologne of my ancestors or the Double of my childhood. One could compose a poem by writing down the names, just the names, of the forests: Chaource, la Dombe, Brocéliande, la Chaise-Dieu. What do they mean to me? It would take me many hours to express it in fifteen lines.

But this is not about me. In the last thirty years I have seen the Celtic forests of the Morvan disappear. I represent that district (in the National Assembly) and I was unable to do anything to protect it. What can be done against a coalition of law, administration, and indifference? Fight! Most certainly fight. I organized numerous debates and discussions to arouse public opinion. I joined the rare groups and committees which attempted the impossible. The General Council of the district of Nièvre devoted several sessions to studying the problem, called leading experts in as consultants, pledged itself financially to assist projects for safeguarding the forests. Paris replied only by firing broadsides of axioms. Economy! First and foremost, economy! What profit was there in those oaks that require a hundred years to reach maturity, those beeches whose fibers refuse to be absorbed by any profitable technology for conversion into cellulose, those ashes, hornbeams, aspens, birches? Each week, hundreds of acres of that forest of light fell under the assault of bulldozers. Make room for conifers! What can one say to local small landowners? From 1946 to 1973 the forestry financing organizations reserved loans and subsidies for trees that grow fast. Speed, speed! Earth and sap and wood must adapt their cycles of maturity to the rhythm of rushing man. Big companies buy our hillsides, lay bare our horizons. I received a prospectus from my bank in Paris, vaunting the profits to be made from the imminent shearing of the Forêt de la Gravelle near Château-Chinon. The National Forestry Department encourages this trend. Its short-term policy consists in destroying some 350,000 acres of deciduous trees and producing paper pulp to take their place. As a long-term policy (but what do fifty years amount to?) some 500,000 acres are to be destroyed. Nobody is concerned by the effect on the flow of water in springs, on the acidity of the soil, or by the inevitable changes of climate, the game that has fled and the birds that have ceased to sing. The rocks of Beuvray have been scraped bare: I looked in vain for the sunken paths bordered till recently by the tall trunks of the beech forest—reminders of a history older than Caesar.

When the fine weather comes, the helicopters appear. They let loose their chemistry on the scents of spring, like that man in a newspaper filler whose favorite pastime was training his dogs to bite children. It is thanks to the war in Vietnam that technology has given us this new way of killing our trees. When there is a little wind the defoliant is sprayed over our fields, mingles with the rain water already heavily polluted by fertilizers, adulterates the milk of our cows, and settles as a gray film on the fruit in our gardens. The mayor will know about it only when he hears the helicopter overhead, unless, of course, he has received that same morning a letter with an illegible signature announcing this visit. This is exactly what happened last year in a village in the Nièvre.

The forests are dying everywhere; copses and hedges and green places too. Superhighways, cities, big-time profiteers, and even worse, the simple desire to wipe out the work of time, to assert one's power over the humble order of things, to extract from transience a feeling of eternity, are accelerating the process.

My readers know that I am not one of those who take up the tune of the moment; that I am more likely to repeat a refrain whose burden can be found in previous chronicles; but it is quite true that, at a time when there seemed no hope of being heard, the choir of ecologists raised its voice to a shriller pitch, and this particular trumpet seems to be shaking the concrete walls of Jericho.

I do not like that menace, the systematic mind. For to me everything is connected. And planting a tree on the sixteenth of April implies a political choice. It is not mine. And forests too are included in the problems that face society.

MONDAY, APRIL 18

I have just reread my notes of yesterday. I might alter them if I had time. I do not believe in fate or in inevitable disaster. Should I succumb to their contagion, I would at once seek remedies. I have just discovered one in this quotation from a book which has recently been reprinted, *Men Drunk with God (Les Hommes Ivres de Dieu)* by Jacques Lacarrière. "Who can fail to see that the world is on the decline, that it no longer has the strength and vitality of yesteryear? Less rain falls in winter to nourish the seed. The sun is less hot in summer to ripen the fruit. Spring is no longer so pleasant, nor autumn so fruitful. The quarries, as though weary, produce less stone, and the gold and silver mines are exhausted. The fields are not tilled, no navigators sail the seas and the armies have no soldiers. There is less innocence at the bar and less justice among judges; friends are less close; there is less industry in the arts and less discipline in morals . . . Thus it is that all things, already now, hasten toward death, are affected by the general exhaustion of the world . . ."

The earth has turned on its axis many times since Saint Cyprian of Carthage, who lived in the third century A.D., wrote these doleful lines to his friend Dimitrianus: "The earth has turned and man also. But our old world is still new."

THURSDAY, JULY 9

Two motionless hours of silence and summer at the home of Dominique and Frédéric Pardo. Frédéric is painting and Dominique (Sanda), who is to play Lou Andréas-Salomé in the film that Liliana Cavani is preparing to make, is reading *My Sister, My Spouse (Ma Soeur, mon Epouse)*, Peters' beautiful book devoted to Lou. The portrait sitting over, round a cup of mint tea—Dominique's speciality—we talked about that strange personage who fascinated Nietzsche, Rée, Rilke, Freud, and of course Andréas. But not Tolstoy! I recounted to my friends, who did not know it, the story told by Boris Pasternak, the great writer's very last secretary, about the visit paid by Lou and Rainer Maria Rilke to Isnaya Polyana. The two travelers, who had come from Germany in a freight train, arrived exhausted and took a troika from the station to the estate. Andrei, the eldest son, opened the door, admitted

Lou, then shut it in Rainer's face. Tolstoy wandered in, greeted her, and went out again. Meanwhile his wife went on taking papers out of a desk and sorting them, taking no notice of anything else. In the next room a child was crying. Tolstoy, talking to himself, came back to console it, then went out again. When he returned, he invited his visitors to go for a walk with him, during which he uttered no more than a few stray words, his mind elsewhere. However, he did advise Rainer against writing poetry. "Occasionally he would stoop, tear up a handful of forget-me-nots and press them to his face," Pasternak notes. "He seemed to be in the grip of some intense emotion and quite unaware of everything going on about him."

THURSDAY, AUGUST 4

Sitting up late one evening at Latche, I hear, all around me, talk of life and death, the origins of the world and the existence of God, the beyond and nothingness. The battle rages in both camps. What certainties on either side! They demonstrate, decide definitively, assert authoritatively. I listen and think that though I like those who ask themselves questions, I am wary of those who find answers.

FRIDAY, AUGUST 12

In the plane to Athens I started rereading *The Young Joseph* by Thomas Mann—one of the books which delighted me most in my twenties, now reprinted. After the first few pages a sentence made me pause. It said that, at the dawn of Creation, God's messenger on earth, Semhazaï, desired the virgin Ikkara and attempted to rouse her feelings. Ikkara took advantage of her tempter's weakness to extract from him the Name of the Eternal; armed with this secret (secret or talisman) she extricated herself from her dilemma by rising forthwith to Heaven, where Yahveh welcomed her with these words: "Since you have known how to avoid sin, we will give you a place among the stars." A place which since then has been called the constellation of Virgo. Semhazaï, unable, because unworthy, to return to Heaven, remained in the dust till the day at Beth-El when Jacob, son of Isaac, had a vision of Heaven's ladder. "With the help of the ladder, he was able at last to return to his fatherland, discomfited at having been reduced to rise on the wings of a human dream," wrote Thomas Mann.

I laid the book on my knee and looked through the plane's window. We were flying over Cephalonia. A mist rising from the sea blurred the sharp contours of the islands and I thought of Semhazaï who, in order to find his way back to God, was constrained to wait until a man dreamed of Him.

SATURDAY, AUGUST 13

Roger Garaudy was talking of "The Future of Socialism" when I entered the assembly room of the Orthodox Academy of Crete near the monastery of Gonia where a symposium on "Socialism and Culture" was being held. Sitting at varnished oak tables set in a semicircle round the dais, fifty or so guests from ten countries of Europe and Africa listened in well-mannered silence. We were on the north coast of the island, on its western side, and through the windows the incandescent blue of the Aegean was so dazzling it hurt our eyes. Three pictures hung on the wall, dominating the dais: in the middle a modern icon, a crudely painted Christ with a sullen expression; and to the left and right, enlarged photographs, one of the Patriarch Athenagoras, luminous forehead and white beard against a background dark as night; and one of the Provincial Metropolitan Kyrillos, hieratic in his wooden armchair. The symposium had started the day before. "General Problematics" had been discussed in the morning, centered on the reports of

Illias Illiou, the great leader of the little EDA, and of Avangelos
Papanoutsos, the Greek writer and member of Parliament. The
afternoon had been given over to "Socialisms and Cultures"—in
the plural. The debate had been opened by Pavel Apostol, professor at the Academy of Sciences in Bucharest. Unable to leave
Paris sooner, I had missed the first day and the beginning of this
one. My arrival provoked a certain discomfort and I had the feeling I was upsetting, however slightly, that complicity of initiates
exuded by any human group, no matter how recently formed.
During a break following Garaudy's lecture, I confided this feeling
to Claude Manceron and told him how, because of a cold, my
parents had postponed for a day my arrival in the lowest grade at
the school of Saint-Paul d'Angoulême, where I was to remain till
the end of my high-school studies. That accursed cold! That one
lost day! It took me weeks before I felt really integrated into that
society and its established order, constituted the day before: I
mean, desk in the classroom, bed in the dormitory, row in the
study room, place at games, and membership in playtime groups.
From the farthest edge, where I felt an unjust fate had cast me, it
took me weeks to break through the concentric circles which separated me from the choir of the ancients—as though in twenty-
four hours the walls of habit had been built and barred, the circles
of friendship closed. It is true that I now know that my timidity
invented obstacles. But later on I was able to verify that a moment
shared creates a relationship which cannot be communicated to
those who have not lived it. Claude smiled but did not laugh at
this reminiscence, which reminded him of similar emotions and
set us both off on the trail of old memories.

When the session was resumed, Jacques Attali took up arms in
his habitual penetrating manner, constructing a thesis on art, the
artist, and society in which he mingled logic and intuition, clarity
of speech and the obscurities of an oracle, full of brilliant ideas
and sparkling formulas. His basic argument was that the crisis of
art expresses the crisis of society. In a society which does not
know to whom it is speaking, the artist has no message to trans-
mit. But a day will come when each individual life will become a
work of art and then the artist—as we imagine him now, an exceptional creature and an irreplaceable creator—will disappear as

such. May he hasten to prepare the way for his own uselessness! It is up to socialism to bring this about. Attali forged ahead, perhaps too fast. On thinking it over I realized that his clarity had deceived me with *trompe l'oeil*, whereas the oracle—once unraveled—elucidated an idea whose sole, temporary weakness was being too far ahead of experience, though transpiercing appearances—with what mastery—in search of reality. His comments on a quotation taken from Carlos Castañeda's book on the Yagui Indians, *The Teachings of Don Juan*, set the discussion going again. Castaneda ascribes to the wisdom of an old Indian sorcerer of the Mexican border, Don Juan, the revelation of the four enemies every man must confront if he is to attain understanding: Fear of knowledge, which closes eyes, ears, and spirit to the universe and to oneself; the knowledge which is never quite knowledge, but contents the spirit without fulfilling it and persuades it to be satisfied; the power given by knowledge which must then be abandoned ("if a man has been dominated by power, he dies without knowing how to use it"); and finally death, which always wins, even though one has won everything else.

Garaudy interrupted him to say, "Let us pause here, with your permission, and talk of the second enemy pointed out to us by old Don Juan. The knowledge which is not knowledge creates too much havoc for the false practitioners of any law to be left in peace. For much of my life, I have been in contact with those whom I call Marx's fools: dogmatists, high priests, Cabalists. Marx was thinking of this type of person when he said to Lafargue, "What is quite certain is that I am not a Marxist." He then reminded us that Marx condemned those scientists who appropriated for themselves one of the fundamental tenets of historical materialism, that is to say "necessity," while deliberately leaving the other tenet, "initiative," hidden under a bushel basket. Garaudy repeated: "No, no. Man is not a 'marionette whose strings are pulled by structures' any more than conscience is 'a passive reflection of man's existence and history, but a moment in the existence of history, the active moment, the germ and the plan of the future.' " Carried away by the subject, he tossed off quotations pell-mell: "What is written in *Das Kapital*? 'The history of man is different from that of nature in that we made the former and not the latter,' or, 'What differentiates the worst architect from the most expert bee is that he has built the cell in his head before building it in the hive.' Or from *The 18th Brumaire of Louis Bonaparte*: 'Men make their own history, not arbitrarily under conditions chosen by them, but under conditions directly given by and inherited from the past.' And from his *Critique of Political Economy*: 'The problem is not in understanding that Greek art and epic poetry are linked to certain forms of social development. The problem is that they still give us aesthetic enjoyment, and that under certain circumstances they still have value as norms and as inaccessible models.' "

Pavel Apostol broke in: "I do not say that you are wrong; many misguided interpretations of Marx erred in that direction. But you must beware of falling into the opposite error. To recognize only initiative and deny necessity opens the way to even more serious deviations." Garaudy reflected for a moment, then speaking slowly, replied, "Yes, you are right. One must not let go of the other end of the chain. To say that men make their own history and to be content with that proposition can lead people to believe that anything is possible at any moment. That is where Sartre went wrong. But I still maintain that Marxism cannot be reduced to an economic doctrine, and that it lays genuine foundations for a philosophy of the act: Man participates, as a creator, in the making of history."

This discussion took up the whole evening. "Shouldn't we grapple with the problem of power, that mortal threat to all understanding? Your 'new philosophers' have written interesting, excellent things on the subject which interest us enormously in Greece. I have read your articles and your chronicles and you have not mentioned them yet. Does that mean that you don't think much of them?" It was Andreas questioning me, Andreas Lentakis, editor-in-chief of the newspaper *Elleniki Aristera*, one-time companion of Mikis Theodorakis in prison and in torture. The question got lost among many others. The last group broke up late, but when I got back to my room I tried to sort out in my mind the thoughts it had aroused. The new philosophers interest me more for their literature than for their philosophy. I knew Bernard-Henri Lévy when he first entered the Ecole Normale Supérieure. I flatter myself for having sensed that this serious young man would become a great writer. One danger threatens him: fashion. But suffering—that friend of the strong—will save him. Everything is preparing him for it. I am not worried by the desire to please that possesses him and at the moment is leading him away from his real territory. When he realizes that he has within himself that which he has gone outside himself to seek, he will turn back to meet it. Even if he wanted to, he could not escape from the fire that consumes him. One can already discern ashes in the eyes of this dandy.

Perhaps I am wrong. Perhaps he will succumb to the temptations of this world beyond their allotted time. That would sadden me. I can accept his continuing to make a show of a great deal of pride before I start calling it vanity. I brought with me from France a copy of *Barbarism with a Human Face* and am taking notes on it for my chronicle. Arrogant and naive. Arrogant by virtue of its language, the internal rhythm, the bitter certainty that only uncertainty exists. Naive by virtue of the object of its quest, which escapes him each time he approaches it. What is the point of concluding with this slogan: "Resist the barbarian menace from wherever it comes" if it is true that "the Master is the other name of the World" and that "as soon as one is dethroned, another takes on the trappings"? Abstaining from fighting the power in place, because "the red princes are already there, pawing the ground in the ante-chamber," forgetting that this power, like any other, "comes from the bottom, returns from the edge, rises up from the dregs of the world," that it always rejects "the set of rules, norms, taboos, and bars to which it anchored itself" rather than give up its exercise of power, that at the first alarm it will gallop back to its own natural law; in other words, refusing to see that it bears within itself Fascism as a fruit bears rot, cancels the demonstration. In spite of this, the dialectical impulse rises high. It reaches its culminating point in the chapter headed "Twilight of the Gods and Twilight of Men," a long passage in which the author maintains that "the crisis of the sacred is primordial, decisive" and that society deprived of transcendence exhausts itself: a great luxuriant tree with its roots cut. And, after Freud, he sweeps clean the political arena encumbered with the rubble of a doomed order. This is why I am not alarmed when I see the idol of Tout-Paris acting as a partner to clowns. Bernard-Henri Lévy, pampered, adulated, promoted, ground to bits by the media—must we say farewell forever to your smile of complicity, the birdlike gestures of your friendly hands, your understated language? No. Simply: *au revoir.*

But Lévy by himself does not constitute the whole group. Even if he has overtaken it and eclipsed it to the point of seeming the leader of the school, do not ask Glucksmann, Benoit, or Jambet if it is a case of usurpation. In the competition for brilliance they are well provided for. One sees and hears nothing but them. The ruling classes yawn with contentment. Philosophers come to the rescue! The salons are wonder-struck. Just imagine—Glucksmann is a Communist, Lévy a Maoist—and they wear such odd clothes, and are so deliciously rude. But let us be serious. I do not blame the new philosophers for having discovered Stalin rather late, or for following the trail of blood in the footsteps of socialism. All power aims at absolute power, "the descent and decadence that are its fate." In the face of the gulag, no aid is to be despised.

MONDAY, AUGUST 15

To get away from the heat after a torrid day, we dined last night in a village in the interior which clung to a hillside overlooking the Aegean. The table was set in front of the inn, on the square lit by an electric light. We were the only guests. The innkeeper introduced himself: "I'm Alexander," and his wife: "I'm Roxane," and she took an armful of carnations out of a vase and gave them to us. The wind was so strong that, calling Alexander to witness, I said, "There's going to be a storm." "No," he replied. "It's always like that up here, even when there isn't a breath of wind lower down." Where did it come from, this never-ceasing wind which rang like a hunting horn through the shutterless and windowless house opposite, sounded like a fog horn as it rushed into the dark opening of a stone staircase, and howled above our heads in sudden gusts? The summit of the island just behind us was less than a thousand meters high. On the other side lay that other sea which stretches all the way to the flat coast of Libya. Someone in our group said that he had observed the same phenomenon in many parts of Crete and added, I can't think why, "The power here is the wind." I listened to that awesome clamor in the motionless sky as though it were an oracle issuing from some deep mouth and imagined that, from their last refuge in the entrails of the Mother Island, the gods still spoke to men—unless it was to the stars and to the stones.

With roots well anchored in the wall bordering the path, a disheveled tamarisk twisted and turned on itself. Peaceably lying on a stout limb, a cat was watching us.

TUESDAY, AUGUST 16

A Chinaman said to the Devil, "Before going to hell I want to know what it is like." "Very well, I'll take you there," the Devil answered. And he led the Chinaman to a high-class restaurant, and there, in front of a table groaning beneath the weight of lobsters, spiders' nests, sea cucumbers, fish sweet and salt, glazed duck, suckling pig, piping hot rice, cakes oozing with cream, liqueurs of every color, sat twelve sad, thin Chinamen with their heads hanging down. They could not eat! How could you manage with chopsticks two yards long? They stretched out their arms and tied themselves in knots like contortionists in an attempt to reach their mouths. In vain. Yes, that is hell!

Some time later, the same Chinaman said to a passing angel, "Just in case I ever go there, I'd like to know what heaven is like." "Easy," replied the angel. "Come with me." And the angel led the Chinaman to a high-class restaurant, and there, in front of a table groaning beneath the weight of lobsters, spiders' nests, sea cucumbers, fish sweet and salt, glazed duck, suckling pig, piping hot rice, cakes oozing cream, liqueurs of every color, sat twelve plump Chinamen exuding good cheer. They ate and ate, and enjoyed their food, and didn't even have time to exchange the amiable words which came to their minds. They too had chopsticks two yards long. But each man fed the one opposite him. "That is heaven," the angel said.

Roger Garaudy stopped talking, looked at us and burst out laughing. "The missionary priest, a Marist, who told me that fable insisted that it preached Christian charity. I contended that it preached in favor of collectivism." "Let us not argue about it," he said. "In any event, heaven is love."

MONDAY, OCTOBER 10

Paul Guilbert of the *Quotidien de Paris* is interviewing me. "Are you a thwarted writer or a politician out of spite?" To which I reply, "I am a politician." No doubt because I prefer action. I could never have been an imaginative writer. I observe—and I write. I like the written word. Language, philology, grammar. I believe that real literature is born—and I have said this before— from the exact correspondence of word and thing. I prefer the writer who is able to say exactly what he has seen and felt to the one who lectures and stresses his personal impressions. To what is this due? I was brought up in that classical school where essays in French and recitations in Latin taught me the proper order and cadence of words and phrases. This has structured my style. Sometimes excessively. I am aware that the mold should be broken. Those who shatter herald those who create. Did my background, the country of my childhood, influence me? Surely. They have produced other writers who adopted the same language, the same style. A whole sheaf of good minor authors. Jacques Delamain wrote little commentaries for the *Nouvelle Revue Française* and also books on birds. Jacques Chardonne belonged to the Boutelleau family. Henry Fauconnier was one of their cousins or friends. His novel *Malaisie* won a Goncourt prize in the thirties. His sister Geneviève wrote some beautiful pages with the Double country as background. Oh, those Cognac families where one married into Limoges china and Bordeaux wine! . . . In other words a local literary world existed which, some time before, had produced the Tharaud brothers who divided their time between the Charente and the Limousin; and farther west—where the last hills of the Saintonge become the Aunis and touch the sea— Fromentin. Mauriac was close to us, both in spirit and as a neighboring landowner. He was a friend of the family and my mother asked him to receive me in his home when I went to Paris in 1934. I knew him well and loved him, and I still feel affection for him. Not always without friction—one day after he had attacked me in his column "Bloc Notes" I had called him "our regionalist writer," which he had not taken very well . . .

Guilbert persisted: "Have you an idea of France? And if so, what is it?" A certain idea of France—the phrase is General de Gaulle's. I do not like it and reproach myself for having used it in a book of mine. I do not need an "idea" of France. I live France. I have a deep instinctive awareness of France, of physical France, and a passion for her geography, her living body. For it is there that my roots have grown. There is no need for me to seek the soul of France—it lives in me.

I spent my childhood where the Angoumois, the Périgord, and Guyenne meet. I need no stories about France. What I feel for her can do without eloquence. I lived whole seasons amid nature, part of a large self-sufficient family. The seasons always return, until the day of our death. Later on I had to get used to other aspects of France—mountains, industry, mining towns, suburbs. I approached them with the same desire to know the country—my country—so diverse, so varied, yet always true to itself, always one. But if I am not to lose my way, I must keep the rhythm of the days, see the sun rise and set, feel the sky above my head, smell wheat and oak, feel the hours passing. That is why it is so hard for me to find my way in this land of concrete that France has become. But then, it is still France, so I feel at home there.

WEDNESDAY, OCTOBER 12

I have just finished reading, for the second time, Philippe Robrieux's most recent book, *Our Communist Generation*. He had already sent me the proofs this summer and I had annotated them page by page as I am extremely interested in the intellectual, sentimental, and political adventures of these children of the century who adhered so fervently to the Communist Party, only to leave it eventually, sometimes broken, and always so strongly marked that it took them years to erase its imprint.

Among the incidents which give to this recapitulation of a life the weight of testimony and a historical and literary value, a few lines make me pause and suddenly reawaken in me the memory of a cruel period. Writing about Rajk, the under-secretary general of the Hungarian Communist Party who had been condemned to death at the time of the famous trial in 1949, Robrieux says: "By evoking the superior interests of the Communist Party, by threatening to torture his wife and children, by promising him a sham execution and a calm retirement with his family to an isolated dacha on the Black Sea, should he, out of loyalty to the Party, agree to play their game, they had obtained his confession. The bargaining had been conducted by the then minister of the interior, a certain Kadar. But the promise had not been kept, and when Kadar had learned of Rajk's execution, which was quite real, he had fainted. He had been arrested in turn." Seven years later, Hungary had driven out Rakosi—fallen from Moscow's favor too late. His memory, even today, is bathed in a trail of blood. Imre Nagy, an historic head of state for the same reasons as Rakosi, but loved by the people, formed a government; Janos Kadar was at his side. He was now secretary general of the Party and a universally respected leader just released from the prisons of the previous regime. The system was breaking down and the entire country was in a turmoil. Man-hunts were organized against the agents of AVH, the gruesome political police, who, once caught, were shot out of hand. The inflexible senior officials of the apparatus had gone into hiding in the provinces or taken refuge in Russia. Within a few days the movement had carried everything before it and Nagy was on the point of proclaiming the neutrality of Hungary. That a country of the East should leave the Warsaw Pact was unthinkable. Khrushchev ordered Soviet troops to enter Budapest. As soon as Hungary had been brought back into line, Nagy was arrested and hanged. But the man who took his place, judged him and condemned him, was Kadar.

These memories, and our grief and powerless anger were on my mind, when, twenty years later, on May 28, 1976, Janos Kadar, by then one of the most long-lasting heads of state in the world, received me in his office in the Parliament building on the banks of the Danube.

Did that day make me modify my judgment of the man, if not of history, even though the background of events strikes me differently now than it did at one time? I admit it. The day before our meeting, one of his ministers had told me about Kadar's arrest, at the same time as his own, the day after the Rajk trial. They had been taken away and without being given any explanation, placed in solitary confinement and put to such cruel torture that they still bear its marks. Nobody knew a thing about them. Neither their families nor their Party comrades. Nobody, nothing. For five years. Thanks to this tragic story I was able to understand this remark made by Kadar, talking as though to himself: "Which is more terrible in a man's life? To be made to suffer by one's friends or by one's enemies? Prison under Horthy or prison under Rakosi? Torture under Rakosi or torture under Horthy? The worst is to doubt one's friends. Horthy deprived me of my physical freedom, but over and above that, Rakosi deprived me of my moral freedom." Then he added with a half smile, "I know of a worse trial—to govern for twenty years knowing what I know."

Janos Kadar is much respected in the Soviet countries. The Russians treat him with great consideration. He is said to be a sage. He looks like one. A simple man with a sad face, dressed in ordinary looking clothes, who says what he has to say in a soft voice and does not live in the official palaces. He refuses any personal protocol and has never succumbed to the cult of personality, either in its coarser or its more subtle forms. He is seldom seen in public. His name appears in the press only when the news actually demands it. Without a doubt he is obsessed by the events of 1956. His first words were, "I want to explain to you what happened. Yes, the revolt was justified and Rakosi was a dictator. But Nagy let himself be carried too far. I backed him as far as possible. But overthrowing the Communist regime was impossible, unacceptable. The balance of power did not permit it, either within the country or outside it. By flattering certain hopes the Americans had insanely exposed their friends—and others . . . Denouncing the Warsaw Pact was the ultimate mistake. Who could think that Russia would remain a mere spectator?"

During the lunch which followed, one of the most highly placed members of the Party had stressed this point: "The USSR could not have acted differently. I am a patriot, passionately, as we are in Hungary. But, except for a very few brief periods, our country has never been a free country. Around us, three empires have dominated Central Europe: Turkey, Austria, Russia. We are a small nation, and however proud we may be of our history, we have had to submit to their tutelage. Happy enough to be allowed to live, to remain on our own land, albeit amputated, to develop our own culture. We have succeeded only at the cost of inevitable sacrifices. Today the empire is Russian and Communist. We are Communists too, which gives us a chance. We are neither Russian nor Slav, so we must practice the virtue of patience. We do not have—will we ever have?—the means to pursue an autonomous policy. Russian divisions are on our soil, in greater number and better equipped than our own army. So we endeavor to obtain internal concessions in return for our external alignment. That is the whole extent of our policy. And I think we are succeeding. Though not entirely satisfying us, economic activity is developing at a good clip. We are diversifying our international exchanges, especially with the West. And at home we are beginning to breathe the air of freedom."

Kadar had emphasized the point, as though the present justified the past. "Two years after Nagy's execution, once an amnesty had been declared, there were only a few hundred political prisoners left in Hungary. There is not a single one now." What strange paths history takes!

THURSDAY, NOVEMBER 17

Lunched with Stepan Chervonenko at the home of a mutual friend. As Russian ambassador to China, it was he who informed Mao Tse-tung that Khrushchev had been disgraced (he said "shelved"). Mao had clapped his hands in delight and remarked, "It should have been done sooner." Hour by hour, Chervonenko lived the rupture between his country and China. Mao, perpetually away, traveling in the depths of the provinces but managing to make his absence from the official palaces felt like an obsessive presence—organizing, maintaining, neutralizing ambitions and rivalries from a distance—kept in constant contact with him by telephone.

The ambassador placed the responsibility for the Sino-Soviet crisis entirely on Mao, who was obsessed by two convictions: the superiority of China and his own personal superiority. He was convinced that nobody in the Communist world other than himself had the mission, the ability, or the authority to map out the paths of Revolution. At this point in the conversation Chervonenko told us with an absolutely straight face that in 1957 Mao had asked Moscow to send him an expert who would go through the complete edition of his works with a fine-tooth comb to verify their conformity to doctrine. Lyubin, an eminent member of the Academy of Sciences, was sent off post-haste. For three years he worked side by side with Mao and the intimacy which resulted prompted Moscow to nominate him ambassador on the spot. From that moment on, Mao gave up seeing him. Two years later, when Lyubin left Peking for reasons of health, without having seen the master of China again, the latter saw to it that the best doctors were consulted and chose one of them, as well as a hand-picked medical team, to accompany the sick man to Moscow aboard a special luxury train. In the Kremlin, the China experts interpreted this gesture as the preamble to a thaw in diplomatic relations. Plans were outlined, but brought to a sudden halt by a note from Peking: the bill.

SUNDAY, NOVEMBER 20

On the death of Stalin. A stroke, no doubt, made of him a man with eyes staring into space, puffing and groaning like a buffalo floundering in the mud. Those around him watched and waited. His breath on a pocket mirror still bore the weight of an empire. On the wall to the right of his bed hung a color print, the only picture to have followed him wherever he slept: a shepherdess feeding a lamb from a bottle.

1978

TUESDAY, MARCH 7

On my way to Blanzy, where the fourth and last public meeting of the day awaits me, I made a brief halt at Chalon-sur-Saône. Pierre Joxe had suggested I stop there long enough to visit the House of Culture, where an exhibition, "Labor and Invention," had gathered together sculpture, paintings, drawings, and graphic representations depicting the history of labor in that mining area. From the artisan of the Renaissance to "the poor laborer condemned to remain a laborer" who, by the end of the seventeenth century "played no further role in the affairs of his trade" (Parias), and in the nineteenth century melted into a "multitude functioning in concert, at the command of capital, in the same space, for the purpose of producing the same type of goods" (Marx), the organizers had remarkably summed up the evolution of the relationship between art, labor, leisure, technology, and creativity. But in spite of the high quality of the works exhibited—two Le Nains, "The Interior of a Forge" by Coclers, "A General View of the Forge at Commentry" by Sabatier, "A Foundry at Le Creusot" by Chassériau, "The Interior of a Forge" by Rosine Giraud-Parran, "The Strike at Le Creusot" by Adler, "Miners" by Steinlein, "The Monument to Labor" by Guillot, and above all, Bonhommé's large canvases, "Iron Founding at Le Creusot," "View of Le Creusot in 1867," or "The Interior of the Great Forge at Fourchambault," I am haunted by two photocopied texts enlarged and mounted on mural panels.

First of all, articles I and II of the law of March 28, 1841. They read as follows:

> Children may be employed only under the conditions prescribed by the present law: In mills, factories, and workshops where engines, either mechanical or with continuous combustion, are used, and in their outbuildings, in all factories employing more than twenty workers gathered together in workshops, children must be at least eight years old to be admitted—between the ages of eight and twelve they may not be employed at actual work for more than eight hours out of twenty-four, divided by a meal—between the ages of twelve and sixteen, they may not be employed at actual work for more than twelve hours, divided by a meal. This work may take place only between the hours of five in the morning and nine at night.

Then came a speech, or rather two extracts from a speech made on January 11 of the same year, before the Chamber of Deputies, by Monsieur Cunin-Gridaine, minister of commerce, during the reign of His Majesty Louis-Philippe I. Judge for yourselves:

> The admission of children to the factories by the age of eight represents for the parents a means of supervision; for the children the beginning of an apprenticeship; and for the family additional earnings. The habit of order, discipline and work must be acquired early and most industrial handiwork (sic) requires a dexterity and an agility which can be acquired only by fairly long practice, and can never be begun too soon. . . .

And this:

> A child who has entered the workshop at the age of eight, who has been trained to work and has acquired the habit of obedience and the first rudiments of primary education will reach the age of ten with a greater resistance to fatigue, more skill and more education than a child of the same age brought up in idleness, who dons the laborer's smock for the first time.

Children of twelve trained like ferrets to curl up in a hole—three cheers for agility! Taught to handle a pick at the end of a narrow gut with their noses in the coal and lying on their backs—long live dexterity! And all that for eight hours a day at a depth of 1500 feet underground. Let us hail the honorable memory of Monsieur Cunin-Gridaine, minister of commerce of good king Louis-Philippe! But Monsieur Cunin-Gridaine is not important. Nowadays he would no doubt be a progressive democrat, or a Social Democrat, or a Socialist Democrat, or something of the sort—a reformer, for example, since before him those same children were working fourteen hours a day. No, Monsieur Cunin-Gridaine is of no importance. It is society that matters. It has changed neither its structure nor its nature, it moves forward only under constraint, gives way only in the face of rebellion. This evening, tomorrow, four days still to go before Sunday's polling, and afterward, for as long as necessary, in hours of doubt and weariness: never forget this.

SUNDAY, MARCH 19

Before the cock crows.

Politics so often obey the laws of physics that I now expect—in accordance with the principle of Archimedes—a sum of doubts, resignations, insolence, and insults exactly equal to the sum of congratulations, pledges of alliance, and promises that the opposite movement would have earned me.

WEDNESDAY, MAY 10

Have just reread my notes of April 30, begun in Madrid and continued in Córdoba during a brief visit arranged by our Spanish friends. Yesterday we were told that Aldo Moro was dead; poor corpse flung into the street, exposed to every eye. I feel an intense pity for this man, despoiled of everything, even his loneliness, and I suffer for his violated modesty.

But I hear someone whisper: "What a lot of fuss over one more death!" The memory comes back to me of those long processions of martyrs that have punctuated my life. I was born during one war: ten million dead. I fought in another: thirty million. And in between: Stalin, Hitler, Franco, and others. And after that? The list would be long, and anyway, you know it, ever counterpointed by that boundless shadow which yet bears a name: gulag, Indonesia, Chile, Argentina, Cambodia—and all the rest. F. tells me that such is the way the Montoneros kill—I approve of their cause—and such is the way that those who kill the Montoneros kill—I despise their cause. The last dawn of a condemned man is not concerned with "whereases" and "wherefores," or with who was judge and who counsel for the defense, or in the name of what right, or in the name of what force of history. How can this atrocious tangle be straightened out? The simplest way would be to return to the simple things which give meaning to the days, to light, to hope. All societies at all times have produced their revolts. Sometimes they were necessary. But in the name of what values? I know of none that justify crime. Violence for violence, fear for fear, blood for blood—each one loses, loses himself. In the Middle Ages men built walls to keep out the plague. Are any walls on earth high enough to keep out the sickness of the spirit?

SUNDAY, MAY 14

Cluny. As it had done last year, the house at Milly opened its doors to us again. It was so late that we had merely glanced through the wrought-iron gate and were discreetly returning to our automobiles, when the young owners, Robert and Jacques Sornay, invited us in. I asked them to tell us the history of the property.

With the exception of a real-estate agent who had bought it in 1860 with the intention of reselling it, this beautiful house, built of the golden local stone a century and a half ago by an ancestor of Alphonse de Lamartine, has changed hands only once. Monsieur Daux, a notary at La Roche-Vineuse, which was then known as Saint-Sorlin, a small town near Milly, bought it in 1861. It has been in his family ever since; to be more exact, in the hands of his direct descendants.

> But soon an outlander, a stranger to the village,
> Will come, gold in hand, to lay claim to the place.

The voice of our teacher at the little village school of Jarnac used to break as he read us these heart-rending lines. "Do not allow, O Lord, this sorrow and this outrage." That outlander and his gold, how we hated them!

I recounted these youthful emotions to our hosts. They corrected them after all these years. "Yes, that is exactly it. Our grandfather, who had wept along with everyone else on reading 'Milly, or the Native Soil,' was still so much under the spell of the poem that, once the deed of sale had been signed, he wrote to Lamartine, offering to sell the house and its outbuildings back to him, on the same terms as he himself had bought them. But the poet, after a series of fortunate inheritances, had acquired title to several estates in the neighborhood and settled at Saint-Point, visiting Milly only for the grape harvest and the accounts. He thanked the notary warmly and in a letter still in the possession of the Sornay family, he declined the offer in these terms: 'Buy it without fear of offending me. Once the shell has been broken the sparrow does not return to the egg.'"

In a previous chronicle, I recalled that Lamartine's imagination, if not the exigencies of prosody, had led him to place ivy where, in fact, wisteria grows, near a stoop of three steps, which really has five. I would not dwell on these details had Robert Sornay not pointed out to us that ivy now climbs up the back of the house, and that it had been planted, later on, by Alix, Lamartine's mother, her piety not tolerating any deceit, however poetic, from her beloved son.

SUNDAY, MAY 28

Four points to the credit of Giscard at the UN: First of all, he was there. Second, he was there to talk of disarmament; and third, he challenged the Russo-American hegemony. All of which is not negligible. I will mention the fourth point later on.

On the debit side I would record the underlying philosophy of the project. Through the mouth of its president, France has declared to the world: "Do what I say. Don't do what I do." I do not suppose that this language misleads anyone, but I am embarrassed that it should have been used.

"Do what I say." France does not (yet) have any satellites—the latest thing in advanced military technology. Russia and the United States do. From the outer reaches of the sky, four hundred kilometers above our heads, small devices delve, search out, and photograph the slightest fold in the earth's crust, take unaware the housewife shaking her linen out of the window, the little girl picking forget-me-nots, and record the flight of a heron for its end-of-the-world archives. Needless to say, its universal curiosity does not end there. A speeding automobile, two men whispering, the glint of steel, the muzzle of a cannon, the outline of a periscope cleaving the water, all interest that little gadget up there that lays photographs as some demented insect lays eggs. Giscard's idea is that the controller should be controlled by a space agency where France would have a seat. A good idea. Providing that inspection becomes the rule in all fields. However, France is absent from Vienna, from Geneva, absent from all those places where somebody might ask her to submit to this same control herself.

"Don't do what I do." We are arms merchants. To ask those who buy our goods to pay a tax—even one for the benefit of the Third World—will seem odd to anyone who has noticed that Valéry Giscard d'Estaing is very careful not to request that those who sell them should also be taxed. No objections where logic is concerned, Your Honor! But if it is a question of morality, or quite simply of peace, or even more simply of life—then you must excuse me! Our Mirages kill very nicely for someone else. Not a war on earth that does not bring us some money. Excellent subject for a speech on the balance of trade. A less good one on disarmament.

"Do what I say." Americans, go home. Russians, stay where you are. Cubans, Ethiopians, Algerians, and Libyans, stop meddling in other peoples' affairs. But the echo answers: Chad, Zaire, Sahara. "Don't do what I do."

The fate of the human species hinges on nuclear proliferation, a fact which is beginning to be realized. According to the Institute for Research on Peace, in Stockholm, on July 1, 1976, the United States had at its disposal 2,124 nuclear and strategic weapons delivery systems, 1,054 intercontinental ballistic missiles in the ground, 665 missiles aboard 41 nuclear submarines, and 414 bombers able to launch 8,500 guided nuclear warheads. At the same date, the Soviet Union had 2,404 strategic devices capable of delivering nuclear warheads, among them 1,452 intercontinental missiles, 812 missiles aboard 60 nuclear submarines, and 140 to 150 bombers able to launch 400 guided nuclear warheads. All this without counting, on either side, tens of thousands of tactical nuclear weapons, most of them more destructive than the Hiroshima bomb. As far as the accuracy of these weapons is concerned, it is instructive to learn that a run-of-the-mill one can hit a target 13,000 kilometers away with a 300-meter margin of accuracy. An added detail: The explosive capacity of the most highly perfected nuclear warhead is equivalent to 200,000 tons of TNT, whereas the maximum force of the Hiroshima bomb was twelve kilotons. "Imagination will sooner weary of conceiving than nature of providing." Valéry Giscard d'Estaing is right to be concerned. He is not the only one. "Do what I say." The two great powers are playing at outsmarting each other. The treaty on the limitation of underground testing has not been ratified. Nor has the treaty on peaceful nuclear explosions outside testing sites. The Vienna talks on the reduction of armed forces in Central Europe have reached a dead-end. The negotiations that would forbid the manufacture or stocking of chemical weapons have failed. The agreements on the nonproliferation of nuclear weapons are ineffectual. As I noted the other day, in 1990 fifty countries will have the means of blowing up the globe. Valéry Giscard d'Estaing is right to complain and to propose that the problem should be attacked in the most concrete manner possible, that is to say through a regional approach. (By way of proof—and this is the final positive point I mentioned at the beginning of these cogitations, he has at last endorsed the treaty of Tlatelolco, which forbids nuclear armament in Latin America, and therefore in French Guiana.) But other than that and up till now, France has not signed anything, is not signing anything. And continues to reinforce its military technology. And goes on selling its civilian technology. "Don't do what I do."

TUESDAY, JULY 4

Russia has no business in the heart of other continents. Its own is enough to keep it busy. It knows by experience how easy it is to get lost there and that power exists only at the portals of space. And what a saving in time! On earth there live men, those worrisome creatures. This explains why I look elsewhere while the West dithers and panics over Zaire: at the sea and its shores, the sea and its passages. This applies to our Europe. Were I responsible for my country, I would focus all my attention on Tito and his Adriatic, or on the Aegean and Turkish ambition. This applies to the Middle East and to what is called the Horn of Africa. Russian soldiers in Ethiopia, war in Eritrea, a simultaneous coup d'état in both North and South Yemen, a change of regime in Kabul, would warn me that the hour is near. The pincers are closing on the Persian Gulf. And when I see, as everyone can see, Brezhnev's troops camping at the borders of Germany and China, I think first of all of Iran.

Should I accuse Russia of making trouble? It treads warily. When you are big you have to. What should I say of America?

FRIDAY, JULY 7

During the presidential elections of 1974 I had felt the need for serious reflection which would allow me—allow us—to get closer to the problems set by data processing, the modern science of communications, and to evaluate its field of application. By May 1976 I had obtained the necessary elements thanks to a symposium organized by the Socialist Institute for Study and Research, whose guiding light is Jean Pronteau. A perfect introduction to the debate centered on the Nora-Minc * report. This document which records its proceedings is still eminently up to date. I wish to take this opportunity to send a friendly greeting to those who devoted their time and labor to it and now suffer at hearing their party dismissed as no more than an electoral machine.

The contribution made by the Nora-Minc report is quite remarkable for a number of reasons: the detailed analysis of the new relationships taking shape between technology, culture, and the industrial system; the veiled though merciless denunciation of the setbacks suffered by French industrial policy in the realm of data processing; the study of the threats to which telecommunications expose our national independence and the future of our freedoms. Once our main networks have been connected by satellite to American data banks, our industrial apparatus will, in fact, depend on foreign technology, while the concentration of power will be increased, not by the force of arms, but by the force of secrecy.

Moreover, inequality will be increased between those who cannot manipulate the data-processing tool, and between those who control its development and those who must submit to it. Finally, increased automation will lead to the elimination of innumerable jobs, chiefly in the white-collar category: post office, secretarial, and office workers. Nothing in the official proposals prepares for these transformations.

* The Nora-Minc report, by Simon Nora and Alain Minc, documented the computerization of society.

However, we must remember that data processing, which arouses the same mistrust and the same ambitions as printing, railways, the telegraph, and the automobile did in the past, can just as readily constitute—in a Socialist society—the decisive instrument of liberation. There will be fewer repetitive tasks, more direct responsibility, greater productivity, and a new upsurge of expansion. Providing, naturally, that a coherent political and cultural program is able to embrace this technological revolution, to define its uses, and master its development. Data processing, biology, nuclear physics: The great fields of knowledge are open to conquistadors setting out in the name of democracy.